T0144982

BITE

—

Recipes for
Remarkable
Research

BITE

Recipes for
Remarkable Research

EDITED BY:

Alison Williams
Heriot-Watt University

Derek Jones
The Open University

Judy Robertson
Heriot-Watt University

SENSE PUBLISHERS
ROTTERDAM/BOSTON/TAIPEI

A C.I.P. record for this book is available
from the Library of Congress.

ISBN 978-94-6209-582-3 (paperback)
ISBN 978-94-6209-583-0 (hardback)
ISBN 978-94-6209-584-7 (e-book)

Published by:
Sense Publishers
P.O. Box 21858
3001 AW Rotterdam
The Netherlands
https://www.sensepublishers.com

Printed on acid-free paper

All rights reserved © 2014 Sense Publishers

No part of this work may be reproduced, stored in
a retrieval system, or transmitted in any form or by
any means, electronic, mechanical, photocopying,
microfilming, recording or otherwise, without written
permission from the Publisher, with the exception
of any material supplied specifically for the purpose
of being entered and executed on a computer system,
for exclusive use by the purchaser of the work.

Whether you are a PhD student, professor or decision-maker, these recipes, case studies and papers invite you to consider research habits, approaches and environments in interesting and different ways.

The recipes present research and advice from a wide range of subject areas in an instantly recognisable format. Each recipe enables the reader to take practical steps to understand and develop their own research at all levels, from the personal to the institutional.

This book is a joy to read. The advice is grounded in the latest creativity scholarship, and also in years of hands-on experience, from this international team of leading scholars, designers, and architects. The book provides concrete recommendations for how to enhance your solitary work as well as your group collaborations, and valuable advice about how to design physical spaces that support effective research. It should be read by experienced researchers, aspiring young scholars, and academic leaders."

Keith Sawyer
Morgan Distinguished Professor in Educational Innovations, University of North Carolina at Chapel Hill.

Most academic texts offer theories; the best also offer practical, evidence-based instantiations of ideas and innovations. This book offers something unique and experiential: a rich tasting menu of complex and nuanced ideas grounded in the vast knowledge and experience of creative designers Alison Williams and her collaborators. To imbibe this wisdom of creative syntax is to enjoy a feast of many senses, founded on solid good sense. Take a bite!"

Lizbeth Goodman
Professor, Founder/Director, SMARTlab, the MAGIC Gameslab, & the Inclusive Design Research Centre of Ireland. Chair of Creative Technology Innovation & Executive of the Innovation Academy, University College Dublin.

A playful, humorous but surprisingly practical and meaty approach to a serious issue."

Cecilia R. Aragon
Associate Professor, Department of Human Centered Design & Engineering, University of Washington, Seattle. UC Berkeley Distinguished Alumni Award 2013.

ACKNOWLEDGEMENTS

Many amazing people
have contributed to
this volume.

We want to thank firstly the many contributors to the SPIRES project: Morag Burgon Lyon for getting it off to a sound and remarkable start; the many speakers and presenters at the SPIRES events for their inspiration and scholarship; our sister projects PATINA and SERENA for their contributions, both to the events and to this volume; the Travel Scholars who brought back their observations and learning, as well as their host institutions; and our PI Ruth Aylett, the Steering Committee and the Finance Officers who have supported SPIRES throughout its three years.

We especially thank the authors of the papers, case studies and recipes for their enthusiasm in trying something different. We had always intended this volume to look and feel special, even if we only had notions of how that might happen. Our design team took this vision and brought their own unique ideas and perspectives: Sean Moore for his incredible mind and agreeing that we might have an interesting idea here; Vince Robbins for his proofreading, editing and (most of all) patience; Eri Griffin, whose brushstrokes have added an extra dimension to this volume; Matt Robinson, whose design ability and approach to collaborative design processes inspired us to even greater things, and Tony Bibby who made the perfect introductions.

On a personal level we would also like to thank Mairi, for always saying exactly what she thinks using swearwords, and Professor Lizbeth Goodman of SMARTlab for her passionate and balanced approach to remarkable research.

DESIGN
Matthew Robinson
cargocollective.com/designbymatt

ILLUSTRATION
Eri Griffin
erigriffin.com

EDITOR BIOGRAPHIES

Alison Williams

Alison Williams's portfolio career includes Fine Art as both maker and teacher, manufacturing design, organisational creativity and university lecturing. She now specialises in the impact of physical space on creativity in the workplace, including research environments. In her academic career she was awarded her PhD for a visuospatial *Grammar of Creative Workplaces* by the University of East London in 2013. The grammar permits people to audit their own workplace in terms of its ability to stimulate and sustain their creativity at optimum levels, and the collected grammar data are contributing to a global benchmarking database. Alison's international collaborations include University College Dublin where she is Designer in Residence to SMARTlab, University of Washington Seattle (Human Centred Design & Engineering) and PKAL (Learning Spaces Collaboratory). She has held honorary posts at Strathclyde and Abertay Universities, and is research administrator and coordinator on the SPIRES project.

Derek Jones

Derek Jones is a Lecturer in Design with The Open University and module chair for *U101: Design Thinking*, the innovative and award winning Level 1 entry course for the university's Design and Innovation degree. His main research interests are: the pedagogy of design and creativity, Design Thinking and theory, and virtual design environments. Derek is a qualified architect with 15 years of experience in the construction design and procurement industries, most recently as the BIM Manager for Keppie Design. In his spare time, Derek is an Associate Lecturer with the Open University (and this is probably his favourite job).

Judy Robertson

Judy Robertson is a senior lecturer in Computer Science at Heriot-Watt University. She is an experienced computer science researcher with a passion for designing technology to address societal problems. She was awarded her PhD in educational technology in 2001 by University of Edinburgh. Since then she has published 15 international peer-reviewed journal papers and 24 peer reviewed international conference papers. She specialises in technology innovation to improve education, and more recently technology to encourage people to increase their physical activity. In order to evaluate the real world effectiveness of such applications, she employs rigorous research methods and regularly collaborates with colleagues from a range of disciplines including psychology, education, public health and sports science. She is also an influential computer science educator, nationally and internationally.

CONTENTS

INTRODUCTION

WORKING SOLO

RECIPES

ACADEMIC PAPERS

WORKING WITH OTHERS

RECIPES

CASE STUDIES

ACADEMIC PAPERS

WORKING ENVIRONMENTS

RECIPES

CASE STUDIES

ACADEMIC PAPERS

CONCLUSIONS

INTRODUCTION

EDITORIAL INTRODUCTION

AUTHORS

Alison Williams
Derek Jones
Judy Robertson

RESEARCH IS HARD

We are researchers. We know that research is hard. And captivating, infuriating, rewarding, and addictive. It can be daunting, too, for new researchers. Much of 'how' to go about the act of research is unspoken. Methods may be explicit, but they don't deal with the detail of what to actually do when things go wrong or with our own reactions to the process – especially the emotional ones.

We work on our own, we work in groups, and we work within the context of our institutions. At the same time we navigate the unspoken, the implicit. We buy into group norms, even when we don't know what the group norms are. We rely on the informal support of colleagues, peers, fellow students and mentors. We work in an academic environment where the impact of personal reactions and emotion is largely unacknowledged.

Research takes place in appalling cupboards, airless offices, beautiful purpose-built labs, the canteen, the bus and the bath. Like the implied conditions under which we learn how to research, our physical research spaces are taken for granted - often grumbled about but rarely confronted. Researchers and research can thrive in the most unlikely and impoverished working environments but this ultimately has a personal cost.

There are practical steps you, as a researcher, can take to make a difference to your own working environment and that of others. The first step is becoming aware that things aren't ideal, and indeed can be hindering your thinking. The next step lies in realising that you can do something about it. Creativity researchers, architects, psychologists and others have been studying this issue for some time. Each of us as a researcher is an expert in our own research environment and how it does, or does not, support our creative and analytical thinking. This book captures some of that wisdom and presents it to you in a digestible format – the recipe. The final step is taking action and these recipes suggest ways of doing this.

The wisdom comes from you. The contributions in this volume come from individual researchers from the newest postgraduate to emeritus professors across a wide range of disciplines: computer science, art, architecture, construction, psychology, writing and comedy, human-computer interaction, health studies, linguistics, biology, mechanical engineering, narrative and story-telling, cognition and learning, anthropology, and multiple sub-sets of each. The contributions are grounded in researchers' ideas, observations, experiences and their formal research.

WHO WE ARE

Who we are matters to what we do.

Your editors are a wise and child-like creativity specialist, an iconoclastic architect and a deeply human computer scientist. Our personalities are part of our research (you can tell we are not positivists). We have had enormous fun editing this book and writing our contributions to it. We remain friends in spite of various philosophical spats on the way (Go on then! Convince the computer scientist). For a taste of these sorts of debates, refer to the *Why recipes?* section following this introduction.

Sometimes our arguments revolved around the type of recipe we should accept: Did it have to be based on research evidence? Or were personal experiences of prime importance? What should we do if there was a conflict between these? These questions go to the heart of 'How do we know what we know?'

We are from three different backgrounds, with very different approaches to knowledge. Two of us have had long careers in commercial settings before turning to academia, while one of us has never had a proper job, according to her mother. Our architect has a pragmatic approach to knowledge, recognising that simple explanations and activity count just as much as complex theories and convoluted ideas. He does, however, have a disturbing yet genuine interest in epistemology. Our creativity specialist has a grounded curiosity and inquisitiveness, seeing the creation of knowledge as posing a question and exploring what emerges. In her view, the minute you pose the question you change the field (but she's not a relativist). Our computer scientist is seen as "softer than soft" by some of her colleagues, but she has a healthy respect for research findings from empirical studies and the more rigorous the better. She has been keeping us honest. Our common passion is creativity as a discipline, that is, as a rigorous process; and how it can be demystified and supported in the research environment.

SPIRES, the network which brought us together, has been funded by EPSRC to support people who investigate research environments: their physical, social and technological aspects. Over the three years of the network SPIRES members have explored these different themes through networking, seminars, workshops and travel. SPIRES travel scholars have visited four continents and researched in both commercial and academic research institutions.

PROCESS OF WRITING

This volume was planned during a writing workshop at Edinburgh Zoo where travel scholars and other friends of SPIRES considered the best way to capture and disseminate SPIRES legacy of knowledge to the research community. We wanted a format which was easy for readers to use in their day-to-day practice, and straightforward for the contributing writers. Accordingly we worked around a design statement of:

> Design a [**WHAT Noun**] that allows [**WHO**] to
> [**WHAT Verb**] in effective places for research.

This encouraged participants to complete the missing elements, while at the same time considering the users and the output in use. We contemplated, among many options, 'join the dots', for 'the public', and a 'colouring-in book' for 'administrators to 'moodle' [sic] 'the future'.

Out of the many different contributions the group chose:

*Design a **RECIPE BOOK** that allows **RESEARCHERS
AND DECISION MAKERS** to **DESIGN, CO-CREATE,
HACK AND SURVIVE** in effective places for research.*

This final design statement sums up the group consensus developed at the workshop. It was tested by attendees for credibility and potential by writing trial recipes. It became clear that this format and approach would indeed be accessible to researchers and decision makers from a wide range of backgrounds, and that the form itself allowed the variety of active methods set out in the design statement.

As the form of the recipes themselves took shape we ran 'shut up and write' workshops with other network members, travel scholars and members of other networks. We badgered colleagues, SPIRES members and friends (and complete strangers – never sit next to Alison on a plane) to contribute to the book you have in front of you now. Travel scholars presented their experiences at the workshops in the form of PechaKuchas and these formed the basis of the case studies and some of the recipes. We invited papers from SPIRES network members, guests, and our sister projects PATINA (www.patina.ac.uk) and SERENA (www.serena.ac.uk).

We recruited a great team around us: a talented book designer, an illustrator, a copywriter and a long-suffering proof-reader. Each recipe, case study and paper was edited by at least two editors and reviewed by all three. Some of the recipes and papers involved working closely with authors to develop their ideas for this volume, providing a unique opportunity for collaborative learning.

Many of the recipes were based on direct experience and, as such, we felt it important to retain the voice of each author, reflecting the importance of individual perspectives.

WHAT'S IN THIS VOLUME

The volume has three sections that emerged from the submissions, reflecting the researchers' different focuses – *Working solo, Working together* and *Working environments*. The papers, case studies and recipes in each section reflect the concerns and observations of the research community in SPIRES and beyond.

Working solo is about the trials, tribulations and joys of the individual researcher, focusing on techniques for improving personal productivity and re-examining (and breaking) old habits of thought and practice.

Working together explores the often difficult territory of collaborative working, with attendant emotions, processes and encounters with the unexpected. It focuses on how a group can build trust and work productively without losing its capacity to challenge each other and thus avoid groupthink.

Working environments explores the variety of physical places in which research can take place – many of which might be surprising yet familiar to many readers. Working environments can affect our thinking to a significant extent and this is all the more important because we are rarely fully aware of it.

The volume also contains what we call 'anti-recipes' - mischievous recipes that are at the same time quite serious. They look at the shadowy side of research practice; at how effective research can be limited and sometimes destroyed by inappropriate bureaucracy, apathy, or simply appalling spaces. The aim of these recipes is to raise awareness of situations that we may be taking for granted and to spur us to action.

HOW TO USE IT

The body of knowledge presented in this volume is contained in the academic papers, case studies and recipes brought together in each section. The book can be read as an edited collection of contributions to foster remarkable research.

But this is also a recipe book – so you can use it like a recipe book. We hope it will stimulate your curiosity and interest and encourage you to dip in and see what looks tasty.

For a starter recipe you might be intrigued by *It's OK to have a stationery fetish* or *Hack your head*. If you are a frugal sort of person and like making do with what you have, *Intimacy* and *Just describe* help you to see what is in the fridge, as it were, and *Make do and mend* and *Work that space* are recipes for spaces that might be perceived rather as left-overs that you can do great things with against the odds.

To push the metaphor a bit further, you can look through the recipes as if you were planning a dinner party. Perhaps you want to identify a specific goal for yourself, or your research group? For example, to make sure things run smoothly, look at *Version control: managing collaboration on academic documents* and *Research group as extended family*. For good planning try a helping of *How might we* or *Visualising the problem* and for improved communications you could do worse than sample *Sharing food* and *Broadcast your mind*. Cravings? Identify the problem and then tackle it with recipes like *Tina says 'push'* when you feel abandoned by your supervisory team or *How to keep loving your thesis (even when it hates you)* when you feel the springs of inspiration have completely run dry. To get you started we have also provided a couple of menus below.

But most importantly we hope that you will put some of them to use. Finding time to consider small changes can save a lot of time in future work – whether this is a change to practice or simply a reflection that confirms and extends existing practice. More importantly it can make you *feel* better, something that is often overlooked in research practice.

We have had great fun as well as challenge in editing this book, and are in awe of the extensive range of perspectives that inform it. We hope that you will enjoy it too, and will find – as we are already doing – that each recipe, academic paper and case study that supports the whole, makes your research life more vivid and your research outputs all the more remarkable.

SAMPLE MENUS

Starter
(you're new into the team)

Connecting with colleagues: *Sharing food*
Negotiating a good working environment: *Working in a shared environment*
Developing your thinking skills creativity: *Hack your head; Prepare your mind*

—

Main course
(your contribution)

Working in the virtual realm: *Digital scholarship – start here*
Collaboratively develop ideas: *Visualise the problem*
Take control of your space: *Beam me up; Work that space*

—

Dessert

Keeping your cool: *Defocus your thinking*

EARLY CAREER RESEARCHER MENU

Starter

Refreshing thinking and practice: *Roll the dice; Think with your hands*

—

Main course

Looking after your students: *How to nurture a PhD student*
Develop effective working habits: *How to love several projects at once*

—

Dessert

Having fun: *Research interest visualisation*

WHY RECIPES?

AUTHOR

Derek Jones

INTRODUCTION

This volume is one of the main outputs from the SPIRES network project – an EPSRC network of international researchers looking at research spaces (see editors' introduction). The project used three principal lenses to view creative research activity: physical, social and technological spaces. As such, the project is dealing with "...the 'halfway' between people and things" (Koskinen et al., 2011), and that immediately makes it complex.

The richness of events and experience that can be described is subjective, emergent and subject to factors that go beyond the physical or even measurable, leading to "...multiple readings of reality" (Charmaz, 2000). There are no simple answers to the question: 'How do our minds, social factors and physical environment affect the way we think?'

A further essential aspect of this work is the way in which this information could be disseminated and presented as a final output – how to describe a range of research artefacts (observations, analyses, case studies, research positions, academic ideas, etc.) from a range of disciplines (architecture, science, arts, psychology, social sciences, etc.) to demonstrate things (objects, places, spaces, behaviours, structures, processes, etc.) that are useful or valuable (beneficial, productive, create agency, engender creativity, feel good, etc.) to people (PhD students, researchers, project leads, administrators, etc.)?

Moreover, we wondered how this might be achieved in a way that allows the improvement of such spaces by the people using them.

Given this, how might we approach such a complex research landscape? More importantly, how might we do this in a way that is accessible to an audience as complex and diverse as the subject itself?

The most obvious way is to try and organise the overabundance of information and knowledge in some way to allow it to make sense – to adopt previously used approaches, such as typology, frameworks, or patterns.

Typologies, types and classification

We might have approached it by considering the rich and diverse history of typology in academic practice. In architecture, for example, we might have chosen to make use of form, space and order (Ching, 1979); function (Forty, 2004); socio-cognitive interrelationships (Roderick, 1987); archetypes (Thiis-Evensen, 1987); politico-historical perspectives (Jan van Pelt & Westfall, 1991); phenomena (Norberg-Schulz, 1980); or even American farm types (Dandekar, 1994).

If we were considering only the architectural aspects of research environments then we could conceivably have done this. But where, then, would the psychological and social factors fit – factors that continued to become more important as the project progressed? Some of these typologies do incorporate such extended elements but there are none that cover all aspects. Each academic discipline has its own approach to how these fundamental areas of knowledge should be approached, even before we consider how they might be combined to create a meta-typology.

Types and typology are difficult for multiple readings of reality. Ultimately, a typology has to say X is a type but Y is not. As such, they cannot hope to deal with the blurred boundaries and uncertainty inherent in a subject being viewed through multiple lenses.

Franck and Schneekloth sum it up perfectly with respect to types in architecture:

> "Type will always be a prison and a promise because it will always be open and closed at the same time." (Franck & Schneekloth, 1994, p. 35)

Ultimately, what we wanted to produce was a knowledge output that would allow positive change to be made. Types and typology can be useful tools for the knowledge, but their purpose is classification and description – not active knowledge to generate spaces of remarkable research.

So types had to go.

Frameworks

Researching or working in any area where people and things meet is complex and tangled in the Rittel and Webber (1973) sense of 'wicked problem'. In this often cited paper, there is a clear and stark recognition of this:

> "...the classical paradigm of science and engineering ... is not applicable to the problems of open societal systems." (Rittel & Webber, 1973, p. 160)

As with typologies, frameworks are essentially descriptions of 'things' but whereas a type tends to focus on the object (or characteristic of that object), a framework provides a description of the 'place' of that object in relation to other objects, attempting to deal with the difficulties identified in the previous section. This does provide a wider opportunity to explore the complex landscape described above and the reader only has to look at the effectiveness of Williams' framework (see *The creative footprint* later in this volume) used to explore the physical spaces of research.

But even if you can squeeze everything into the framework it is entirely possible that in doing so you have actually changed the nature of what is being 'squeezed'. More importantly, the frame we apply to a wicked problem necessarily affects the problem itself – at the very least, it influences how we state, view or approach that problem (Schön, 1987; Waks, 2001). In other words, as we frame something, we necessarily change the way we look at and understand it. This is most effectively summed up by Wittgenstein's ladder metaphor:

> "6.54 My propositions serve as elucidations in the following way: anyone who understands me eventually recognises them as nonsensical, when he has used them – as steps – to climb up beyond them. (He must, so to speak, throw away the ladder after he has climbed up it.)" (Wittgenstein, 2010)

Frameworks are also essentially descriptive, and in some ways passive when it comes to their application. They may be used very successfully to describe and organise elements but, as with typology, they are not necessarily useful in effecting change.

During the first design workshop, a few framework topics did emerge but all of these were either very general or (most importantly) there were always artefacts that didn't 'fit'. Once again, the second imperative (to generate a practical fieldbook) was difficult to achieve with a perfect framework in place.

So frameworks, despite their benefits, had to go too. At this point bridging the gap between theory and practice started to emerge as an essential aspect of the knowledge.

Pattern language

With this in mind, we might have turned to patterns and pattern language, mainly as developed by Alexander as 'design patterns' which ultimately combine to form a 'pattern language' (Alexander et al., 1977). The key advantage of patterns is their ability to deal with the complexity of grammar, syntax, objects, behaviours and the entire gamut of elements we must consider. Patterns do not rely on typologies or frames in that they can be rich collections of information presented in a particular way – they are in many ways descriptions or narratives of common problems and solutions that emerge from real-world cases

> *"Each pattern describes a problem which occurs over and over again in our environment, and then describes the core of the solution to that problem" (Alexander et al., 1977, p. x)*

The creation of patterns ideally requires a pattern grammar or at least some consistent method of approach, and the notion of a 'pattern shepherd' has been identified as crucial to the identification and extraction of patterns (Harrison, 1999). The subtleties of recognising the pattern beneath the observation are important here to extract the essence that Alexander claims "...you can use a million times over".

Within the scope of the project this was a significant challenge which was not necessarily desired. The richness of the individual writing from researchers was something that was valued in and of itself, the qualitative 'voice' of the different frames we bring to method and knowledge are often embodied within those methods and knowledge domains. This was considered to be an important aspect of the knowledge itself.

Moreover, there is no universal agreement about what a pattern (ultimately) is. Questions around whether a pattern has to be 'positive' have not been resolved – for Alexander it was clearly always a positive outcome, a view that is still generally prevalent in design-based pattern research. In computer science, however, patterns of failure (anti-patterns) are as useful as successful ones. Alexander himself was ultimately sceptical of the translation of patterns to other domains, suggesting that the elements of morality, coherence and emergence were difficult to transfer to certain disciplines (Alexander, 1996).

Something that most pattern researchers do agree on, is that the application of patterns in practice has had limited success – especially in knowledge domains such as architecture (Mor, Warburton & Winters, 2012).

Kruft sums this up (perhaps a little bluntly) by stating that Alexander's patterns:

> *"...by virtue of their very generality, have a certain validity but which can scarcely be turned to practical account." (Kruft, 1994, p. 443)*

So pattern language came very close, to the extent that Jim Hensman's academic paper *Connecting design in virtual and physical spaces* proposes patterns as a framework for analysing recipes prior to translating their basic principles from the physical to the virtual. But as a way of organising what we have called the overabundance of information and knowledge, pattern language had to go.

EPISTEMOLOGICAL FAIL

As editors, we had a dilemma in the absence of a typology, framework or pattern language. We had a series of case studies – some undertaken within a framework (Williams, 2013) and others that were not. We had traditional research artefacts created within their own domains (subjects and epistemologies). We had a diverse group of authors, from a range of subject backgrounds, all ready and waiting to take the next step. This body of knowledge was no less valuable simply because it wouldn't fit into some meta-knowledge system.

In trying to apply definitions, frameworks or patterns, we are perhaps conflating what we can say *about* something and what we know *of* something. As Coyne suggests, the knowledge of location is often conflated with knowledge *of* something (Coyne, 2013). This conflation of information and knowledge is one to be aware of in any research. It is entirely natural to take what we can say *about* something to make a *definition* of that thing. In doing so, we risk misunderstanding what we think we know *of* that thing.

At the other end of this spectrum we might then decide that since there are no absolutes we must accept the opposite position – that everything is relative and subjective. But this can lead to the 'relativist trap' – by accepting that everything is completely relative we can end up saying nothing at all. The application of relativism starts with the rejection of absolute truth – not the acceptance that everything is relative.

It is worth noting that the elements of knowledge discussed in this paper were all debated at the first SPIRES writing workshop. Without perhaps realising it, the group were looking for some way of making sense of the mass of information being shared via a snowstorm of sticky notes. At the same time, the group realised the difficulties in actually achieving some overarching structure – there were always a few sticky notes left over. This difficulty makes any notion of a normative or deterministic approach effectively impossible. As Schön observed:

> "If the situation is unstable or uncertain or unique you can't do research" (Schön, 1980, p. 3)

In order to move forward we were able to turn, once again, to the second objective of the work – an output that would allow readers to improve their research in a practical way. We needed a grounded approach to the knowledge.

ALL IDEAS HAVE BEEN GROUNDED

Despite 'failures' of epistemology, life still seems to go on. People still do things despite the difficulty of actually formally (and completely) generating 'ultimate truths'. Between epistemology and ontology there is some kind of 'reality' that we mostly inhabit.

This middle ground is perhaps best articulated by the pragmatist tradition in philosophy, from Peirce and James, through Dewey and more recently to Schön (among many others). In recent decades, constructivist and grounded methods of research have informed many areas of knowledge. Most recently, Cross (2007) sums up this landscape of epistemology in design research by considering the study, methods and values in the practical knowledge systems of sciences, humanities and design - setting out a spectrum of epistemology with design between the subjective and objective extremes of humanities and science respectively (Cross, 1982; 2006). This is not to be taken in any way as a 'better' approach – it is simply a recognition of some middle ground within which useful knowledge can be found.

Inhabiting the middle ground, so to speak, is a necessity borne out of the complexity and tangled nature of the subject we are considering. It was to this middle ground that we turned in order to move forward. Switching to a grounded method, and in particular focusing on the second objective (how to disseminate the research), immediately allowed the group to move forward. By running a design process, the group were able to explore and expand rather than trying to think of everything and find the pattern.

From this, the group came up with the design statement:

> Design a RECIPE BOOK that allows RESEARCHERS AND DECISION MAKERS to DESIGN, CO-CREATE, HACK AND SURVIVE IN effective places for research.

In design practice, there are those moments when you just know it's going right, similar to Csikszentmihalyi's flow (1996). A similar event occurred at the first writing workshop at this point.

As soon as the design statement was expressed, there was a change in attitude and approach from almost all participants. There was an immediate recognition of the potential of this as a way to approach the knowledge. Going back to Csikszentmihalyi, the group was definitely 'in flow'. The recipe was clearly a conceptual metaphor that the group shared.

THE EPISTEMOLOGY OF RECIPES

The recipe is an instantly recognisable form and this matters a great deal. The power of analogy and metaphor should not be underestimated, and indeed, it may underpin both ontology and epistemology (Lakoff and Johnson, 1980).

By using metaphors to translate elements of information and knowledge, recipes allow summaries of research and observation. Looking at the recipe components, *Background* can provide context, experiential reporting, observations, positioning, proposing, relevance, and importance – all the things one might, in fact, expect as the necessary preconditions for some piece of research in context. *Ingredients* can describe elements, artefacts, items, and other things, and can include conceptual elements such as attitudes, approaches, and ideas. As with the background, the ingredients can form a natural language of organising research items. *Method* can provide steps for replication, recreation or simply description. More importantly, since this is a recipe metaphor, it can also allow for 'maybes' and 'possibilities' – not simply the definite elements.

Reviewing the previous argument, it is clear that recipes do actually contain many of the features of types, frameworks and patterns – despite the rejection of these as methods in themselves.

We do have some typology: the sections are divided into *Working solo, Working with others* and *Working environments*. But these features emerged from the process of collecting and editing the recipes – moreover, they emerged iteratively. We could have continued to rearrange the recipes *ad infinitum*.

We have a framework in that the recipe itself is, in effect, a framework containing objects, processes, conditions and other framing elements. But the individuality of the recipes means that not all of these elements are consistently applied. The framework is, therefore, one of linguistic structure and form, with the flexibility to adapt to whatever elements should (or should not) be included.

The recipes are also in some ways patterns: they predominantly describe potentially positive outcomes from an observed or researched source. But we also include anti-patterns in a 'designerly' way, patterns that could be applied to negative effect. Moreover we have not developed a pattern language or even considered the scalability of the recipes as patterns – many of which are too person- or context-specific to be generalised to the 'millions' of repetitions required by Alexander.

An overall point is that the sum of the recipes is incomplete – both in terms of content and process. That the content is incomplete we hope is self-evident – there are many instances of research practice to yet record (see *Conclusion and invitation* if you wish to help with this!). Even the process is incomplete – the recipe itself in culinary terms has evolved, from the transfer of knowledge through practice to websites where the search terms 'chicken' and 'custard' might provide new ideas and insights to the questing cook. By approaching knowledge-in-context in this way, theory and practice can sit together allowing ideas and their realisation – an effective combination for a fieldbook on remarkable research.

SUMMARY

There is, perhaps, one final benefit of writing recipes – they are fun to do.

Don't dismiss this lightly. In the paper *It usually takes three of us, a few beers and a lot of imagination*, a clear theme emerges consistently in their investigation of research activity: that the personal aspects of research matter much more than we perhaps think. Moreover, we perhaps do not even acknowledge and discuss these aspects of our work as much as we should.

Recipes have a clearly defined structure that, once learned, allows you to very quickly create the starting point for an idea. This means that you can immediately begin to write without grammar, structure or semantics getting in the way. An absolutely critical aspect that the majority of researchers into creativity and design agree on is the ability of the creative mind to *act*.

The idea in the mind is nothing until it is expressed in some way. The valuable difference between simply thinking creatively and designing is perhaps recognising that creative thinking requires another step to become an idea. Einstein could have happily continued to stare at the light filtering through the trees in Bern; Fleming could have simply thrown that Petri dish away...

The fact is that they did not – they acted on the thought, expressing it in some way and went on to do the work needed to see the idea through.

This structure is also very malleable – as anyone who has followed a food recipe will understand, there are always slight changes that can be made: personal taste can be accommodated; different options can be suggested; even the balance between ingredients and method can be altered depending on the circumstances and intention.

If we do think in metaphors (Lakoff & Johnson, 1980) then the recipe is a powerful tool for thinking – for the creation and adaptation of thoughts.

One of the problems the editors shared was that of stopping writing recipes.

IT USUALLY TAKES THREE OF US, A FEW BEERS AND A LOT OF IMAGINATION

A qualitative exploration of what it means and takes to do research

AUTHORS

Madeline Balaam
Rosamund Davies,
Martyn Dade-Robertson
Mike Fraser

INTRODUCTION

In September 2010 we started on project PATINA (www.patina.ac.uk) with a diverse group of collaborators consisting of computer scientists, archaeologists, media theorists and practitioners, and architects among others. The idea of the project was to investigate new digital practices and their insertion into the more grounded material practices of research across our different fields, in order to develop both new technologies to support researchers and new understandings of how to design effective research spaces. Although diverse, we were, we thought, at least connected by the fact that we were academics working within recognised research institutions. Our understandings of what constituted research would be broadly similar. We were wrong. In the many meetings which followed, very little commonality emerged about our practices, approaches or the status of knowledge within our fields. While we all described what we do as research, what we were actually doing was difficult to conceptualise within a single framework. It became apparent that the term 'research' was so broadly constituted as to always require further qualification. Such qualification, however, tended to lead to disagreement or misunderstanding.

There are, however, common practices and common conditions of research if we look beyond arguments of epistemology and view research as a human practice from the position of the individual and the experiences, motivations and meanings that people see in their work. When a researcher is asked not what they do or how they do it but what they experience and how they experience it, a rich description of research practice appears which is not distinguishable in terms of subject domains and epistemologies but requires a different index.

In this chapter we lay out the evidence of a study on researchers and their practices based on this premise. We conducted 12 interviews and obtained 12 first-person written narratives on the subject of the experience of research within academia. The interviews were conducted with a group of researchers independent from those who contributed narratives of their research practice. All participants were academics from a range of disciplines, including architects, archaeologists, computer scientists and biologists working in the UK, the US and Sweden. Our approach parallels the study by Sellen, Murphy and Shaw (2002) of how knowledge workers used the Internet, as it emphasises the desire to understand the everyday experiences of academic researchers in detail.

SEMI-STRUCTURED INTERVIEWS

The semi-structured interviews explored researchers' experiences of doing research within academia. An interview schedule was developed to guide the interviewer. Questions were asked around the following themes:

> The research process (e.g. "Tell me about a typical day of research", "Describe your last moment of insight").

> Experiences of sharing research (e.g. "How do you feel about sharing your research with others?", "How much do you know about the research that your colleagues are doing?").

> The researcher's space and objects (e.g. "Tell me about your workspace", "What would you carry with you if you didn't have a permanent research space?").

> The researcher's experience of technology (e.g. "How do you use digital technologies in your research?").

> Each interview lasted for roughly an hour and where possible was conducted in the interviewee's research environment. The resulting interview data was audio recorded and transcribed.

First-person research narratives

Researchers were asked to write about their experience of research. The unit of a day was suggested, because it seemed contained enough to permit and encourage close and intense observation and note taking on the part of the researcher, and so allow texture and detail to emerge. Researchers were asked to choose, as far as possible, a typical day of research, and to note down their activities, where and when they took place, and, above all, what they were thinking and feeling about these various elements. They were then asked to write up these notes at the end of the day as a narrative of the day. The writing up of the narratives was chosen as an alternative to interview in order to bring into play an extra level of conscious narration and 'meaning making'. The aim was to see how, unprompted by specific questions, people actually reflected on and wrote up the intimate experience of research as process, compared to how they work up research material for publication. Researchers wrote in total 40 pages of narrative.

A qualitative, inductive analysis was applied to both datasets, with themes identified through iterative reading and interpretation of the data.

By using these methods we provide an account and a tentative set of conclusions, questions and further directions of study, which might pave the way for a new reading of research practices in the context of experience rather than epistemology. This reading, we will suggest, may have implications for the way we conceive and design new types of research spaces and technologies as we reflect on the researcher and their personal experiences of research.

COMING TO KNOW

At the heart of research is the need to come to know, to articulate something to your community that is new, or to provide a new lens through which to explore an established concept. Before moving on to describe the processes, environments and experiences central to this it is worth briefly describing how the researchers talked about the mechanisms by which they come to know.

The researchers who engaged with us either through interviews or by providing narratives conducted research through design, drawing, experimentation, reading and writing. The methods and experiences are variable and eclectic. However different the process, each of the researchers experimented with ideas and concepts in order to begin to understand them. As one might expect, those participants who work within the sciences derive much of their 'coming to know' through experiments within the laboratory, happily working through a number of small experiments until with one experiment they make a breakthrough that allows their work to progress.

Interviewee 10:
"I think as a rule of thumb now you'll try about ten experiments and one will work. One sort of keeps going along that line, so if you can get someone who is quite happily operating on ten different little things one of them will work ... the other nine will just stall, then that one that's working would stall and they will be able to progress the other one and that tends to be the way things operate."

Perhaps more surprisingly, there is also evidence of experimentation by those who work with words, with features of word processing software facilitating experimentation within their writing practice.

Interviewee 3:
"...I'll write three or four sentences all of which have two or three clauses in and sometimes it's useful to swap the clauses about as you're writing. But it's also useful then because, when it comes to the bit where you've had a go at sketching it all out and you're then looking for the thread, you can start to cut and paste paragraphs around so it's all because of cut and paste."

In experimenting, the common view of research might imply that a researcher moves through a series of logical and linear steps until new knowledge or understanding is constructed. However, our interviews indicated that even those doing fairly fundamental science do not perceive this to be the case.

Interviewee 10:
"Some of it is guess work. Most of it is just that looks like a good direction to go with, it will make sense if we try this, a little bit of instinct perhaps but, but most of it is blind luck."

In addition to experimentation, the externalisation of knowledge and thinking is a crucial element of most researchers' work. In one sense, by externalising new knowledge and understanding, the researcher is able to find out what they think about a particular subject or problem.

Interviewee 4:
"If you can type without looking at your fingers, you're looking at the screen, so I conceptualise it as seeing what's in...trying to see what's in your brain. You see the words and you can keep changing them. I don't know quite how I think of it but it is, yeah, so if you could see what's in your head that's what you're seeing on the screen aren't you?"

Writing is one way of actively interrogating an idea. By writing, the researcher is able to fully interrogate the idea and identify holes in the logic, as well as make connections between these new ideas and his or her prior knowledge and experience. It is clear that research is a very active, durational process. The researcher only comes to understand a particular concept or model through working with it, talking about it, and clarifying it for themselves or others. Research takes time, concentration, and persistence.

Interviewee 6:

> *"As I say it's quite a consuming, quite a total process. It's not just something you can park and move on to something else. You've got to live it all the time."*

But this research 'lived all the time' is lived at various levels of intensity and focus. It is not always a sustained and goal-oriented linear process, but also about maintaining a state of openness or awareness.

Narrative D:

> *"I read stuff from professional journals I receive monthly, and also read quite a lot from Twitter (I follow a number of professional colleagues, who post links to useful stuff, which I bookmark generally). I also review quite a lot of papers. This is my 'unfocused reading', and it leads to ideas being generated, which I usually don't write down...it's very much a continuous activity. I am never in the situation of: today, I have explored all my research ideas, let's go and find something new to do. I maintain a continuous pipeline of things to work on."*

Researchers are involved in many different and sometimes conflicting tasks, from writing research proposals, and completing administrative tasks, through to teaching, and mentoring other less-experienced researchers. This often results in researchers, particularly senior ones, struggling to find time in the day to do research. Those who participated in our study tended to snatch moments early in the morning, or at the end of the day when interruptions are few and they can feel they have time and the headspace to do research.

Interviewee 1:

> *"I tend to concentrate better in the morning, so I tend to actually assign the tasks that require a bit of cerebral effort first thing in the morning and that usually sort of coincides with the fact that the student body by and large is still in the land of nod and hasn't surfaced. So there's normally a sort of an hour or two hours grace in the morning where you're not likely to be disturbed, so you can actually do some reading and some constructive work there."*

Perhaps in part due to the time pressures felt by most researchers, along with the intense concentration necessary to 'come to know', the interviews contain a number of examples of the researchers seeking just the right tools with which to do their work. For some, this need was fairly extreme, with one researcher being thrown into an existential crisis when his favourite notebook stopped being manufactured. But, for others, the role of the technology (or other research medium) was simply to facilitate the research. Deviation from this role was intolerable.

Interviewee 3:

> *"I try to find things that don't interrupt the reverie, you know, something about just you and it without something in the way so it's me and the words and I like the computer to not be in the way and it's me and the piece of tracing...me and the drawing and I don't like the pencil or the tracing paper to be in the way and quite often I suppose one of the reasons I'm a new-technophobe is that the learning...learning things tends to get in the way of actually doing anything."*

ATMOSPHERE AND REVERIE

A number of our interviewees described how they created or sought particular atmospheres in order to be able to complete their research. As indicated in the previous section, certain stages of research demand intense concentration by the researcher. Some researchers describe the experience associated with constructing their own understandings as all-consuming, almost prayer-like, and even like giving birth.

Interviewee 2:

> "When I'm making an argument I can't sleep in bed...very...so I wake up let's say six o'clock or seven o'clock, normally I wake up at eight o'clock or something and then I have to run to my computer and continue so that it's like my machine of praying is in its way..."

As might be inferred from the above quote, interviewee 2 required absolute silence and no interruption during these times, but it is clear from our participants that this is not the case for all researchers. For instance, some of our participants explicitly sought places where they know there will be people and some quiet chatter, such as cafes or communal work areas.

The creation of an atmosphere conducive to research and thinking goes beyond the physical and environmental, becoming also something that is cognitive and emotional. Specifically, some of our participants described the importance of being in the right state of mind in order to 'do' research.

Interviewee 3:

> "It just doesn't come so if there's too much rubbishy happening stuff or,
> you know, I've got three letters to write for the practice or whatever it is, I can't do it. So it needs everything else to be at a low, you know, not...I've always got a list that's got twenty things on it but needs everything else to be reasonably under control for me to be able to have the space to write..."

In addition, a number of our participants specifically sought out (or constructed) places for research that would provide a sense of intimacy, security, and comfort.

Narrative K:

> "I need to hibernate almost...I also do what I refer to as 'duvet' computing (sometimes quite literally) and rarely find it easy to begin a paper in an office or in a formal environment – it is as if, like drawing, the intimate process of giving birth to an idea needs to happen in an intimate and personal space. I can frame or begin to frame an idea anywhere...but the shift to a position where these become more refined and more focused is a personal and private one that tests the patience and a different series of skills."

Such places may be carefully selected by the researcher (as outlined in narrative K) because those places support the feeling and atmosphere that the researcher needs, but researchers also actively use tools to make places that support these feelings.

Interviewee 4:

> "...I create an acoustic environment...for me the acoustic environment makes a difference on how I feel. It's seems to, I don't know if it relaxes me and I also think it also focuses. I think of it in that sort of way as if it makes a sort of separate sound world and then I feel good in there, I feel, I don't know what it does physiologically but I often feel nice, I feel and it sometimes it makes me feel really good, you know, some pieces they stir you in some way and...I think some of that is good for me...it's sort of refreshing or soothing or whatever it is, it's nutritious, does that make sense?"

Physical activity was also recognised by some as being particularly important, especially during times of difficulty. Equally, a change of scene was considered useful to the thinking processes.

Narrative G:

> "Always try to start the day with a long burst of physical activity - at moment ride (very wet today!). Tend to think through niggling research questions rather than processes when doing so."

Researchers also mentioned the liminal times and spaces involved in travel, e.g. trains, planes and airports, as conducive to what we might term reverie: carving out uninterrupted periods of time out to think, read and write in an otherwise busy schedule.

Narrative F:

> "I feel more relaxed whilst reading on the train, and I often feel that I get more reading done on the train than at home or in the office at University."

Particular objects in a researcher's working space also seem important in creating atmospheres, and particularly atmospheres that enable a researcher to overcome a difficult phase of research.

Interviewee 2:

> "This is only for inspiration so sometimes when I'm a little bit like down I look at it and I think yes I will look at it and think I will use this architecture in my PhD so it's sort of an inspirational pile and I have a similar inspirational pile about pictures, about books, about things which I haven't read yet and they are sort of my future."

A number of our researchers used items such as their notebook, or the state of their office to ascertain the state of balance between their 'work' and their research.

Interviewee 4:

> "The discomfort comes from the mess, you know, these piles here and the stuff down there and all this. ... But that's the reflection of not being quite on top of it and having more things to do than I'd like to."

EMOTION, EXPERIENCE AND SELF

The experience of doing research is often a personal one. Individual researchers describe their experiences of doing research in ways which suggest they associate their research with their sense of self as well as also performing their sense of self through their research activities. When listening to the interview recordings, it is compelling that many interviewees paused and laughed when asked to articulate what they considered to be the best thing about doing research, as though this simple question was causing the researcher to articulate something that is often not expressed. It seems that, for many, the element of research that researchers enjoy most is the ability to spend their career exploring areas that are of particular interest to them.

Interviewee 10:

> "Satisfying my curiosity. Really that's why I do the research. I want to understand how it works sort of and saying I like to take it apart and put it back together and there's an understanding that side so a biological system."

But, the self is entangled with the research to a much greater extent than just driving the general direction of their research. The researcher and their growing amalgamation of experiences as a researcher leads to what they consider to be worth knowing next, what they consider will make a useful contribution to their field and in general how they will progress their research agenda.

Interviewee 6:

"My own personal understanding which is drawn out of twenty five, thirty years of intense engagement in Mediterranean archaeology based in Spain and in Italy and from the way I read what's been published and some of the work I've done and other people have done there are a series of issues that I think are relevant and so it's all around that understanding that I then started to direct onto the project to answer questions that I think are important."

It seems that a number of researchers identify the self as researcher to the extent that one's professional status can also adversely affect one's whole sense of self.

Narrative K:

"Having failed to achieve promotion because I did not have the 'research credentials' and sensing an academic life that was limited by a lack of understanding
or 'the wrong kind of education' I went through a very difficult personal time having to reframe my understanding and professional identity."

It is also insightful to consider the language used by interviewees when discussing research and the parts of their day that are spent doing research. Interviewee 9 talked about being 'allowed' to do research, while other interviewees described having an 'urge' to do research, or finding research to be an 'indulgence'. This use of language indicates that research is an incredibly personal activity as well as perhaps being something more than doing work, and more like a vocation.

Notions of the self seem to strongly drive research, which introduces complex requirements in the regulation of emotion within the day-to-day lives of researchers. On the one hand, it seems likely that the importance and interest attributed to research is central to enabling the researcher to complete the hard, sustained work of research. An interesting example of this is interviewee 4, a rather prolific author, who in order to write visits a selection of cafes around a city. He conceptualises his research activity as being about writing, but also attempts to create a sense of indulgence around this activity.

Interviewee 4:

"I enjoy it. It [research] seems it always feels like an indulgence, you know, it's a little bit of self-indulgence... You know if you go and sit in a cafe it kind of feels a bit like indulgence, somehow. But maybe it has to be to work. Maybe that's what I'm...maybe that's one of the things that I'm setting up for myself... the possibility that I'm going to find it enjoyably self-indulgent."

But similarly, the centrality of the self to the research gives rise to a whole series of emotional responses which need to be managed by the researcher.

Interviewee 4:

"I was...yesterday I was...was it yesterday, yeah and the day before I had
I got a bit stressed about doing it and I don't know why... I was really asked to talk about my work in anthropology and how it relates to architecture and in a way that's quite a personal thing because it's a personal journey for me to have strayed into another discipline and see what I can learn and I felt, I don't know, not defensive at all but I just wanted to make sure it went well..."

In part, when a researcher shares their research and ideas with others they are putting their reputation as a researcher and as a knowledgeable person within the field up for scrutiny. As interviewee 9 describes, the researcher really needs to be able to trust in the work they do since when forging truly new ways of thinking within a field others are unlikely to immediately fully understand these new ideas.

Interviewee 9:

> "So the reviews we got we had like, I don't know, six reviews and you know written, long essays and they had apparently had a long discussion about this and so on so that was... that means that you are on to something where people are like 'we don't get it' you know. If you're fairly, you know, if you trust yourself that yes, this is interesting then that kind of reaction is cool."

Persistence is an additional factor to research which is central both to working through times when research might feel hopeless, but also so as not to be distracted by interesting sidelines that appear throughout the work.

Interviewee 6:

> "The one thing I would say about research is that it's a...it's very, very hard and it seems to be one of the qualities that you need is a lot of persistence and you know you've just got to try very, very hard. It doesn't come easy. How can I say? It's very easy for people to get sidetracked."

CONCLUSIONS, QUESTIONS AND AREAS FOR FURTHER STUDY

These interviews and narratives indicate that research is a prolonged experience that involves persistence, well-regulated emotion and trust in both oneself and others. The self and the way one sees the world are intimately tied up in the research choices that an individual makes. This entangled and reciprocal relationship between the self and research results in research being (at times) an all-consuming almost vocational endeavour. Research is so often considered, discussed and designed for as though it is a logical, linear and objective experience, yet the interviews and narratives we have presented only serve to illustrate that it is (even within the 'hard sciences') messy, situated, emotional and subjective. Our dataset is relatively small and in contrast the domain of research is both large and diverse, and therefore unlikely to be fully accounted for in the descriptions we have provided. Nevertheless we believe the description of research provided here will be helpful, both in terms of providing inspiration for a new focus on the design and development of research spaces and in conceptualising the experience that is research. We would emphasise, in particular, the affective nature of research and the space in which it takes place.

The affective research space

A salient element of how researchers manage their affective experience resides in how they step into the role of research and how this might be seen as construction of a space for research. Researchers, and particularly those who are senior, perform a wide variety of roles in their working lives, from doing research, to teaching and supervising work, through to completing administrative tasks, and writing proposals to support their research and potentially their research group (Leshed & Sengers, 2011). Our thematic analysis shows the distinct work that our researchers do to move out of these roles and into the role of the researcher (e.g. someone who is creating or articulating new knowledge). In particular, we have found that a number of our researchers need to construct the right atmosphere in order to do the hard work of refining an idea, or coming to know. At the simplest and perhaps most strategic level, by separating themselves from the environment where the researcher does their 'urgent but not important' tasks, they are able to reduce the possible disruptive effect of these tasks on their ability to think and articulate new understandings and ideas. But, for a number of our researchers, there is more to this change in environment than simply reducing possible disruptions. To even begin the process of 'coming to know' many researchers expressed the need to have their cognitive environment clear and uncluttered, for example by making sure that they had completed administrative tasks to create an appropriate thinking space. Researchers also use different environments to create a feeling of intimacy (narrative K) and nourishment or of 'indulgence' (interviewee 4). Such environments are often constructed ritualistically by the researcher going through a set of actions to reshape their existing environment – such as tidying up, laying out a particular set of objects, arranging a room in a certain way. In carrying out these physical actions, the researcher is reconfiguring their cognitive and affective as well as their physical space. There is further work to be done in investigating more fully these research practices in relation to the wider body of literature concerned with the 'practices of everyday life' as part of the social production of space and of power relations (drawing on de Certeau (1984), Lefebvre (1991), Deleuze and Guattari (1987) among others).

Researchers also move to particular physical spaces to carry out research. The types of environments that were conducive to research varied between researchers and between tasks and stages of research. Our interviewees sought out solitude but also environments with noise and activity. Liminal and transition spaces such as cafes, airports and trains also appear to have significance (narrative F). Studies of the built environment would describe such environments as 'non-places' (Coyne, 2007), and while non-places are considered to be the negative result of design neutrality and homogeneity they do seem to function as effective research spaces. Picking apart the values of non-places that support research warrants further study and may extend other work on place and the mobile worker (Coyne, 2007), situating it within broader questions about the relationship between space and place (Tuan, 2001). It is also necessary to investigate and understand the interrelation between time and space. At a preliminary level, we can observe that many of these choices of place, cited above, indicate the need to find a time as much as a space to step away from other responsibilities and into the role of a researcher. The change and management of space is a practical and symbolic way of managing the less tangible, but equally important element of time (Shaw, 2001). Moving into a 'non-place' means moving away from the usual demands on one's time, which tend to accrue within a particular place, whether the office, or at home. Designing effective research spaces means designing effective 'timespaces' for research.

Beginning to see research as less formal and as a less directed process also has implications for designing for the periphery. While we described the importance of persistence in the previous section, it also seems that peripheral research activity and at times a lack of focus can be healthy for the researcher. Many researchers described having a central research focus, but also having many other peripheral research activities occurring alongside it. This less focused activity could at times become more centrally focused helping along the progress of the researcher. For example, interviewee 10 described how a successful lab researcher would often run several different experiments in tandem where only one experiment was the main focus of their work. This meant that when the researcher's main experiment met an inevitable roadblock the researcher could utilise some of their peripheral lab activity to help them work around the problem. Similarly, in the case of narrative D, the researcher surrounds himself with ambient information consisting of, amongst other elements, his Twitter feed and the unfocused reading of research papers, which can at a point in time inspire new thinking around the research at the centre of their focus. Trying to come up with a general model for this practice is likely to be impossible, but certainly the importance of the periphery to sustaining the research process needs to be better understood and designed for.

This alternative reading of research practice needs to be considered in a broader context of the policy and design of our research spaces and research technologies. Often research spaces are considered in terms of their utility with an emphasis on facility and productivity of research. Similarly the history of research technologies is tightly bound in the relationship between the researcher and the intellectual object of research. Rheingold (1985) cites Licklider's early contributions *Libraries of the Future* (1965) and, perhaps, one of the earliest recognisable HCI papers, *Man-Computer Symbiosis* (1960) in which Licklider conducted an analysis of his own research process revealing that many of his decisions on what to research were the result of "clerical feasibility not intellectual capability". Computer systems and our physical research spaces, thus often organise our research objects with this facility in mind (particularly in highly programmed spaces such as libraries and laboratories). While these spaces serve the facility of research practice they don't necessarily provide answers to the experiences described above. The process of research involves a more complex lived experience. While technological (and we could include building and software here) artefacts tend to treat research as formal and structural phenomena, we contend that research practice actually involves creative and often idiosyncratic methods and that the relationship between our spaces and research practice is rich and complex.

By moving to new locations, creating a fracture in experience, our researchers indicate, perhaps, that the institutional places and tools of research do not support the researcher in stepping into the affective timespace necessary for coming to know. Alternatively, we might view the experiences recounted by researchers as evidence that such institutional places and tools cannot and should not seek to encompass and contain the experience and practice of research within their confines. Either way, it is important to acknowledge, in developing research strategies and designing research spaces, that researchers' cognitive, affective and spatial surroundings need to be configured in a specific way before they feel able to focus on their research practice. Thus the facilitation of research and research space by institutions needs to be informed by a holistic view of the timespace of research. How can the researcher be supported to move into the role of research and in the creation of his or her own research spaces? In short, in designing our research spaces we need to consider not only facility but the facilitation of the researcher's affective needs.

Acknowledgements

The Arts and Humanities Research Council (AHRC) and the Engineering and Physical Sciences Research Council (EPSRC).

WORKING
SOLO

WORKING SOLO

"A man's mind may be likened to a garden, which may be intelligently cultivated or allowed to run wild; but whether cultivated or neglected, it must, and will, bring forth. If no useful seeds are put into it, then an abundance of useless weed seeds will fall therein, and will continue to produce their kind." (Allen, 2007: 11)

The mind is your primary research environment; your garden where creative ideas grow. In celebration of this idea, we have cultivated a set of recipes which focus on improving habits of the mind to complement the subsequent sections in the book which consider connections with other people and the physical environment.

The authors, seasoned gardeners of their own minds, present you with various techniques for preparing the ground for creative thought. *Prepare your mind, Defocus your thinking* and *Let your mind wander* are informed by concepts from creativity research: the importance of connecting and divergent thinking, defocussed thinking as well as the unconscious period of 'incubation' in which ideas germinate. The powerful idea of imposing restrictions on one's ideas by forcing choices or presently concepts extremely concisely is introduced in *Constraint as a seed for creativity. Get into the flow* introduces Csikszentmihalyi's famous concept of flow, and explains how researchers can encourage it to flourish.

Once you're pursuing an idea, there is no substitute for hard mental effort. *Hack your head* attempts to bully you into regular cognitive effort so that you cannot avoid getting better at what you do. If you find it hard to sustain attention during these periods, *Instant willpower* provides some tips on how to prevent yourself getting distracted online. When you're exhausted from your labouring in your mental fields, try losing yourself in natural surroundings as described in *Relieving Attention Fatigue.*

Most researchers' minds are not perfectly ordered gardens of rational thought. There are jungles of anxiety, self-criticism, boredom, and fear to be tamed, particularly for those new to academia. *My work is not me* helps students detach themselves from their work to increase confidence and emotional robustness. *Tina says push* is a bracing yet comforting recipe about how to make progress in the absence of your PhD supervisor. *How to nurture a PhD student* is a call to supervisors to take care of their students to avoid them resorting to such recipes in the first place! *Keep loving your thesis (even when it hates you)* advises PhD students on overcoming the anxiety of writer's block. Another approach which may help some individuals 'unblock' is described in the *Automatic writing* recipe. For those reaching the next stage in their careers, *How to love several projects at once* offers some thoughts on how to manage your time when you are required to select and work on multiple projects simultaneously.

Researchers rely on tools, physical, digital and mental. *It's ok to have a stationery fetish* focuses on the connection between physical artefacts and thought, while *Think with your hands* celebrates the importance of movement and senses. Some people find music a useful tool to help them think, but as *What to listen to as you work* points out, general background noise is generally detrimental to concentration. Talking of which, if you are finding your office mates' chatter distracting, *Working in a shared environment* has some practical tips for making shared offices more harmonious. *Digital Scholarship - start here* offers some tips for those wishing to become online academics with digital tools. Mental tools can be useful too, and the recipe authors offer suggestions for shaking up your mental habits and establishing more effective working patterns. *Roll the dice* recommends appraising your own research activities with respect to a set of creativity related criteria and experimenting with new ways of working. For a more intensive project on evaluating your work environment and your role in it, consult *Just Describe* and *Intimacy* which are different takes on the fascinating idea that you can improve your environment by using research methodologies.

There are no case studies for the Working Solo section, on the grounds that the SPIRES network did not fund travel scholars to visit other people's minds. We felt that the funders would not look kindly on telepathy. There are, however, two papers. Williams' paper *The creative footprint* describes her grammar of creative workplaces which was used by SPIRES scholars to audit the workplaces they visited. She presents results of these audits so far, ending with the intriguing finding that playfulness and exploration appear to be (in researchers' eyes) key factors in producing remarkable research.

Creating sensory-sensitive spaces for remarkable research by Williams and Barrett analyses the recipes in this volume in terms of Barrett's three design principles of naturalness, individualisation and level of stimulation. It comments that the recipes concentrate "on those areas where individual researchers and research teams can be empowered or empower themselves to make changes that directly benefit their creative research". That is, researchers can improve their working environment through personalising it and tailoring it to their individual requirements.

Using the recipes in this section, it is possible for your research to flourish even in uninspired physical surroundings.

#01

AUTHOR

Derek Jones

—

SERVE TO:

Anyone wishing to improve their creative thinking

COST

Low

TIME

PREPARE YOUR MIND

Feed your mind to increase your creativity

BACKGROUND —

This simple recipe is an often-overlooked classic, central to all creative cognitive processes. It follows from research that considers creativity to be a simple outcome of a functioning conscious mind (Craft, 2001; Heilman, Nadeau & Beversdorf, 2003; Sawyer, 2011) – something that designers have been aware of (consciously or otherwise) for some time.

In his little book 'A Technique for Producing Ideas', Young (2003) considers the mind of a designer to be interested in all things; inquisitive, questioning, explorative. Take every opportunity that comes your way to do this and you will naturally engage in connecting and divergent thinking, which are two central cognitive functions for creative thinking (Heilman, Nadeau & Beversdorf, 2003; Abraham & Windmann, 2007).

INGREDIENTS

- Anything and everything which could be of interest to you. Start with books, magazines, posters, pavements, doorways, dog behaviour, cloud shapes, etc

- Expand to things you would not normally look at...

METHOD

1. Expose yourself to new ideas. Don't stick to your own specialist area of knowledge – it gets boring after a while and you run the risk of reinforcing pathways of thought. Give your brain a break by thinking differently.
   a. Pick up Concrete Quarterly, the publication for people interested in concrete.
      Then read it.
      All of it.
   b. Have a look at anything at all on www.brainpickings.org.
   c. Go to a library and BROWSE! (It's like using Google but with a bit more paper.)
   d. Go up to a stranger in your institution and ask them what they do. For once, don't try to get what you do into the conversation...
   e. Go into a newsagent's and pick a magazine at random. Don't judge the magazine – just read it and see what happens.

2. Communicate your own ideas in different ways. You know a lot about your subject but when was the last time you saw it from someone else's perspective? Write about your knowledge in a completely different way to see it afresh. For example, how would you explain your knowledge to :
   a. A 10-year-old child
   b. Someone who doesn't have much time
   c. Someone who likes pictures
   d. Someone who despises creativity
   e. Someone who really doesn't understand why researchers need to do so much thinking...

3. Generate your own new ideas. For 10-15 minutes each day, look around you and question the physical things you see. This has nothing to do with your subject but everything to do with thinking and research methods. So, pick an object or observe a behaviour and ask:
   a. Why is it like that?
   b. Who uses it and why?
   c. What would I change about it?
   d. How could I make it better?
   e. Now, see if you can change it...

4. Take it to the next level. Don't just speculate and think –
    act on your thinking. Try to:
    a. Take up a brand new pastime – something you
        would not normally try (different thinking leads
        to new ideas...).
    b. Have a pet project that only you know about
        (such as making the world a better place by
        adding stick-on eyes to things to give them a face).
    c. Record your observations of things – take pictures,
        notes or videos. Doing this extends your thinking
        into recording.
    d. Have a "Say 'Yes!' to Everything" day.
    e. Have a go at the digital storytelling MOOC, DS106
        (Groom, 2011).
    f. Take an adult education class in something
        completely new.
    g. Attend a lecture at your institution that you
        wouldn't normally attend.

COOK'S TIPS

This recipe can be
challenging if you are not
used to trying new things –
some people feel
intimidated or nervous
about this. That's absolutely
fine. You can still do this
by taking on something that
you feel OK with. Start by
having a look at the
examples above and see
where you think would
be a good place to start.

WARNINGS

This is preparation,
not research. Do not
confuse familiarity with
a subject with knowledge
of that subject.

RELATED RECIPES

This recipe is a great
appetiser for any of the
recipes that follow.

#02

AUTHOR

Judy Robertson

SERVE TO

Individuals

COST

Low

TIME

HACK YOUR HEAD

Improve your cognitive skills through deliberate practice

BACKGROUND —

Many of the recipes in this book are about manipulating the physical environment or changing the way you interact with your colleagues in the hope that it provides inspiration.

But in the end, even the most perfect surroundings will not by themselves produce a masterpiece of knowledge. Effective research takes skill, and skill takes practice. If your head is your most important research space, what hacks can you make to improve it?

INGREDIENTS

- Basic level of expertise in your area

- Discipline

- Regular time slots devoted to skills development

- A calendar

METHOD

1. Set a goal for an area of study which you want to master. Newport gives the example of a difficult mathematical paper he devoted considerable time to understanding in depth (Newport, 2012). It is particularly effective to pick a paper which is well known to be important, but difficult to grasp. If you put the time into grasping it, then you have a considerable advantage over your peers who understand it at a superficial level. It's important that you find the topic challenging.

2. Devote regular, intense time slots to understanding your topic. Use strategies for active understanding, such as writing summaries or solving example problems. Allocate a target time to spend on this activity and be strict with yourself about keeping to this. If your mind tries to wriggle away from the difficulty, firmly bring it back to focus. You may want to try the Pomodoro Technique in which you set a timer for 25 minutes and refuse to allow interruptions during this period (see: pomodorotechnique.com).

3. Keep a diary of hours spent in this kind of deliberate practice. Set a realistic target for the number of hours you would like to spend each month practising and try to keep to it.

#03

AUTHORS

Ema Findley
Judy Robertson

SERVE TO

Individuals in search
of creative solutions

COST

Low

TIME

LET YOUR MIND WANDER...

Incubate your ideas before you go to sleep

BACKGROUND

Do you find that your mind wanders as you work? If not, you're kidding yourself; recent findings indicate that people have around 2000 mind-wandering thoughts each day, but are only aware of half of these (Sawyer, 2011). This sobering thought might be more palatable if you consider the hypothesis that those of us more given to mind wandering are more creative. The reason behind this comforting notion is that there is evidence of an 'incubation effect' in many studies of creativity. In Wallas's model of the creative process (Wallas, 1926), there is a period of incubation followed by an 'Aha' moment of illumination where a creative solution suddenly appears in your mind. When your mind is wandering, perhaps it is incubating a wonderful new idea.

Sleep and dreams often crop up in historical accounts of creativity. Poets and organic chemists alike attribute their genius to sleep. Indeed, a study from 2009 suggests that REM sleep (during which dreams occur) is more effective at enabling problem solving than non-REM sleep or a period of quiet thinking time (Cai et al, 2009). Perhaps your mind continues to wander as you dream.

The period just before sleep is perfect for mind wandering. Can you exploit this magical time for the sake of your research?

INGREDIENTS

- Comfortable quiet surroundings (ideally a bed!)

- A prepared mind which has the necessary information to tackle a problem

- Writing or drawing materials of choice

- Sleeping attire to taste

METHOD

1. When you are drifting off to sleep your brain is working through the day's activities, thoughts and problems to make sense of them. This often (but not always) throws up some thoughts which may be useful later.
   As these thoughts surface, write them down on the notepad next to the bed, and draw any images that come to mind. You could also use a voice recorder, smartphone or tablet computer.

2. This method can also be used to clear your mind of unwanted thoughts to make room to solve the research issue of choice. To do this, write lists to take things from your head before you sleep. This enables you to get to sleep, and also clears the mind to tackle the problem solving while you are sleeping.

3. In the morning, have a look at the notepad to see if your brain came up with anything sensible. The stage after illumination in Wallas's model is verification; checking to see whether the creative solutions are in fact valid.

NOTES ON INGREDIENTS

To prepare your mind to tackle the problem, marinate it in literature for approximately eight hours during the working day.

WARNINGS

Your boss might not appreciate sleepy mind wanderings in meetings.

RELATED RECIPES

For thoughts on how to school your unruly mind, see the *Hack your head* recipe.

#04

AUTHOR

Derek Jones

—

SERVE TO

Individuals

COST

Low

TIME

DEFOCUS YOUR THINKING

Relax your brain to make deeper connections

BACKGROUND —

Remember the taste of that moment of inspiration, eureka, confluence, serendipity? Think it happens by accident? This recipe encourages a cognitive function required to allow this moment to happen – defocused thinking (Dietrich, 2004; Sawyer, 2011).

Here's the science: your pre-frontal cortex (PFC) is (probably) the bit that tells the rest of your brain what to do when you have a task to complete (Reverberi et al., 2005). Sometimes, this is easy – if you are asked 'what is 2 x 2?' your PFC 'knows' which bit of the brain is good at that sort of thing, fires it up and gets an answer. Job done.

But if you are asked 'what colour is 2?' your PFC has a bit more trouble. In this instance, it 'tells' the rest of your brain to try to make connections. Effectively, the PFC 'defocuses' and lets the rest of your brain do some thinking. When the other bits of your brain get a chance, 'deeper' connections can be made leading to creative innovation – something that is aided by reducing stimulation and arousal (Heilman, Nadeau & Beversdorf, 2003).

INGREDIENTS

- Pre-frontal cortex
- The rest of the cerebellum
- Distant objects
- Bed, bath, bus
- Ambient sounds or
  soundtracks (rain on
  a tin roof is good)
- Candles, fires, clouds
  – any complex dynamic
  (time-based) physical
  system that can be
  perceived visually,
  audibly, or tactilely.

METHOD

1. *Relax*...There is a reason that many creative people talk
   about having ideas in the bath or as they fall asleep – they
   are in a low arousal state that allows the rest of the brain
   the chance to make connections. Low arousal leads to
   deeper connections. You will only ever engage in 'deeper'
   brain connecting if you give yourself the time and space to
   do it. Low arousal requires that you reduce sensory input
   and mental stress.
2. Make the most of those 'in between' moments –
   bed, bath, bus are repeated as classic examples
   of interstitial times during which it is possible to shut
   down your PFC. Staring out of the window of a bus or
   train and defocusing your eyes (see below) lets your
   brain have some time to think...
3. Your environment (physical and emotional) has a *huge*
   effect on your ability to defocus and engage in deeper
   cognitive connections. See Anthes (2009) for some
   examples in education.
4. *Defocus your eyes, ears and brain.* There is a reason
   why the creative individual staring out of a window is an
   appealing image – but actually it has nothing to do with
   what's really going on. When you defocus your eyes, you
   reduce the level of aroused processing in your brain.
   In actual fact, staring at anything about eight metres or
   further away has the same effect.

5. Stare out of the window – but make it a nice(ish) view. Good things to look at are: sky, trees, water, lots of stones, flocking birds, grass being blown in the wind. If you don't have the luxury of these items in your view and it's a really poor view then obscure it with translucent film. Defocusing the view might defocus your mind...

6. Chaotic patterns can induce defocused thinking – but they have to be the right patterns (chaos and randomness are not the same things at all). Stare into a fire or a candle flame. See that semi-relaxed, weird thing that happens to your eyes and brain? That's defocused thinking. Look back at the things that are good to look at out of windows – they all have this in common.

7. *Do something else.* You can actually teach yourself to make deep connections in a high arousal state – designers still have to come up with ideas to deadlines. But they are also good at recognising when this doesn't happen. It's like a crossword puzzle - if you don't get it in the first 10-15 seconds, you will simply have to wait for the rest of your brain to come up with the answer – so you might as well do something else...

8. If it's not happening, don't try to force it (unless you know how to). Break the pattern physically and mentally - get up from where you are and go somewhere else. Just breaking your focus can help.

9. Defocusing your mind works at many levels - not just the cheap parlour tricks mentioned above. For example, when you walk with no purpose or destination you are engaging in a cognitive process - exercise helps this type of thinking (the 45km of neurons in your body are also part of your thinking system).

COOK'S TIPS

The important point here is reduced arousal. If you stare out of the window and see a building site that's on fire with people shouting at each other, your arousal state will probably increase...

WARNINGS

Do not defocus while operating heavy machinery.

RELATED RECIPES

Serve with *Prepare your mind* or *Let your mind wander.*

#05

AUTHOR

Diana Bental

SERVE TO

All researchers who use the Internet for their research

COST

Low

TIME

INSTANT WILLPOWER

Improve your concentration by blocking out distractions

BACKGROUND —

There are many technological temptations competing for your attention: social networking tools, news sites, endless videos of cute cats. To avoid distractions, many productivity books advise closing down your web browser when you're working. But what if your work depends on using the web, for example searching the literature or consulting technical documentation? What you need is *instant willpower* in the form of software which records your good intentions about which websites you would like to avoid and enforces these as a safeguard against your weaker moments. Such software gives you a reminder, a gentle nudge back into work time. You won't feel resentful, because it is very much under your own control – you set it up, not your boss, to suit your own needs and preferences.

LeechBlock is an example of software that stops you from sliding into tempting distractions without consciously considering it. It makes it a conscious choice: 'Do I really want to spend time on this?' So as well as stopping you from doing what you shouldn't do, the program makes you aware of what you are doing. It is a technological solution to a technological problem.

INGREDIENTS

- LeechBlock, a Firefox plugin available free (with an optional small contribution to the developer) from www.proginosko.com/leechblock.html

- Similar plugins are available for other browsers (see note below)

METHOD

1. Download and install Mozilla Firefox if you don't already have it. Download and install LeechBlock.
2. Configure LeechBlock with the sites you would like to block and when they should be blocked. BBC News, Facebook, your email server, and Twitter would be a good starting list.
3. Set up rules for how much time you will allow yourself to spend on various sites e.g. 'I don't want to go to these sites between nine in the morning and five in the evening.' Or 'Block them for the next hour, or the next 10 minutes.' Or 'Make sure I don't look at it for more than, say, 10 minutes at any time, or over the whole day.' If you try and go on a site you're not supposed to, it shows you a red No-Go sign with a wriggling leech in the centre.
4. To avoid cheating yourself, you can even set it so that you can't turn it back on again until your time is up.

“

Do I really want to spend time on this?

”

NOTES ON INGREDIENTS

See this article in the Economist for examples of similar software on other platforms: www.economist.com/node/16295664. See also the 'Taming Your Tools' section of Glei (2013).

WARNINGS

This tool is intended to help you with your addiction to technology; don't get addicted to it.

#06

AUTHORS

Derek Jones
Pawel Orzechowski

SERVE TO

Anyone wanting
to broaden their
creative thinking

COST

Low

TIME

THINK WITH YOUR HANDS

Use your body to think and enhance
creativity

BACKGROUND

We think with our hands. In fact, we think with many parts of our bodies. By this, I do not simply mean that our brain uses our body to think – actual cognition takes place in our bodies as well as our brains (Wilson, 2002).

This might be surprising to some, but consider: the human body has about 45km of nerves, and these nerves are composed of neurons. Those neurons are not just sending signals to the brain – they are cognitively active.

Even if we forget the science for a bit, in practice-based disciplines, the importance of *physically doing* is understood as an essential aspect of the creative process. However, in other disciplines, we typically underestimate how important the sensory world is to our thinking (Hatwell, Streri & Gentaz, 2003; Damasio, A., 2006), especially our hands and how they help us to think (Wilson, 1998).

INGREDIENTS

- Your body parts
  (especially hands)

- A pencil and paper

- Objects for fiddling with

METHOD

1. *Fiddling*. Play with objects that can be balanced, squashed or moulded into shapes. They should have no other meaning connected with whatever task is at hand. For immersive fiddling, use a rocking chair, have an office chair race or learn to juggle. Possibly technological smart objects could be used here (smart objects that have impact on the light or sound in the room)

2. *Doodling*. Do you doodle? In meetings? While you are on the phone? Doodling is not idle activity. If you stop looking at the doodle and actually consider what is happening in the mind, it turns out that it can be an extremely effective way of engaging particular brain activity – especially for creative thinking (Schott, 2011; Brown, 2011). At worst, it helps you to retain information in meetings (Andrade, 2009).

3. *Take up knitting.* As with fiddling, knitting engages the hands but allows you to concentrate on other things too. Many universities have knitting groups – and it has a particular place in mathematics (Belcastro, 2013). The slight difference between knitting and fiddling is that with knitting you are making something useful at the same time. See which works best for you – at the very least, it might have a positive impact on your health and well-being (Riley, Corkhill, & Morris, 2013).

4. *Sketching and diagramming.* Like knitting, this is an extension of doodling but with a bit more direction. The trick is not to make it too directed – when we sketch, we are actually thinking (Garner, 2008). Designers make use of this simple activity as a way of exploring ideas and thinking – the sketch emerges as the thought does and the sketch has an effect on the thought. In fact, it is sometimes unclear which comes first.

5. *Marginalia.* Ever noticed that you prefer reading a paper that's printed out instead of on the screen? Do you make notes at the side? Why is it not the same with marking up a pdf? This is because you are engaging in motor acts and that requires different parts of the brain. Don't print off everything, of course, and if you can, try using digital tools to mark up electronic documents. Remember, one of the greatest achievements in maths started with a margin note... "I have a truly marvellous demonstration of this proposition which this margin is too narrow to contain" (Singh, 1998, p. 66).

NOTES ON METHOD

All these activities have one thing in common: they are motor acts. We use such acts naturally to counteract cognitive states such as boredom, impatience, frustration, etc. In acting physically, we allow our brains to return to a default state of arousal: either from too much or not enough (Schott, 2011). The right cognitive arousal level is absolutely essential for certain modes of creative cognition (Heilman, Nadeau, & Beversdorf, 2003).

COOK'S TIPS

Start using a sketchbook in meetings instead of a lined book – doodle right to the edges.

Use colour to inject a further dimension into your thinking.

WARNINGS

If you are caught 'playing', make sure you respond by quoting the literature. Under no circumstances should you play the game and feel guilty.

Similarly, if someone is doodling while you talk, there is a possibility that they are paying significant attention to you and remembering your words.

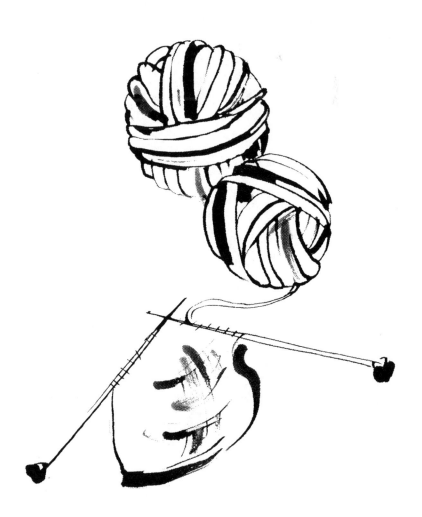

#07

AUTHORS

Pawel Orzechowski
Derek Jones

SERVE TO

Individuals and
teams needing to
generate output

COST

Free

TIME

CONSTRAINT AS A SEED FOR CREATIVITY

Inject innovation into your thinking by
limiting your choices

BACKGROUND —

Do you ever get the feeling that your head is bursting with thoughts and ideas? This can actually be counter-productive for your research. When it gets too much, your thinking might need to converge to help you move forward.

Think about haiku: three lines, five-seven-five syllables. Haiku are very restrictive but lead to such creative output that it is worth considering why. While abundance can be an interesting and (apparently) effective environment in which to work, the truly amazing comes from limited resources.

In architecture, there is an urban myth that the best architecture comes in times of recession: fewer projects and limited resources encourage more time and thinking applied to what is available, leading to significant innovation. *Jugaad, jua kali* and *rasquachismo* are all international flavours of 'make do and mend' cultures that have existed since the start of humanity (U101 Course Team, 2013). Similarly, research shows that limiting choice can have a positive effect on the creative process (Costello and Keane, 2000; Stokes, 2001; Sellier & Dahl, 2011).

"

...the truly amazing comes from limited resources.

"

INGREDIENTS

- A lot of ideas in one head

- A research idea, project
  or thesis

- Pen and paper

METHOD

1. With research, project or thesis ideas, trying to condense these can really help us to focus on what matters. Even just externalising ideas helps sort your head out. Get out pen and paper and try these:

2. Write the idea(s) as a newspaper headline piece – start with the text of the idea, make the strapline (one short sentence) and then the headline. Have a look at how newspapers do this and go for pithy and meaning-filled headlines.

3. Make a presentation slide – just one slide – to explain your research (this is not a research poster – the less you put in, the better).

4. Imagine the world is about to face disaster and you have been asked to provide a sentence that will be preserved for future generations when they emerge again – what sentence would sum up your knowledge/problem/idea?

5. Write a problem or design statement to focus your
    ideas. Try to include the reliable 5W1H: Who, What,
    Where, When, Why, How. Then create sentences
    such as 'How might we...', 'Design a ...', or 'If ... then ...'.
    Using specific templates like these can help you work
    out what doesn't work.
6. Write down the problem you are working on. Now ask
    yourself 'is this the problem or is it a symptom of another
    problem?' Now write down the problem that lies behind
    the first one and repeat until it gets silly. Somewhere in
    between these extremes lies the 'Goldilocks zone' of
    your problem.
7. If you are working with a lot of different ideas,
    try to set these out spatially and see what patterns
    emerge. For each idea, note it down on a sticky note or
    paper – summarise it (step 1) and use one or two words
    as a title for the idea. Put ideas that seem to relate to
    one another into groups and re-summarise these (this is
    a sort of cheap synthesis).
8. For the hardcore minimalist, create a cartoon
    communicating your idea (with not more than three
    frames) or write a haiku as an abstract. Go one step
    further and check that someone else can 'read' it.
9. Kill your darlings, your initially favoured ideas, (slowly) by
    having an area in your notebook or on your whiteboard
    where you dump ideas that don't fit. Leave them there
    for a few weeks. If nothing comes from them, get rid of
    them (but put them into storage – you never know...)

COOK'S TIPS

Remember, this is not just
about creating difficulties;
it is about embracing them
to engender innovative
thinking.

It's also an iterative process
– if you're getting stuck with
one method, move on and
try another. The ones that
don't work will tell you more
about what does.

WARNINGS

It can be difficult to strike
the right balance between
limitations and divergent
thinking. Ensure that
someone is charged with
keeping an eye on the bigger
picture to make sure that a
good balance is achieved.

#08

AUTHOR

Sapna Ramnani

SERVE TO

Individual thinkers
interested in their
mental well-being

COST

Free

TIME

AUTOMATIC WRITING

Explore your unconscious

BACKGROUND —

I was first diagnosed
with tinnitus a year
before I started my PhD.
My audiologist said that
the condition was
permanent, nothing could
be done to stop the noise
and it would get worse with
time, and indeed it did. For
two years I lost the ability to
function and communicate
on a daily level, far less to
continue with my PhD
research. I then met
David Corr, a UKCP (United
Kingdom Council for
Psychotherapy) Registered
Psychotherapist and a
hypnotherapist experienced
in the treatment of tinnitus.
Over the next few years,
I would learn about how to
encourage the subconscious
to reveal information that
had been buried so deeply
in the subconscious that it
was forgotten at a conscious
level: the root of my tinnitus.
Part of this process has
been the use of automatic
writing.

"Automatic writing in
the simplest form may be
defined as script which the
writer produces involuntarily
and in some instances
without being aware of the
process, although he may be
(and generally is) in an alert
waking state" (Muhl, 1930).

In other words, in automatic
writing the subconscious
is able to express itself
through the written word
and the conscious can,
for a change, take a back
seat. I discovered automatic
writing by chance as I was
browsing online and
happened across an article
on the subject. After further
research, I developed the
ability to write automatically.
This method has enabled
me to unlock memories,
thoughts, feelings and
emotions that were once
hidden and out of bounds to
my conscious self. Similar to
dream analysis, this method
has been invaluable to me as
I recover from tinnitus.

This recipe looks at how
automatic writing could have
the potential to empower
individuals to take control
of their own mental health
and well-being. The use of
this recipe will vary from
person to person and should
be implemented with care
and at your own discretion.

INGREDIENTS

- A quiet place to work

- A paper and pen

- A regular time of
  day when you will
  be undisturbed

METHOD

I have been practising automatic writing almost every day and, for the most part, twice a day for approximately eight months. Here is the method I use, and I hope it will work for you too:

1. *Be consistent.* I usually write automatically at the same time each day so that my subconscious becomes accustomed to revealing itself on a daily basis. The environment in which I write is usually quiet with a calm atmosphere which is essential for me during this process.
2. *Don't peek.* Make sure that the pen and paper are in contact with each other and that the paper is hidden from your view. Due to having a disability, I am unable to use my hands to write and so I dictate what I want to write to my personal assistant who types as I speak. For those who can use a pen, don't look at the paper or the pen when writing.
3. *Relax mentally and physically.* The first time I tried automatic writing, the lights were turned off and I relaxed for a few minutes to slow down the conscious thoughts. I felt my mind going blank while also feeling the sensation of losing control of what came out of my mouth as spoken words. I then began to speak aloud the first thoughts that came to me. For those who become used to automatic writing, this preparation stage will become easier and faster to perform without so much time needed to relax.
4. *Use distraction techniques.* If necessary distract yourself by perhaps watching television or listening to the radio while your subconscious takes over. Recently, I have been trying this method and find that the writing produced is much deeper and therefore much more surprising to me when I read it back. I often do not easily recognise the writing in front of me since it feels like it has been written by another person.
5. *Work with another person.* Perhaps at first, another trusted person could ask questions to your subconscious while you are distracted by another activity. Although this may seem a little strange, it is an effective way of ensuring that what comes out is more or less not under the influence of the conscious.

NOTES ON INGREDIENTS

As with all the recipes, this technique may or may not work for you – try it and see. I'm now back on track with my PhD work.

COOK'S TIPS

On my first attempt I wasn't sure what, if anything, would come out, but something did emerge. Having never written poetry before, I was more than a little surprised when the automatic writing came out in rhyme! Since then, the writing has become stronger and deeper in content.

WARNINGS

After undertaking an automatic writing session, I may feel extremely mentally exhausted and often feel the need to sleep or, at least, rest.

DEDICATION

This recipe is dedicated to David Corr.

#09

AUTHOR

Alison Williams

—

SERVE TO

Any researcher wishing
to make a breakthrough

COST

Free

TIME

GET INTO THE FLOW

Prepare to experience creative flow

BACKGROUND

—

How do we manage time?
How do we deal with the
pressure of deadlines?
Deadlines can be helpful in
completing work, but stress
can shut down our creativity
(Huppert, Baylis & Keverne,
2005; Treadaway & Smith,
2012). However, when we
are in *flow* (Csikszentmihalyi,
1975; Treadaway & Smith,
2012) we lose our sense
of linear time, and time
expands. We can accomplish
much when we are in flow,
and it contributes to our
sense of well-being
(Seligman, 2011). This recipe
looks at how we might create
physical space, and social
and emotional space that
helps us experience flow
more easily and deliberately.

The Hinman Research
Building, College of
Architecture, Georgia Tech,
has a mezzanine level which
is hung from the ceiling of
the main space, a refurbished
engineering research
laboratory. The mezzanine
walls are about one metre
high and made of metal
mesh, so visibility is complete
both into and from the
space. A postgrad researcher
has crafted her own
workspace there. She gets
the degree of privacy she
needs by filling in the mesh
walls with images, and hangs
her drawing tools on them.
She has everything she
needs close at hand;
she is within sight of her
peers and their shared work.
She can also be private.
She says: "There is
something about being in
a culture where everybody
else is – there is this open
visual connection. You can
choose to close yourself in,
and then you can also come
out of it. And people can
come by and there is ...[a]
community sense."

INGREDIENTS

- Somewhere to work
  without interruption

- Comfortable level
  of background noise

- Something to gaze
  at/zone out with

- A sense of what flow is,
  and how to honour or
  value it when it comes

- Trust

- Openness

METHOD

1. Have a look at the *Just describe* recipe in which you
   will find an observation process for closely examining
   your research environment. Use the suggestions to:

2. *Prepare your physical environment: privacy, sound,
   view.* Create private or semi-private elements in your
   space – a pot-plant can work wonders. Do you have a
   space that allows you to be separate from other people?
   This need not be a different room, but a space where
   you can't see anyone else and they can't see you unless
   you choose to be seen. Fayard & Weeks (2011) talk about
   the balance between proximity and privacy – being able
   to work solo and also access your colleagues easily. Is the
   sound level the quiet buzz that absorbs individual noises
   and acts as an acoustic screen? Do you need noise as a
   screen? Do you need white noise to cancel out colleagues'
   chat? Do you have a view to look out at? A picture to rest
   your eyes on? An internal line-of-sight that is calm and
   uncluttered, but not boring? Create a signal that you don't
   want to be disturbed. Make sure you have everything you
   need close to hand. Shelves, hangers, sticky notes, folders,
   files (paper and electronic).

3. *Prepare your personal cognitive space.* You are working
   for the sheer enjoyment of the quest, even (especially)
   when it becomes difficult. Find out about *flow* and be
   able to recognise it in yourself when it happens. Accept
   the challenge of pushing your understanding of the more
   difficult areas of your research (see also the *Hack your
   head* recipe).

4. *Prepare your social space.* You can train yourself and
   your colleagues to appreciate that there are some times
   when you (and they) need to work without interruption.
   This requires openness for you to be able to explain to
   others what you are thinking and feeling. It also requires
   trust for your colleagues (and you!) to know that you will
   get on with the work in hand and only interrupt yourself
   (and them) when there are real issues to be dealt with.
   Give yourself permission to say NO to colleagues – and to
   yourself – when you need to.

WARNINGS

Flow can become addictive (Csikszentmihalyi, 1975)!

#10

AUTHOR
Inger Mewburn

SERVE TO
PhD students

COST
Free

TIME

KEEP LOVING YOUR THESIS (EVEN WHEN IT HATES YOU)

Overcome writer's block through free writing

BACKGROUND

Maintaining love for your thesis topic can be exhausting, basically because a thesis is such a hard thing to love. A thesis slowly takes shape over a period of years and must be closely attended to for most of the time. Many cooks find this exhausting and impractical, yet for best results, it is wise to keep your eye on it at all times.

A thesis doesn't love you back. It demands a lot of energy and only gives you irregular rewards. Like any long-term relationship, it can be hard, at times, to remember the spark that got you interested in the first place. However, if you want to succeed, it is essential to try to keep the love alive.

One of the reasons we can become so estranged from our thesis is that the pressure to perform can spoil the enjoyment. This recipe shows you how to use 'free writing' to spend quality time with your ideas, without expectations. Free writing is advocated by many writing teachers as a way of overcoming writer's block, but it is used here to help you break your habitual, mechanistic relationship with your thesis.

INGREDIENTS

- A pen and piece of paper, or a computer – whichever you prefer

- 10 minutes of your time

METHOD

1. At the top of the page write 'My thesis will help me...'
2. Set a timer for three minutes.
3. Now do some free writing – write anything which comes to mind, regardless of whether it really makes sense or not. Go fast without stopping to think. Let your pen/fingers do the thinking work, without editing.
4. Stop and stretch. Take a deep breath.
5. Now spend no more than two minutes reading over what you have written, underlining or highlighting anything which seems interesting.
6. Write this interesting thing at the top of a fresh page and set the timer for three minutes. If you don't have anything interesting, try another prompt, like 'My thesis is important because...'
7. Do some more free writing for another three minutes then stop.
8. Read over this second output for a minute, underline or highlight any ideas which are good or worth pursuing further.

*My thesis
is important
because...*

COOK'S TIPS

It's best to do this exercise when you are out of the office. Try it while you are on the road: on public transport, in a waiting room, watching the kids play in the park. The different space will stimulate ideas.

WARNINGS

Don't expect anything to emerge in a particular session; it's the habit of taking time to think out loud about your research, without expectations, which is important.

#II

AUTHOR
Alison Williams

SERVE TO
Troubled PhD students

COST
Low

TIME

MY WORK IS NOT ME

Detach yourself from your work to
safeguard your confidence

BACKGROUND —

It is sometimes difficult for us to take criticism of our work. We are so bound up in it that the work somehow becomes us, and critique of the work feels like a personal attack. This is damaging in two main ways:

1. If I feel attacked when my work is critiqued, then my confidence is likely to go down. I feel that it is not just the work that is inadequate, it is me.
2. If I can't stand outside my work then it is more difficult to make changes and improvements.

This recipe is for people who come out of a meeting with a supervisor feeling completely devastated and stupid, and forgetting that they are in the top 1% of the world's thinkers. Its aim is to help you detach yourself from your work so that even if the work is going badly, your confidence and self-esteem are not irreparably damaged.

INGREDIENTS

- One piece of blank paper

- One glass with a little water in it

- One jug with lots of water in it

- One totally discouraged PhD student

- One puzzled but co-operative supervisor

METHOD

1. The PhD student writes their thesis title on the paper and puts it on the table between them and their supervisor.
2. The student then puts the glass on top of the paper.
3. Next, either the student or the supervisor says 'What is needed to fill the glass?' i.e. what is needed to improve the research work?
4. The student and supervisor answer in the form of 'We could fill the glass by...' for example:
   '....looking into the literature for X';
   '....adjusting the method we are using by doing X and Y';
   '....adding a further testing phase'.
5. At each suggestion, the person who made it pours a little water into the glass. The game is to see if the glass can be filled by the end of the supervision session. If it's full before the end of the meeting, then that's enough work to do on the research project until the next time.

COOK'S TIPS

If you have an allergic reaction to the idea because of a total sense-of-humour failure, here's what to do:

For the student: If you've got to the stage where anything will tip you into tears or bluster, get someone to tell you a couple of dreadful jokes before you go into your supervision session.

For the supervisor:
If you've got to the stage where anything will tip you into cynicism or bluster, get someone to tell you a couple of dreadful jokes before you go into the supervision session.

Swap jokes at the start of the session.

WARNINGS

If you have a supervisor who you suspect won't play, give them a copy of this recipe before the supervision session so that they have time to get used to the idea. Tell them that it is important to you that they play along without cynicism.

#12

AUTHOR
Judy Robertson

—

SERVE TO
Early career researchers

COST
Free

TIME

HOW TO LOVE SEVERAL PROJECTS AT ONCE

Learn to manage your time effectively by being selective

BACKGROUND —

Remember the days when you were safely cocooned with the one true love of your academic life? When all you had to worry about was being loyal to your own thesis?

Things get more complicated when you get an academic appointment. You find yourself conducting affairs with several alluring yet demanding projects at once. How can you manage your time in such a way that every project gets the attention it craves without exhausting yourself?

INGREDIENTS

- Integrity
- Assertiveness
- Realism
- The ability to plan

METHOD

1. *Adjust to your new situation*. The problem is that people who have just got academic appointments are ridiculously high achievers working under considerable pressure to pursue multiple conflicting goals (such as teaching, bringing in grant funding, and publishing). They're used to putting in 100% effort in everything they do, and producing work of very high quality. Unfortunately, the strategy of 'I will work my hardest, do my best and nothing will stop me' doesn't scale because of the pesky restriction of having only 24 hours in a day and a huge number of possible opportunities you could pursue. You simply can't be as committed to all projects as you were to your own PhD. By necessity, you must two-time your projects. Spread your love around.

2. *Turn down some good offers*. The secret is to choose which projects you can commit some time to, and turn down the rest. Learn to say 'No' to the right things. It helps if you decide in advance some specific research goals in the medium term. Tattoo them on your hand. Before deciding whether to take an opportunity, scrutinise your hand. If the opportunity doesn't help you further one of your goals, say 'No'. If I'm busy I sometimes turn down reviewing or conference-organising requests. Once you have a certain number of conference committee and journal reviewing items for your CV or résumé, you can stop taking them on so frequently. It's not particularly fun, and rarely directly furthers research goals. You will find that some senior colleagues will make it their business to give you jobs to do which will 'further your career'. Simply hide under your desk until they go away. Or ask them sincerely which of their other tasks you should drop to enable you to do this new one.

3. *Pick a time management strategy.* The world is full
   of books on managing your time. Pick one, skim it,
   and implement the advice which you think you can make
   work. Boyce (2000) and Allen (2002) are good choices to
   start with. Boyce recommends moderation in working,
   slowly advancing each project with small steps at a time.
   Allen recommends deciding on achieving next actions
   for every project and tracking whether they have been
   completed. Such strategies essentially ensure that you
   keep making progress on multiple projects even when the
   progress is slow. This can work reasonably well, but there
   are two problems with this in my experience. One problem
   is that if you end up trying to complete a project in very
   short time slots (the classic 30 minutes per day) you
   never really experience flow because you don't work on
   anything for long enough. Flow is one of the experiences
   which make academic work enjoyable, so it would be sad
   to miss out on it. The other problem is that it is inefficient.
   In computer science, if you have too many processes
   competing for resources, re-establishing context after
   switching processes consumes all the processor's time and
   no actual work gets done. This is known as thrashing and
   is best avoided. It is well-known in management circles
   that it takes up to 20 minutes after an interruption to get
   back to the level of effectiveness you were at before the
   interruption.
4. *Watch out for guilt.* Guilt is a clear sign that you are
   overdoing the philandering. When you find yourself using
   words like 'should' and 'ought' and 'must' then look at
   your hand, your list of priorities, again. It is likely that what
   is causing you guilt is a project you got lumbered with that
   isn't in line with your research goals. (A secondary emotion
   here is resentment – watch out for this one; it can be
   a real downer.)
5. *Be true to yourself.* Circumstances may force you
   to academically philander, but you can still retain your
   integrity. Be honest in admitting your affairs with other
   projects, so your colleagues know how much time you are
   likely to be able to commit. Don't take credit for others'
   work, even if you are pressed for time. Mastering step 2
   above is the key to achieving integrity. You cannot maintain
   a high quality of research if you are overcommitted.

WARNINGS

Take time management
strategies with a pinch of
salt. Don't get too caught
up with implementing your
time management regime.
Don't spend longer
enforcing it than you do
actually working!

RELATED RECIPES

See also *Hack your head,
Get into the flow* and *Keep
loving your thesis (even when
it hates you)*.

#13

AUTHOR

Derek Jones

—

SERVE TO

Yourself (no one else need know)

COST

Varies

TIME

IT'S OK TO HAVE A STATIONERY FETISH

Make your pens an extension of your thoughts

BACKGROUND

Admit it, you probably already do. It's OK, so do I. I have a favourite make of pen. I have a favourite notebook. I have a particularly favourite make of pencil.

There is an academic myth that, upon realising that his favourite Moleskine notebook was no longer being manufactured, a reasonably famous academic was so upset that he was no longer able to think (see Chatwin (n.d.) for a further example). Although this might or might not be true, we do develop emotional attachments to the tools we use – in many ways they become part of us, our thinking, or our processes. At their best, they become embodied, visceral artefacts – the deepest of ontological elements.

This may seem a gratuitous and frivolous recipe but there are some serious underlying ideas. We often underestimate just how much emotional and sensory attachment we make with the objects we use – a fact that designers make use of regularly. Steve Jobs famously said that one of the design goals of the look of Apple's new operating system (OSX) was that "... when you saw it, you wanted to lick it" (Jobs, 2000).

If you want to get philosophical about it, consider Heidegger "...the less we just stare at the hammer-Thing, and the more we seize hold of it and use it, the more primordial does our relationship to it become" (Heidegger, 1962, p. 98). Or if you prefer the embodied phenomenology of Merleau-Ponty: "The properties of the object and the intentions of the subject... are not only intermingled; they constitute a new whole" (Merleau-Ponty, 1962).

In design, the link between people and object/product is understood as an essential aspect of the value of design, for example Schultz, Kleine and Kernan (1989), Chapman (2005) and Spence and Gallace (2011). It is even argued to be central to genuinely sustainable design (Chapman, 2009). Whichever philosophy you prefer, our world around us is intimately connected to ourselves. Don't ignore the visceral.

INGREDIENTS

- Pens, pencils, paper,
  notebooks, notepads,
  paperclips, sketchbooks,
  etc

- The sense of touch

- A few quiet moments to
  yourself

METHOD

1. Have a look through your existing collection of pens.
   Set them out with your favourites at one end and the least
   favourite at the other. Can you see any patterns emerging?
   Do you prefer heavy or light pens? Thick or thin tipped?
   Most likely, your favourites will be there for other reasons.

2. Find a pen that you really like writing with – one that feels
   like an extension of your thoughts (not just of your hand).
   The chances are that you do more with this pen than you
   realise – make this your special pen and only use it for
   particular tasks. Similarly, assign tasks to your other pens.
   That horrible sales-rep pen? Do your expenses signing with
   that. Imagine the contempt you feel for the system and
   the pen flow through your hand/pen as you sign...

3. Treat yourself to a wander around a stationery shop.
   Don't do this online – it's important that you see the
   objects, feel the thickness of the paper, assess the weight
   of the pen in your hand, and smell the notebook.

4. Now work your way around other favourite objects –
   try to work out which of these are special and why
   (there will be a reason, and it might be a visceral one).

5. Celebrate these objects by using them in particular ways
   (remember your lucky pen in exams?). Keep these objects
   for special occasions. Do you have a markup pen?
   Take your favourite notebook for a walk. Remember
   that feeling of the first mark in a new notebook?

COOK'S TIPS

Make this a treat, not a
gluttonous feast. Try to
limit your choices to just
one or two favourite items,
for example, a favourite
notebook and pen or pencil.

WARNINGS

Don't ever touch my pens.

RELATED RECIPES

This goes really well with
Think with your hands –
doodling is thinking.
Doodling with your
favourite pen is luxurious
intellectualism.

#14

AUTHOR

Anitra Nottingham

SERVE TO

Anyone interested in improving research spaces

COST

Low

TIME

JUST DESCRIBE

'Say what you see' to understand a place

BACKGROUND —

If you want to improve the place where you conduct your research, it pays to fully understand and document the current setting. This recipe works on the idea that the act of *writing* is a 'lab tool' of qualitative social research, and is a practice capable of generating data (Law, 2004), in the same way that a microscope produces data by enabling us to observe realities invisible to the naked eye. Here writing generates a narrative-style description of the field which is then used as data and subjected to analysis.

This dish is the fortuitous result of mixing a lack of human participants, a deadline, and a dash of panic. It springs from theories of the socio-material, in particular *actor-network theory* (ANT). It is based on the idea that objects can be made to 'speak' – to tell us something of what they may contribute to the social – if we describe them well enough (Latour, 2005).

INGREDIENTS

- Research space
  (physical or virtual)

- One willing volunteer
  to walk around with a
  recording device in any
  remote physical spaces
  the researcher cannot
  visit in person

- Internet access to any
  virtual spaces, and for
  sharing data if needed

- Devices to capture
  photographic and
  video documentary data,
  including smartphones,
  cameras and screen
  recording software

- Something to write on
  and with

METHOD

1. To make this method work you must ditch any ideas that
    the humans you see in the space are the most important
    component of the social. You must become open to all
    the material things you see, no matter how mundane and
    seemingly unimportant. For example, the first time this
    recipe was used, writing about the means by which notices
    were taped to a wall over some office waste bins or
    trashcans revealed important insights into the people who
    worked in the space. Just because you are open to the
    non-human things in the field doesn't mean that humans
    shouldn't be described. What are they doing? What are
    they saying? What messages do you read in their face or
    body posture?

2. Firstly gather your documentary evidence:
    a. If a space is virtual, take screen snapshots and/or
        use screen-based video capture to record yourself
        using the site(s).
    b. Walk around any physical spaces and record as
        you walk. Hold the camera at eye level. Try not
        to interfere with anyone in the space as you do
        so. Record the human and the non-human things
        equally. Take your time so that you get as much
        information as possible.

3. Watch the recordings over and over and study any screen
    snapshots. Get your writing tool and start writing about
    each space in turn. Start by describing where you are and
    how you arrived there.

4. It helps to write in the form the recordings take, which is
    as a *walk around*. As you 'walk around' with your writing
    describe everything that you see and whatever activity
    occurs in the space in the order you observe it.

5. 'Just describe' (Latour, 2005) means just that. Try not
    to decide what is important or significant, try not to
    conduct analysis; just do your best to describe everything
    you see and hear. You may find it surprisingly difficult.
    This is because writing a good description is hard work
    and can take a lot of time. You may end up with a LOT of
    data (in the form of words), which you may not end up
    using once the analysis is complete. For instance: look
    at colours, what's on the walls, the materials used, the
    quality of the light, how many people are around, what
    they are doing, and so on. If you can smell, hear, or touch
    anything, describe that too. If anything moves, describe
    how it moves. Don't leave out your reaction to the space,
    describe how it makes you feel.

6. Your writing style should be the best you can manage. Write in full sentences and structure the narrative so that it's easy and engaging to read. A reader should be able to picture the space easily in their mind's eye.

7. Once you have your written descriptions, which might be very long, subject them to analysis depending on what you are seeking to study about a space.

8. It helps to gather literature on whatever it is you wish to study, and to use this to help you analyse how the space might be working.

WARNINGS

This recipe is not for the faint-hearted or those who are unprepared to defend their study methods. Writing as a means of generating data may be discounted by others as 'non-empirical' as it seems to come only from the researcher's viewpoint.

It must be acknowledged that those researchers who privilege the human in their research may initially find this a disconcerting and strange combination. However, those with an open-minded and adventurous approach to research practices will be well rewarded.

#15

AUTHORS

Richard Coyne
Jenny Roe
Peter Aspinall
Panos Mavros

—

SERVE TO

Weary researchers

COST

Low

TIME

RELIEVING ATTENTION FATIGUE

Recharge your mental batteries productively

BACKGROUND —

To concentrate on a task you need to block out distractions. In fact that's what it means to concentrate – to inhibit other instinctual inclinations. Once that blocking function gets worn down by fatigue you are more likely to act on impulse, to run away if something challenges you too much, to take unnecessary risks, to become irritable, and to get distracted from your task by things that are more engaging but less challenging, such as video games, television programmes, or random images on the Internet. These are symptoms of *attention fatigue*.

Attention fatigue is useful. If you kept on with challenging tasks, no matter how important, without a break, then you would be less likely to notice what's going on around you. You'd be like the dysfunctional inventor, scientist, writer or student cramming for an exam who has to be dragged from the laboratory or study desk in order to wash, eat and socialise.

How can you restore your ability to concentrate on the important task at hand? Sleep is one approach, but attention fatigue can disrupt it and can lead to irregular sleep patterns and sleepless nights. The solution seems to reside in taking a rest from direct concentration and instead redirecting one's concentration to things that don't require as much effort, i.e. things we find 'naturally fascinating' that command our attention effortlessly.

There are many candidates for recuperative attention, depending on your inclinations: reading a novel with a suspense element, checking up on whether an email or post has arrived, buying lottery tickets and following the results. Most people are fascinated by animals, so watching YouTube cat videos might do it, or even playing with a real pet.

Most people are drawn to extremes in physical appearance and circumstances. So watching car racing, cartoons and soaps, reading gossip columns, and experiencing unusual architecture may fit the bill. Whether through biological, social or cultural attunement these are sources of fascination for many. They easily arrest and hold our concentration, and offer some restorative benefits, though exaggeration in its own right can have other disturbing effects, a bit like the effects of watching a horror film or movie.

But there's another kind of fascination that maintains our ability to concentrate, willingly, with little effort, and more effectively. This is *soft fascination*, as proposed by the psychologists Rachel and Stephen Kaplan (Kaplan and Kaplan, 1989; Kaplan, 1995). Soft fascination is best for recuperation as it provides opportunities for reflection, is non-taxing, and deals less with exaggeration and its attendant disturbances.

INGREDIENTS

- A tired mind

- An outdoor space

- Another world (fictional or otherwise) to retreat to

- Willingness to leave your smartphone behind

METHOD

1. *Seek out the natural environment.* The natural environment – the outdoors, with plants, sweeping vistas, water, and wildlife, or even just a vegetable garden or a row of indoor plants – is ideal for soft fascination. Kaplan says, "Nature is certainly well-endowed with fascinating objects, as well as offering many processes that people find engrossing" (Kaplan, 1995, p. 174). There are clouds, sunsets, leaves rustling in the breeze, and attending to these patterns doesn't take much effort. We conducted a study using mobile electroencephalography (EEG) as a method of recording and analysing the emotional experience of people walking in three types of urban environment including parkland (Mavros et al., 2012; Aspinall et al., 2013). Our analysis of the data shows evidence of lower frustration, engagement and arousal, and higher meditation when moving into the green space zone, and higher engagement when moving out of it. We human beings have an instinctual inclination towards outdoor activities – as predators, nomads, domesticators, observers, and survivors. Most of us relate well to the countryside. However, the restorative environment should be compatible and meaningful to *you*, so adapt this as you see fit.

2. *Get away from it all.* Spend time in a different environment to the one you are working in. This helps rest your concentration. It's obviously good to get away to the countryside if you can, but Kaplan (1995) suggests that this restorative capability can be accomplished by experiencing an old environment in a new and different way, or even looking physically in a different direction from time to time. Being away involves a conceptual shift. Think of this as entering into an alien environment, or seeing the familiar as alien in some way, a bit like being a tourist.

3. *Find a whole other world.* The restorative environment needs to provide a 'whole other world'. Kaplan says, "It must provide enough to see, experience, and think about so that it takes up a substantial portion of the available room in one's head" (p. 173). Places that evoke memories, stories and histories, including natural environments, provide this. So looking at images at random on the Internet would probably not fit the bill. There's no structure, nothing to be probed in depth as offered up by the natural world.

4. *Consider digital recuperation carefully.* Does the ubiquity of digital media help or hinder this aspect of restorative outdoor environments? Some people are certainly suspicious of smartphones and other digital technologies, and think they provide a barrier between us and the restorative benefits of the outdoors. According to a book on nature and health (Selhub and Logan, 2012), "instead of stroking the keyboard or rubbing the belly of your smartphone screen, you – and the world – will be better served by petting your dog" (p. 138), and "strolling through a park while engaging with a smartphone screen may cause a vitamin G deficiency" (p. 216) where vitamin G is vitamin B2 or the 'green' vitamin. Larry Rosen presents a similar view: "If you are going to use nature as a restorative cure for technologically-induced brain overload, it is best to remove all technology from the scene" (Rosen, 2012, p. 206).

"

Soft fascination is best for recuperation... Seek out the natural environment

"

NOTE

This recipe incorporates some material from www.richardcoyne.com /2013/04/06/ soft-fascination which acknowledges Kaplan (1995).

RELATED RECIPES

See also *Defocus your mind, Off-grid creativity* and (for contrast) *Smart working with a smartphone.*

#16

Judy Robertson

Researchers in a
noisy environment

Low

WHAT TO LISTEN TO WHILE YOU WORK

What you hear affects what you think

BACKGROUND

Background noise can be very distracting, driving even the most placid researcher to rage. Some types of background noise are worse than others and should be avoided. This recipe gives some suggestions about what to avoid based on meta-analytic studies of the effect of audio on cognitive task performance (Kämpfe, Sedlmeier & Renkewitz, 2010; Szalma & Hancock, 2011).

Bear in mind the 'creative footprint' (Williams, 2013). Different people have their own preferences here and it is vital to understand individual differences (Toplyn & Maguire, 1991). In fact, the original version of this recipe was based on the suggestion of a researcher who liked to use *Judge Judy* on the television to help her to block out distractions!

Also remember that once you enter the flow state it doesn't matter what you're listening to, as you won't be aware of it. Have you ever returned from a period of intense concentration to discover that your playlist of favourite songs ended hours earlier without you hearing any of them? This recipe is intended to help you to ignore distracting noises long enough for you to experience flow.

INGREDIENTS

- Annoying background noise

- Earphones and portable music player

- Laptop and Wi-Fi so that you can work elsewhere

METHOD

1. Before you start, *consider the task you are engaged in*. Most research indicates that noise reduces creative thinking for many people but some are able to deal with moderate noise very effectively. Similarly, it is not always the effect of sound on the efficiency of output that matters – if it is motivating you and helping you to keep going then that is important too. Follow the steps below to become more aware of how sound affects you.

2. *First identify the source of the background noise to estimate how much it is likely to distract you.* The impact of noise depends on the task you are trying to carry out, as well as the type, volume and duration of the noise, and whether it is intermittent or constant. Even moderately loud noises cause people to perform worse on cognitive tasks; the accuracy of the work tends to be affected rather than the time it takes to complete the task. Intermittent noise is more debilitating than constant noise, as it is harder to habituate to it. Speech is more disruptive than non-speech, a mix of speech and non-speech sound, or music (Szalma & Hancock, 2011). This is because processing the speech requires cognitive resources and your brain will persist in trying to process it whether you are interested in your neighbours' discussion of the price of milk or not.

3. If you're somewhere with moderately loud, intermittent speech sound, and you are doing a demanding task, *go somewhere else quieter.* Give your brain a chance! Don't tire it out trying to process irrelevant information. Working on the train or in a café puts you at the mercy of other people's background chatter so it is a good idea not to plan difficult work for these venues. Some people claim to be able to work in such environments. However, there is a good chance that they are fooling themselves; people are not very good at identifying when their performance is impaired, because the brain doesn't have spare capacity for metacognition if it is labouring under a high cognitive load (see, for example, Strayer, Drews & Johnston (2003) for evidence of this in experiments relating to mobile phone usage while driving).

4. If you're stuck in a noisy environment, try to *block out the distracting background noise with music* in your headphones. Music has been shown to disturb reading and has a slight negative impact on memory (Kämpfe, Sedlmeier & Renkewitz, 2010), but this may be preferable to other people's conversations. Also, it can have positive emotional effects which might soothe your rage, so experiment with different genres of music (and even ambient soundtracks). There were no clear effects for volume in the analysis by Kämpfe, Sedlmeier & Renkewitz, but there was an indication that tempo can impact the speed of your behaviour while listening to music. This is an open research area, so surprisingly little is known about it; development of more robust methodology and theory is required.

COOK'S TIPS

Remember, this depends on your creative footprint, the type of task you are performing and the type of sound. Work out what works for you and remember that you could be lying to yourself too!

WARNING

It's not just speech which has a negative impact on cognitive performance. Multitasking does too (Ophir, Nass and Wagner, 2009), so stop looking at Facebook while reading this recipe!

RELATED RECIPES

See *Working in a shared environment.*

#17

AUTHOR

Debbie Maxwell

SERVE TO

Researchers who wish to improve their working environment

COST

Low

TIME

ROLL THE DICE

Encourage serendipity by taking a fresh look at your research environment

BACKGROUND

All too often we become habituated to our environments and practices. Noticing, embracing, and introducing ambiguity into everyday working life can enable fresh observations, receptivity to new ideas, and ultimately, serendipity.

INGREDIENTS

- **Willingness to try new ideas**

- **Time to observe**

- **Cardboard and scissors**

- **Group of fellow researchers (optional)**

METHOD

1. Identify your key current research tools and practices. These might be your laptop, favourite software package (e.g. iA Writer), your office space, a favourite cafe.

2. Identify six of your research and working patterns and likes/dislikes: for example, working on the train, keeping a clear desk, where you go for lunch, whether you communicate with co-located colleagues face-to-face or by email.

3. Create a patterns dice. Make a blank cardboard cube (if you have forgotten how, see www.mathsisfun.com/cube.html). Write one of your research patterns from the previous step on each face. If you have lots of patterns, make more than one dice.

4. Introduce chaos by rolling the dice once a day to single out an existing pattern of behaviour. Critically reflect on how you could alter this behaviour today. For example, instead of working on the train journey, use it to observe how other passengers interact, or listen to a documentary podcast. Alternatively, go somewhere different for lunch and make a point of talking to someone new there.

5. Capture your new working practice and generate a 'pool of reflections' for future use, using the keywords below.
    a. Serendipity
    b. Delight
    c. Open-mindedness
    d. Flow
    e. Culture
    f. Digital spaces
    g. Designing for reflection
    h. Ambiguity
    Rate each activity and its relative success in allowing you to think and make connections in new ways against the keywords: what degree of serendipity, delight, open-mindedness etc did this new practice engender?

6. After a week or so, use your notes from step 5 to decide on which changes to your working habits you might like to keep.

#18

AUTHORS

Alison Williams
Judy Robertson

SERVE TO

Early career researchers, or others working in an open-plan office

COST

Free

TIME

WORKING IN A SHARED ENVIRONMENT

Establish office etiquette early

BACKGROUND

This recipe looks at what to do when one person in a shared workspace needs silence, and others want to talk. As one interviewee for this book said: "The difficulty is ... maintaining the context when you are doing different things. There are times when I don't want to be distracted. And especially when you have people who are working on different things. Especially, when you have two people who are talking about project A when you are trying to work on project B which is totally different and you are not getting anything from their conversation. It can be distracting."

Different labs have different ways of dealing with this. A computer science lab in Heriot-Watt University has a sign on the door 'No chatting in the lab'. But some researchers find that unwelcoming. "[It's] upsetting, I don't like it. I have some sympathy with it. But this idea of no chatting at all – I wouldn't like that".

A postgrad in DiLab, Georgia Tech, has a simple sign on his desk made from an upturned coffee beaker and three sticky notes on it in a triangle:

- AVAILABLE

- NOT AVAILABLE

- AVAILABLE FOR
  IMPORTANT INTERACTIONS

The beaker sits on his desk and signals to his colleagues what he needs.

The researcher interviewed above says: "I like to be able to talk to my colleagues in the office (as long as it isn't too much). There is something about having the right number of people in the office [...] working on very related projects. So there were two or three of us at a time. So we weren't distracting anyone else. And it didn't feel bad to say: 'Look, could you guys go somewhere else because I need to concentrate' when you are working with people that you do have a working relationship with."

BITE
Working solo

INGREDIENTS

- One researcher
  in a shared office

Desk, computer and screen

- Pin board, pins and
  reusable adhesive

- Good earphones
  or headphones

- Good working relationship
  with colleagues

METHOD

1. Personalise your desk and assert your territory: introduce inspiring and quirky images and words; change these at least every week. Reach agreement with your office mates about working habits: invent some simple signals, like the DiLab postgrad did, to communicate with your colleagues. For example, a stuffed panda could mean:
   a. 'Please don't interrupt' (e.g. panda turned with back to the room, you put your earphones on);
   b. 'Happy to chat' (e.g. panda sits on computer, you turn your chair round);
   c. 'Stuck – have you any ideas?' (e.g. panda holds large question mark).
2. Work out and agree telephone etiquette such as taking the call in the corridor or having agreed quiet times.
3. Work out and agree conversation etiquette so you can feel fine about asking colleagues to chat elsewhere because you need to concentrate.
4. Hold regular lab/office process meetings where these issues are raised.

COOK'S TIPS

Keep it light and funny whenever you can.

WARNINGS

Tackle irritations early. Imagine a line where your reaction to something is mild irritation at one end, and ballistic at the other. Get into the habit of speaking out at the mild irritation end while you can say things without emotion, and before you go ballistic.

RELATED RECIPES

Try *What to listen to while you work* for further personalisation.

#19

AUTHOR

Derek Jones

SERVE TO

Researchers

COST

Free

TIME

DIGITAL SCHOLARSHIP – START HERE

Dip your toe in digital scholarship

BACKGROUND

Technology has changed a number of aspects of the academic process and workflow and in many ways this has always been so. Reacting sceptically to new ways of working, especially where technology is concerned, is perfectly normal and often stems from the difference between the promise of new technology and the reality (Robey & Azevedo, 1994).

But the chances are that you are already a digital scholar (Weller, 2011a). So why not think about it in other ways – how can this work to your advantage? What can you make of this? How can it work for you? The trick is to realise that digital scholarship is just normal scholarship using different tools.

Digital scholarship can have an impact on all aspects of scholarly activity and this recipe cannot hope to cover everything. The 'pedagogy of abundance' is an important concept to be aware of (Weller, 2011b). So think of this as a recipe for tapas – a way of giving things a try.

INGREDIENTS

- Computer, tablet or
  smartphone

- Access to the internet

- A variety of online tools of
  your choosing

METHOD

1. *Your personal workflow.* As mentioned, you are probably
    already a digital scholar in that you are most likely using
    digital tools. But could you be using them better? What
    else could you get out of them? Have a look at *Tidy Your
    Desktop* for a few tips on this and make good use of
    Unsworth's list of 'scholarship primitives': discovering,
    annotating, comparing, referring, sampling, illlustrating,
    and representing (Unsworth, 2000). For each of these,
    there are a number of digital alternatives you could try.

2. *Your personal knowledge footprint.* Did you know that
    this is a valuable resource, that your notes, searches,
    bibliographies and other research artefacts are incredibly
    useful academic artefacts in their own right? Academics
    have shared bibliographies as knowledge assets for centuries
    but new technology allows this in other ways. Try sharing
    your references with others – most bibliography managers
    support this (e.g. RefWorks, Mendeley, and Zotero).

3. *Blogging.* If you don't blog, why not? This question
    is *not* asked as a challenge – only to get you to consider
    it. Blogging can be used in a variety of ways, ranging
    from note taking and idea formation, right through to
    'proper' academic publishing. It might not be for you
    but have a think about what else *you* could use it for
    (Heap & Minocha, 2012).

4. *Grow your social network.* Weller (2011a) identified his
    social network as one critical difference in his academic
    writing process. By connecting with others you can create
    a significant scholarly resource that can be used in many
    ways. But this takes time to develop and you cannot simply
    rely on it happening by itself.

5. *Start with your physical research network.* Are your
    academic contacts already making use of particular social
    media channels? By starting with an existing network you
    can quickly grow your own, so find out what networks exist
    in your discipline.

6. *Academic social networks.* There are a number of
    specific academic social networks, such as Academia.edu,
    Mendeley, and Zotero. These can lack the momentum of
    mainstream social networks but they can also fulfil a useful
    function in your discovery or representation of
    work stages.

7.   *Social networks.* It's not for everyone but you don't have to be a broadcaster if you don't want to – there are still a number of very useful sources you can follow in all main social media streams. Again, ask around and try things – the chances are that many of your colleagues will have strong preferences for different social media. As a starter for ten, follow your institution, colleagues or national education resources. Or start with 101 Twitter Accounts every PhD should follow (Online PhD Program, 2013).

8.   *Others.* Remember, YouTube, Flickr, SlideShare, Prezi and most online resources like these are also social media. Start with one that you are familiar with (such as SlideShare) and see what connections you can make.

9.   *Don't underestimate the humble mailing list.* It's still going strong! OK, some are better than others, but there are a few good ones out there. Have a look at JISCMail (www.jiscmail.ac.uk) as a starting point.

10. For the researcher wanting to take this further, consider Weller's borrowed formula: 'Fast, cheap and out of control'. Seek out these technologies and approach them with the frame of mind discussed in the recipe *'How might we …' space*. Find a few key ed-tech people to follow – they tend to be the first to find new technologies. Try things, find out what they can do and then reflect on and evaluate the results. This should be an embodied process – forget the 'tools versus purpose' debate and realise that both go hand in hand.

NOTES ON INGREDIENTS

Start with Weller (2011a) and if you want to take your digital scholarship further, try Goodfellow & Lea (2013)

.COOK'S TIPS

If you're a post-grad doing the PhD thing, give #phdchat a go on twitter. You are not alone.

WARNINGS

There are social norms in social media too – make sure you are aware of these and don't be afraid to ask.

OTHER FLAVOURS

It's definitely a good idea to start with *Tidy your desktop*.

CREATING SENSORY-SENSITIVE SPACES

Identifying key parameters for research environment design

AUTHORS

Alison Williams
Peter Barrett

INTRODUCTION

It is acknowledged that the sensory elements of physical space, including factors such as light and colour, air quality and temperature, impact upon people's performance in the workplace (Brill, Margulis & Konar, 1984; McCoy, 2000; Williams, 2013) and pupil learning in schools (Heschong Mahone Group, 1999; Jindal-Snape et al., 2013). However, there is little research on the impact that these sensory elements may have on performance and learning in research environments. Researchers in the emerging field of interaction between workforce and workplace agree that "there is limited knowledge on how the physical space actually enhances creativity" (Kristensen, 2004, p. 89) and that "the spatial dimension has been largely neglected in the literature when focusing on creativity or innovation" (Haner, 2005, p. 291) despite the fact that the link has been perceived for some time (McCoy & Evans, 2002).

As a contribution to addressing this issue we draw upon the recipes in this book, analysing them through a three-part model of design principles based on an interpretation of broad neuroscience structures (Rolls, 2007). The model is derived in principle in Barrett & Barrett (2010). It has to date been successfully tested in primary schools (Barrett et al., 2013) and proposed as potentially informing the design of secondary schools, offices and care facilities for older people (Barrett et al., 2013).

In the first part of this paper we set out the three-part model, its derivation, and its related matrix of design principles/practical options (Barrett & Zhang, 2009; Barrett & Barrett, 2010); in the second part we analyse selected field book recipes using the design principles/ practical options matrix, and present our findings. Finally, we suggest what the learning might be for the design of new research facilities, the improvement of existing ones, and how individual researchers and research teams might 'hack' suboptimal research spaces when no official improvements are forthcoming.

THE THREE-PART MODEL OF DESIGN PRINCIPLES, AND ITS DERIVATION

Although we experience physical space through our senses, we make sense of it in a holistic way in our brain. Barrett's (2010) model of key sensory design principles (Fig. 1) is built upon Rolls (2007) neuroscience work on "primary and secondary reinforcers" that ultimately motivate human survival behaviours. Rolls argues that human needs such as clean air, an even temperature, light, shelter, food hoards, appropriate levels of stimulation/response and an absence of natural dangers govern human behaviours and emotions. Raw sensory data about our external world is processed by the brain's orbitofrontal cortex where the value of environmental stimuli is assessed. Rolls describes "built-in" primary reinforcers which form the basis against which the external data is initially interpreted. This leads to learning through pattern-matching (Rolls, 2007, p. 148), where alternative strings of neuronal associations are built up and progressively and continually updated. These learned responses become "secondary reinforcers" (2007, pp. 62-67) as the situational elements are linked to the primary reinforcers. For example, the taste of food is a primary reinforcer, while the sight of food is a linked secondary reinforcer. Owing to the overwhelming volume of sense data we experience, Rolls stresses that an individual's response to a space is strongly implicit/emotional. That is, we react to spaces often without realising what is happening.

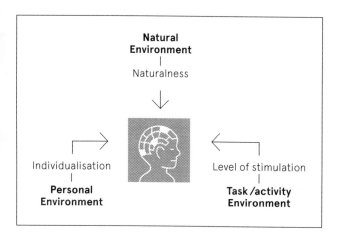

Figure 1:
Key sensory design principles

Extrapolating from the broad features of this neuroscientific base, three themes of the physical environment emerge (Fig. 1) which inform a holistic approach to good design, and can have "profound impacts on human functioning" (Barrett, 2010, p. 187). These are, firstly, that as our primary reinforcers have evolved through the "person-in-nature" there is a strong human response to the positive dimensions of *naturalness*. For example, recipe #15 *Relieving attention fatigue* describes a study in which mobile electroencephalography (EEG) recorded and analysed people's emotional experiences while walking in three types of urban environment including parkland (Aspinall et al., 2013; Mavros et al., 2012). The data analysis showed that when moving into the green area there was evidence of lower frustration, engagement and arousal, and of higher meditation states; higher engagement was noted when moving out of the parkland. Secondly, the brain functioning described by Rolls (2007) underlines how people use pattern-matching to make links. Each complex set of secondary reinforcer patterns is unique to each individual, given that each person will respond differently to their environment depending on their previous experiences in that and other environments (Franck, 1984). Taken in conjunction with memory's situated nature, a highly individual response to spaces, supported by personal-value profiles, results in the second important theme, that of *individualisation*. Finally there is a recurrent theme of appropriate *levels of stimulation* for given situations.

It seems fair to suggest that naturalness is generally required for positive human functioning. In addition, it would seem intuitively obvious that spaces designed to support creativity and innovation should be individual and stimulating. In this context however, the literature on innovation indicates that, for effectiveness in practice, cycles of divergent *and* convergent behaviour are needed (Osborn, 1953; Cougar, 1994). This is shown in the innovation model (Fig. 2) which is based on Van de Ven et al. (1999).

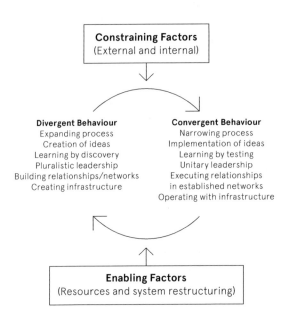

Figure 2:
Innovation Journey (based on Van de Ven et al., 1999)

This is not a linear model, but suggests that these cycles repeat at various stages, and that the ability to switch gears is intrinsic to successful innovation. In simple terms, the divergent phase would seem to call for an individualised/stimulating environment, but the convergent phase for a more calming and deliberate context. Ideally spaces for innovation should support both modes of working, and moreover, switching of behaviour as the creative work progresses should be enabled by cues both in the built environment and the affordances provided (Gibson, 1977).

The model given in Fig. 1, therefore, takes the three elements and relates them to different aspects of the environment: natural, personal and task/activity. The scope of the model is driven by the concept of a person in a space, experiencing sense data and computing (pattern-matching and creating) a holistic response. As such it goes far beyond the normal, measurable internal environment quality aspects of heat, light, sound and air quality to become a holistic/comprehensive analytical framework.

DESIGN PRINCIPLES AND PRACTICAL OPTIONS: BUILDING THE MATRIX

The model has been tested extensively (Barrett & Barrett, 2010) and used as the basis for identifying the impact of primary school design upon pupils' learning (Barrett et al., 2013). To operationalise the concepts, the three themes informed the building of an analysis matrix (Fig. 3). This was done through an initial iterative exercise which linked the sense dimensions of naturalness, individualisation and level of stimulation (along the top axis of Fig. 3) to practical design alternatives (down the side axis). This was driven by placing evidenced propositions regarding sense impacts from the literature in the matrix cells and collapsing the subcategories making up the axes until all major aspects had a home, but no columns or rows were completely empty. The cell numbers in Fig. 3 relate to section headings in Barrett and Zhang's (2009) study, for example 3.1.1 refers to the section on light, 3.3.2 to the section on colour and so on.

		Practical options							
		Plan & envelope					Spaces		
		Location	Orientation	Layout	Appearance	Windows	Rooms	Circulation	Outdoors
Level of stimulation	Texture								3.3.3
	Colour				3.3.1		3.3.2	3.3.2	
	Complexity				3.3.1				
Individualisation	Connection	3.2.3						3.2.3	
	Flexibility						3.2.2		
	Choice				3.2.1		3.2.1		
Naturalness	Air quality		3.1.4	3.1.4		3.1.4			
	Temperature		3.1.3	3.1.3		3.1.3			
	Sound	3.1.2		3.1.2			3.1.2		
	Light	3.1.1	3.1.1			3.1.1			

Figure 3:
Design principles against practical options for primary schools (Barrett & Zhang, 2009)

Using this framework, a study of 34 primary schools successfully isolated a powerful impact of spaces on the learning rates of the 751 pupils involved. In this work, the built environment aspects have been shown to account for up to 25% of the variability in the pupil learning rates observed (Barrett et al., 2013).

In the second part of this paper we now use the design principles/practical options matrix as a basis for analysing and interrogating the field book recipes.

RECIPE ANALYSIS THROUGH THE DESIGN PRINCIPLES/ PRACTICAL OPTIONS MATRIX

There are 62 recipes in the SPIRES field book. We have analysed those recipes that directly or indirectly reference the physical environment: 7 of the 19 recipes in Section 1: *Working Solo*, 9 of the 22 recipes in Section 2: *Working in a Group*, and 18 of the 21 recipes in Section 3: *Working Environment*. The remaining 28 recipes make no mention of the physical environment so do not, therefore, form part of this analysis.

Table 1 sets out the high-level meaning ascribed to each cell from the research environment recipes, some holding direct references from the recipes and others indirect. It is immediately noticeable that the three *individualisation* columns have the highest number of direct references; we will return to this shortly. In the four *naturalness* columns, light, sound, temperature and air quality get only passing mentions in the recipes. Apart from windows where views and natural light are referenced, and location, where good light is indicated, the other 30 of its 32 cells are either empty or with an indirect mention only. In the three *level of stimulation* columns, 18 of the 24 cells are either empty or contain indirect mention only. The complexity column is referenced predominantly as affordances (Gibson, 1977) that give researchers the possibility of making connections with other people, with information and with ideas (Williams, 2013). Affordances in the recipes range from the small (plenty of paper and pencils in #6 *Thinking with your hands*) to the large (rail carriage or banquette seating in #32 *Serendipity on the back of a napkin*) or the middling (large whiteboards in #36 *Visualising the problem*).

			Practical options							
			Plan & envelope					Spaces		
			Location	Orientation	Layout	Appearance	Windows	Rooms	Circulation	Outdoors
Level of stimulation		Texture				Rich environment		Rich environment	Rich environment	Indirect
		Colour				Indirect		Indirect	Indirect	Indirect
		Complexity	Inherent complexity and interest		Stimulating layout	Affordances connecting people, ideas, info	Indirect	Affordances connecting people, ideas, info	Easy connection between spaces	Good connection between outdoor spaces
Individualisation		Connection	Ability to move easily between spaces		Supports ease of connection between people and between information etc	Isovists that encourage connection	Connecting to outside	People can connect with others, with ideas and info	Connection between people and between information etc	Connection between people and between information etc
		Flexibility	Location is flexible – can be altered		Supports furniture etc being moved around	People can make changes in the rooms' appearance		Can make changes to the rooms	Can make changes in the circulation areas	Can alter the outdoor spaces
		Choice	People can choose where they work		People can choose how the space is laid out	People can choose what appearance they like	People can choose to be close to a window	People can choose the rooms they work in	People can choose to use the circulation spaces	People can choose to go outside
Naturalness		Air quality				Indirect				Indirect
		Temperature				Indirect				Indirect
		Sound	Indirect		Indirect	Indirect		Indirect		
		Light	Good light exists	Indirect	Indirect	Indirect	Views		Indirect	Indirect

Design principals / Design elements

Table 1:
Direct and indirect references from the recipes analysed cell by cell

Colour is referenced indirectly, and texture appears as part of a rich environment described by Franz & Wiener (2008, pp. 577-578) as "*complexity* (implicating diversity, entropy, richness) and *order* (comprising legibility, clarity, coherence)".

The cells of *individualisation*, however, are almost completely filled; only four of its twenty-four cells have no direct or indirect meaning ascribed to them in the recipe analysis. These four are the three *orientation* cells and one *windows* cell. Neither category is something over which a researcher has direct control.

Table 2 shows which recipes populate the cells of the two axes: the x-axis of *design principles/design elements* and the y-axis of *practical options*.

			Practical options							
			Plan & envelope					Spaces		
			Location	Orientation	Layout	Appearance	Windows	Rooms	Circulation	Outdoors
Design principals / Design elements	Level of stimulation	Texture				49, 61		33, 57, 59, 61	32, 34	15
		Colour				36, 49		40, 52, 56, 59	32, 59	15
		Complexity	37, 47		52	7, 9, 36, 49, 61	9	33, 37, 40, 44, 57, 59, 61	32, 58	15, 29, 47
	Individualisation	Connection	4, 36, 61		29, 32, 33, 58, 61	32	9	25, 32, 41, 59, 61,	32, 34, 58,	15, 62
		Flexibility	17, 33, 40, 57, 58, 61		25, 33, 40, 50, 51, 61	17, 18, 25, 33, 40, 51, 56, 57, 61	36, 51	17, 33, 40, 41, 50, 56, 57, 59, 61,	34, 61	15, 62
		Choice	1, 3, 4, 17, 33, 43, 53, 57, 61, 62,		32, 33, 40, 50, 52, 51, 61	18, 36, 32, 33, 40, 50, 51, 52, 53, 57, 61	60	3, 4, 30, 32, 33, 40, 53, 58, 57, 61,	34, 32	4, 15, 52, 62,
	Naturalness	Air quality				56				15
		Temperature				56				62
		Sound	16		32	49		9, 16		
		Light	54	34	49, 60	49, 54, 60	9, 34, 49, 53, 56, 60		49, 53	62

Table 2:
Recipes in each cell by their index number

The attribution of a recipe to a particular cell depends on whether the cell's high-level meaning is directly or indirectly met by the recipe content. For example, recipe #53 *Bus as a research environment* appears in the two cells *light-windows* and *light-circulation* because it indirectly references views and travelling. It also appears in the *choice-location* cell and in the *choice-rooms* cell because it directly references the writer's choice of where she will undertake a research activity: "I have a half-hour journey to and from work and I can read papers on the bus – the bus as a research space".

Recipe #40 *Creative spaces for interdisciplinary research* appears in nine cells: *choice-layout, choice-appearance, choice-rooms, flexibility-location, flexibility-layout, flexibility-appearance, flexibility-rooms, complexity-rooms,* and *colour-rooms*. The author talks about his "ideal spaces for creative investigation, research, and learning" needing "standard university classroom, traditional furnishings removed". Instead he recommends the researcher to "remove all traditional furnishings from the classroom and replace with sturdy, lightweight, durable tables and chairs that can be moved out of the way when necessary".

Through their observations as SPIRES travel scholars or their personal experience as researchers, the recipe writers have a very strong focus on researchers' ability to make changes in their environment. *Individualisation* is referenced 101 times through the recipes, against *naturalness* 22 times, and *level of stimulation* 35 times. We suggest that the design elements of naturalness and stimulation could be said to be hygiene factors (Herzberg, 1959, 1987) and as such are not noticed by the users unless and until they impact negatively (Williams, 2013). This may be compounded in the case of *level of stimulation* by the need for variation between convergent and divergent parts of the creative process, making it potentially less clear cut. It may be that researchers concentrate more on the 'divergent' part of the innovation cycle and take the 'convergent' aspect more for granted.

Focusing on the hygiene factor argument, interviewees in Williams' research, for example, would accept and grumble about high levels of discomfort of office furniture, and not until they developed bad backs would they do anything about it. This is underpinned by the observation that *#56 A recipe for mediocrity* is the only recipe that references *temperature* and *air quality*, and one of only six that reference *windows* and four that reference *colour*. This anti-recipe sets out the authors' observations of the kinds of physical environment and management that work to "stifle your researchers' creativity", and asks if you wish to "stunt their intellectual growth" and "foster apathy where possible". This accords with McCoy's (2000) observation that less creative teams (in the US government offices she was studying) were actively hindered in any growth of team creativity by the limitations of their physical environment and their inability to change it: "Incremental [less] Creative teams have physical environments that hinder communication and collaboration [two prerequisites for creativity]" (2000, p. 242). McCoy points out the tension between the team's need to support, enhance and express its creativity in the physical environment, and the needs of the planner, designer or facilities manager "whose focus is efficiency and cost containment" (2000, p. 254). Or as the anti-recipe writers mischievously put it: "Appoint buildings managers and administrators who love the building more than people, and can therefore be guaranteed to follow your policies rigorously. Impress upon them that their job is to protect the building from the infestation of people who are allegedly necessary for the university's core business".

DISCUSSION

As we saw in the introduction to this book, recipes are based on the learning, observation and direct experience of SPIRES members, travel scholars and guests over the three-year life of the SPIRES project (supported by EPSRC, the UK's Engineering and Physical Sciences Research Council). It is therefore unsurprising that aspects of *individualisation* are mentioned so often. Each recipe is grounded in empirical data and in previous research; each is generalisable to research environments beyond those described. The importance of individualisation in a research environment is supported by McCoy (2000). In describing the highly creative (breakthrough) teams she observed in her US government case study she says:

> *Higher levels of creativity were associated with the team's autonomy and motivation to achieve the required features and properties of the physical setting. This control includes a willingness to challenge and even circumvent the [...] policies of standards and guidelines governing the physical environment at [the government department].*
> (McCoy, 2000, p. 242. Emphasis added.)

McCoy's study demonstrates that creative achievement is enhanced by the degree to which people are empowered (either by their management or by themselves) to adapt their physical environment to their unique needs, enabled to communicate and collaborate freely, and permitted to demonstrate their shared professional focus through the display of team artefacts. These criteria resonate with *individualisation* in which people have *choice* about where they work, *flexibility* in how they adapt their physical space to that work, and autonomy over *connection*: that is, to communicate and collaborate freely with others.

It is noticeable that recipe writers tackle only obliquely (or ironically) those areas of research facilities that are part of a building's fabric. Light, sound, temperature and air quality (*naturalness*) along with colour and to a certain extent texture (*level of stimulation*) pertain to the capital and maintenance costs of a building, and hence to the facilities department. Haner (2005) indicates the economic pressure on commercial companies to capitalise on every bit of floor space; university research facilities are no different, and space allocation surveys are common.

We conclude, therefore, that the SPIRES researchers, travel scholars and guests have – consciously or unconsciously – concentrated on those areas where individual researchers and research teams can be empowered or empower themselves to make changes that directly benefit their creative research. However, there remain opportunities to further enhance creativity and innovation in research by more explicit consideration of the hygiene factors that lead to a 'naturally' healthy environment, and to the more targeted use of factors such as active cues related to visual complexity, colour and texture, that support divergent and convergent working and help trigger appropriate cognitive switching between the two.

LESSONS FOR NEW AND EXISTING RESEARCH FACILITIES

There are three main areas revealed by an examination of the recipes through the lens of Barrett's (2010) three-part model and the accompanying design principles/practical options matrix: i) what might be recommended for the design of new research facilities; ii) what might be recommended for official improvements to existing research facilities; and iii) what can be done to existing ones through users' unofficial 'hacking'.

Taking the last first, the recipes, with their focus on *individualisation*, cover practical options that can be hacked, with the exception of building orientation and windows which cannot. We do not recommend taking a sledgehammer to the walls of a dark office to let in more light and reveal the views beyond! The practical options (*Spaces* and *Plan & Envelope*) for making changes to light, sound, air quality, and temperature in *naturalness* are, we suggest, limited by two aspects: the fabric of the buildings, and researchers' perception and acceptance of the status quo. Researchers' inability to change the preprogrammed air quality and temperature of buildings is self-evident, but there remains room for hacking with light and sound. Daylight bulbs and 'task lighting' can be found out of departmental budgets (see *#60 Beam me up (or down)* recipe), for example, and recipe *#16 What to listen to while you work* gives a selection of approaches that can help to reduce distractions from background noise. *Naturalness* taken in its wider aspect of biophilia (Fromm, 1964; Ulrich, 1984, 1993; Kaplan, Talbot & Kaplan, 1988) appears in only six recipes (Table 2) but hacks can be made that bring the benefits of the natural environment into the research place. That none of the recipes present possible approaches suggests that *naturalness* at an individual or research team level may be a hygiene factor (Herzberg, 1959, 1987) and only noticed when the detrimental effects impinge on people's awareness.

Our analysis of *levels of stimulation* reveals that researchers are aware of, and use, small affordances (Gibson, 1977) such as whiteboards that make a large difference (e.g. in recipes such as *#36 Visualising the Problem* and *#41 Idea room*). The areas under colour and texture are less determined. Going in at the weekend when the building supervisor is away to remove redundant cupboards and repaint the walls or cover them in whiteboard or plastic comes under the heading (courtesy of McCoy, 2000, p. 242) of "a willingness to challenge and even circumvent the [...] policies of standards and guidelines governing the physical environment".

A need for official improvements to existing research facilities is clearly implied by this analysis. Researchers cannot, or can rarely, directly tackle issues of poor ventilation, heating, colour schemes and light, hence the *#56 A recipe for mediocrity* anti-recipe. The impact of these issues on innovation and creative thinking are well documented (among others: Brill, Margulis & Konar, 1984; Knez, 1995; Williams, 2013) but are too rarely taken into consideration in the design or refurbishment of existing facilities. And, as discussed above, researchers and research teams were not often observed being empowered to make the changes they needed.

Finally, design of new research facilities should, we suggest, take into account researchers' preferences, expressed in the recipes, for each of the three main sensory themes of *naturalness, individualisation* and *levels of stimulation*. While *individualisation* remains in the hands of the researchers themselves and is to some extent a cultural (empowerment) issue, the hygiene factors implicit in the other two themes have the capacity to contribute substantially to a healthy environment in which remarkable research can flourish.

THE CREATIVE FOOTPRINT

AUTHOR
Alison Williams

INTRODUCTION

This paper introduces the concept of the *creative footprint* (Williams 2009a; 2009b), and examines its impacts on people's research creativity. The concept states:

> *"The creative footprint is a set of physical [...] elements which together uniquely form an individual's or a group's optimum physical environment for stimulating and sustaining workplace creativity, in changing situations." (Williams, 2013, p. 125)*

In other words, just as we are each different, so our creative needs are different. We use different physical elements at different stages of our creative process and in different situations, and the combination of these elements forms our unique *creative footprints*.

Examples of this impact are provided from this volume's recipes. Additionally I present the *Grammar of Creative Workplaces* (Williams, 2013) and the accompanying questionnaire used by SPIRES to assess research environments' capacity to support multiple creative footprints. I use the lens of the creative footprint to compare the findings from the SPIRES questionnaire with an analysis of the recipes. I examine the recipes' content against the grammar's structure, particularly its *engage/disengage meta-model of creative behaviours* and bring forward one particular area – play and experimentation – that emerges strongly from the findings. Finally, I present the SPIRES database of audited research environments and discuss its benchmarking work.

THE CREATIVE FOOTPRINT AND GRAMMAR OF CREATIVE WORKPLACES

It has long been known that the physical environment has an impact on people's thinking, particularly creative thinking, but substantiating it has been another matter (McCoy & Evans, 2002). As Csikszentmihalyi says:

> *"Unfortunately there is no evidence – and probably there never will be – to prove that a delightful setting induces creativity." (Csikszentmihalyi, 1996, p. 135)*

In researching how workplaces support their users' creativity research, I found that people are able to identify the spaces that work for them in stimulating and supporting their creativity, as well as those spaces that restrict and hinder it. As one interviewee said about her workplace:

> *"The physical confines of the lab [and] the [detrimental] impact that that actually had on you physically, psychologically, creatively, is amazing. You can actually feel – it's as if your whole body just slumps."*

This individual response to workspaces is informed by the interviewee's *creative footprint*. The data also informed the *Grammar of Creative Workplaces* (Williams, 2013), a visuospatial instrument for identifying creativity-supporting physical elements of workplaces, including research environments. These elements are codified into three main groups:

1. The *place* itself: Is it for example an office? A laboratory? A cafe? Is it indoors or outside?
2. The *sensory properties* of that space: Is it, among other things, light or dark? Comfortable or not? Brightly coloured or subdued?
3. Its *affordances*: What are the equipment, tools and materials within the space that support creative behaviours?

Looking at this grammatically (Chomsky, 1957; Lyons, 1970), the grammar's *meaning* is the degree to which an environment supports creativity, its *lexis* contains the discrete elements (place, properties and affordances) that impact creative behaviours, and its *syntax* is people's creative behaviours in that environment (Table 1).

MEANING	LEXIS	SYNTAX
To stimulate, sustain and support everyday creativity in the workplace	Physical environment: - Place - Properties - Affordances	Creative behaviours (deliberate & chance): Engagement with: - People - Information - Ideas Disengagement from people for cognitive engagement with: - Information - Ideas Disengagement from the issue for cognitive refreshment and incubation

Table 1:
Structure of the Grammar of Creative Workplaces

Syntax in this context has at its foundation a meta-model of creative behaviours (Williams, 2013) in which people either engage or disengage with other people, with ideas and with information, and do so deliberately or by chance (Table 2).

ENGAGEMENT		DISENGAGEMENT			
Deliberate engagement with people, information & ideas	Chance engagement with people, information & ideas	Disengagement from others & context through physical movement	Disengagement from others & context through mechanical movement	Disengagement from the issue or context through short distractions	Disengagement from others, the issue or context through longer periods of time

—

Table 2:
Summary of data categories of behaviours that stimulate,
sustain and support workplace creativity

We might, for example, consider how a particular space allows the exchange of creative ideas between workers (meaning). To explore this, we might then look at the place, properties and affordances of that space (lexis) and observe and understand user engagement (syntax). In recipe *#45 Lowbrow powwow,* information and ideas that are outside a researcher's discipline are made easily available and can spark divergent thinking. In *#40 Creative spaces for interdisciplinary research,* unexpected elements such as unusual materials (affordances) and interesting people combine to produce an act of creation (Koestler, 1964). Taken together, these three grammatical elements make up the *Grammar of Creative Workplaces* and this was used as a framework for assessing a research environment's capacity to support *creative footprints.*

SPIRES RESEARCH

SPIRES supports scholars who investigate research environments and SPIRES network members and travel scholars have explored what constitutes best practice in research environments in the UK and abroad. To date SPIRES travel scholars, of whom I am one, have visited over twenty sites, including: the University of British Columbia in Canada; four universities, a private company and a symposium in the US; two universities and a conference in Japan; three universities and a new media cooperative in Australia; and academic, artistic and private institutions in Germany, Spain, Portugal, and the UK.

A condition of the funding was to observe best practice in these institutions, and the travel scholars were asked to use the *Grammar of Creative Workplaces* as a basis for their observations, and a tool to assess the observed research sites. They then brought the learning back to SPIRES, and thus to this volume, contributing a recipe or case study of their observations. The travel scholars were also asked to gather questionnaires from researchers in the audited spaces. These questionnaires aimed to identify researchers' preferred elements of physical space and hence their different creative footprints.

The findings presented in this paper emerge from the 2012 SPIRES travel scholar data, collected from across the world (Table 3).

EUROPE	NORTH AMERICA (USA)	ASIA (JAPAN)	AUSTRALIA
4 sites	6 sites	2 sites	1 site
7 questionnaires	7 questionnaires	9 questionnaires	4 questionnaires

Table 3:
Numbers of questionnaires completed globally

Each travel scholar completed a grammar audit for each site and up to five user questionnaires per site.

The questionnaire (Table 4) listed all the elements of the grammar audit in its three strands of *properties, behaviours* and *affordances*. Researcher-respondents were invited to indicate which elements were important to their creativity. They were also asked to rank the top five in order of importance, but the results from this question were not robust, given language and comprehension difficulties. The questions were presented in English, which created some problems in Germany and in Japan as the respective travel scholars were not fluent in either language and could not rely on subjects being fluent in English. Some answers were written in Japanese including one note to the SPIRES researcher translated as: "Thanks for your patience. You are very kind to us even though we can't understand English much. Good luck!" This paper therefore sets out the findings from the first question only: *Tick all that are important to your creativity.*

The details of the three strands (properties, behaviours and affordances) were derived from data collected in my PhD study from interviews, focus groups and case studies, and are underpinned by the literature. Under *properties*, research subjects identified twelve different senses overall as integral to their creative footprints. These were: the five Aristotelian senses of taste, smell, touch, sight and sound; the neurological senses of temperature, movement/proprioception and spaciousness; and the Steinerian senses of thinking, speech, life/liveliness, and the 'I' (Williams, 2013). *Behaviours* fell into either the *engagement* or *disengagement* meta-categories (Table 2), supported by the relevant *affordances*.

CREATIVE FOOTPRINT ELEMENTS		Tick all that are important to your creativity	5 most important for your creativity
PROPERTIES (what I need the space to feel like)	Fresh smell		
	Fresh atmosphere without being draughty		
	Temperature just right for desk and conference work		
	Lively feel		
	Sound level at a quiet buzz		
	Orderly environment, minimum mess		
	Comfortable furniture		
	Good views of the outside		
	Natural light flooding the workplace		
	No glare from sunlight or artificial light		
	The artificial light is like daylight		
	The colour scheme is cheerful and calm		
	Long line-of-sight inside the workplace		
	High ceiling		
BEHAVIOURS (what I need to be able to do in the space)	Able to personalise my workplace		
	Able to display team information and updates etc		
	Able to hold impromptu conversations		
	Able to concentrate		
	Able to have formal meetings		
	Able to see formal information displays		
	Able to see/find out informal information		
	Able to experiment, play, craft and try things out		
	Able to bump into people by chance		
	Able to encounter unexpected information and ideas		
	Able to encounter unexpected information from outside the work environment		

AFFORDANCES	Able to walk about easily
(what tools and equipment I need for creative behaviours)	Able to exercise strenuously
	Able to think and reflect quietly on my own
	Able to work without interruption
	Able to make my thinking visible to team members
	Able to see what other teams are doing
	Able to think visually with other people
	(e.g. whiteboards, talking walls etc)
	Able to collaborate easily with other people and teams
	Able to have informal conversations

—

Table 4:
Creative Workplace Questionnaire (2nd section)

DATA ANALYSIS 1: QUESTIONNAIRES

The analysis of the questionnaires (Table 5) revealed that respondents' perceptions of the most important elements for their creativity were places that supported creative behaviour to a) experiment, play, craft and try things out (23 mentions); b) concentrate and reflect (22 mentions); and c) think visually individually and together (41 mentions from 3 related questions). The most mentioned sensory property was good views of the outside (21 mentions).

The next most important elements particularly identified by respondents were to have places that a) supported impromptu conversations (20 mentions) and bumping into people by chance (18 mentions); and b) being able to walk about easily (17 mentions). The most mentioned secondary sensory property was a need for comfortable furniture (17 mentions).

The importance accorded to the wish to experiment, play, craft and try things out was unexpected; the element of play and experimentation was a minor finding in my PhD thesis (Williams, 2013). This may reflect the preponderance of research environments in the SPIRES study as opposed to mainly commercial environments in my doctoral study. In general terms, the commercial environments were concerned with small-c creativity (Simonton, 2005; Amabile, 1983; 1996) of productivity and incremental change, whereas the research environments were more concerned with the middle-to-big-C creativity of exploration and step change. The other primary and secondary themes of concentration, visual thinking, impromptu and serendipitous meetings, and physical movement were congruent with the doctoral findings. Good views came high in both studies, but comfortable furniture was a low priority in the doctoral findings. This could be attributed to comfort being seen in commercial environments less as a creative motivator and more as a hygiene factor (Herzberg, 1959; 1987) "and as such not noticed by the users unless [it] impacts negatively" (Williams, 2013, p. 181).

DATA ANALYSIS 2: RECIPES

In this volume, an analysis was done of 34 recipes that deal with creative physical environments, creative behaviours and creative affordances; the remaining 28 recipes are all concerned with issues of virtual space, cognition or affect and hence not part of this analysis. Of these 34 recipes, 30 contained references to elements of the creative footprint (Table 5).

The importance of support for play and experimentation to questionnaire respondents is further reflected in the recipe analysis. It has the highest number of recipe mentions: 13 (Table 5).

Creative footprint elements reported as most important by research respondents	No. of times mentioned in questionnaires	No. of times mentioned in analysed recipes
Experiment, play, craft and try things out	23	13
Concentrate and reflect	22	4
To think visually individually and together	41 (3 questions)	9
Good views of the outside	21	6
Supported impromptu conversations	20	} 9
Bumping into people by chance	18	
Walk about easily	17	5
Comfortable furniture	17	10

Table 5:
Creative footprint elements reported as
important in questionnaires as against recipes

Thereafter the correspondence between the questionnaires and the recipes is similar, except for the relative unimportance in the recipes of concentration and reflection, and the greater importance accorded to comfort. Concentration recipes, however, are more cognitive, and as such are not included in this analysis. Recipe examples for play and experimentation include: "*Fiddling.* Play with objects that can be balanced, squashed or moulded into shapes" (*#6 Think with your hands*); "Spaces are furnished with an array of both physical resources and virtual resources to strengthen collaborative hypothesising and encourage collective creativity" (*#33 'How might we...' space*); and "A dynamic fun space to tinker, fail, and figure things out. It is a space where tinkering is allowed (and expected)" (*#61 Workshop space*). Finally: "Learning in design is often accomplished through physical interaction with materials. Clay, wire, wood, paper, and cardboard factor into these investigations" (*#40 Creative spaces for interdisciplinary research*).

Concentrate and reflect appear in recipes as, for example, "a space where the individual can revisit their own creative thinking and problem-solving process – question their thought processes" (*#41 Idea room*). Thinking visually appears in nine recipes, such as: "The visualisation [...] reveals commonalities among people in their research topics, problems, and methods, prompting *ad hoc* brainstorming meetings, coffee breaks, and beer outings, [...] helping people find each other [and] stay aware of the changing research landscape at a large institution" (*#38 Research interest visualisation*).

The need for good visual links to the outdoors (views and biophilia (Fromm, 1964)) include: "Does the space have lots of natural light? Is it big enough with long lines-of-sight and high ceilings? Does it feel alive?" (*#54 A mobile thinking shrine*) and pragmatically: "Make use of the double affordance of windows – light and view. Power sockets are NOT more important than people!" (*#60 Beam me up (or down)*).

Recipes for serendipitous conversations include instructions for creating a physical space: "Find an area with heavy footfall with spare space for a few seats. This will afford the possibility of a maximum number of chance encounters" (*#32 Serendipity on the back of a napkin*) and making behavioural changes: "Go up to a stranger in your institution and ask them what they do. For once, don't try to get what you do into the conversation" (*#1 Prepare your mind*).

Walking about easily, or as Montaigne put it in 1580: "My thoughts fall asleep if I make them sit down. My mind will not budge unless my legs move it" (quoted in Bakewell, 2010, p. 158), is examined in *#62 Meetings in the great outdoors*: "Why not [introduce] walking meetings?" Comfortable furniture and surroundings appear in several recipes, including *#48 Meat(ing) place* and *#25 Research group as extended family*.

FURTHER EXPLORATION OF THE CREATIVE FOOTPRINT

The breadth of people's creative footprints is demonstrated in the breadth of the recipes. There are different recipes for the same outcome or aim written by different authors, each author observing different behaviours in different research environments. For example, some people need the stimulation of others to generate ideas: Resnick's (2007) iterative creativity or Sawyer's (2003) synchronic interaction. The *#41 Idea room* recipe is for them. Others need to generate ideas on their own (Wallas, 1926) and in flow (Csikszentmihalyi, 1975; 1996) and can find a suggested solution in *#54 A mobile thinking shrine*. Reassessing the habitual – a key component of creativity – appears in several recipes with approaches as diverse as *#17 Roll the dice*, consciously becoming aware of, then breaking, habits of thought (*#47 Don't panic!*), moving furniture around (*#40 Creative spaces for interdisciplinary research; #50 Make do & mend space; #51 Work that space*), and seeking out new and unexpected people and information (*#1 Prepare your mind*).

There are also different recipes for different stages of the creative process, written by the same person. For example, Robertson's *#57 Thinking den* recipe reflects her need for privacy when generating ideas, as against her *#62 Meetings in the great outdoors* recipe when sharing and honing those ideas with others.

The recipes demonstrate the writers' own and others' expressed creative footprints, and their observations of best practice in research environments. This best practice is further captured in the SPIRES database.

SPIRES DATABASE

The SPIRES database is an ongoing project in which assessments of research environments, made using the *Grammar of Creative Workplaces*, are entered, permitting the collected data to be interrogated. The aim was to create a common platform from which the research environments could be compared and contrasted, both with other research environments, and with more general workplaces. The travel scholars' audits were also supplemented by assessments of research environments by UK CIRCLE (Creative Interdisciplinary Research on Collaborative Environments) members, and by the addition of two commercial spaces undertaken as part of the PhD research. As well as benchmarking, the database generates reports on each research environment.

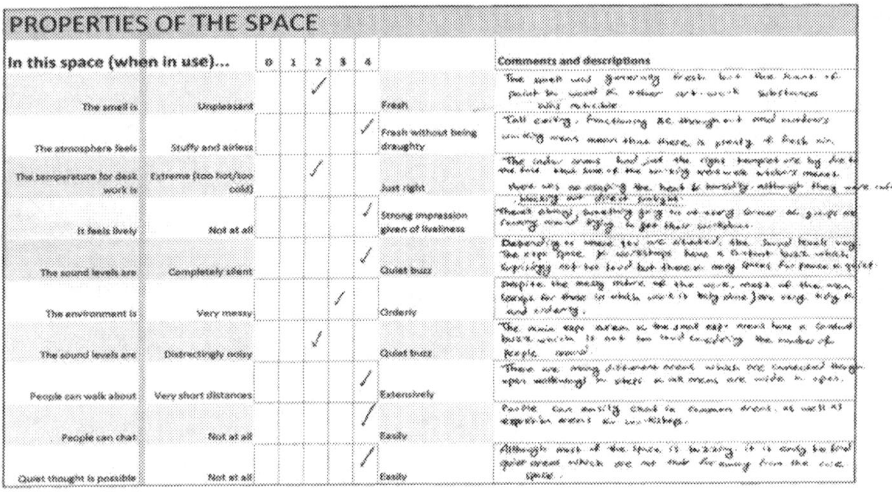

PROPERTIES OF THE SPACE

In this space (when in use)...		0	1	2	3	4		Comments and descriptions
The smell is	Unpleasant			✓			Fresh	[illegible]
The atmosphere feels	Stuffy and airless					✓	Fresh without being draughty	[illegible]
The temperature for desk work is	Extreme (too hot/too cold)			✓			Just right	[illegible]
It feels lively	Not at all					✓	Strong impression given of liveliness	[illegible]
The sound levels are	Completely silent					✓	Quiet buzz	[illegible]
The environment is	Very messy				✓		Orderly	[illegible]
The sound levels are	Distractingly noisy			✓			Quiet buzz	[illegible]
People can walk about	Very short distances					✓	Extensively	[illegible]
People can chat	Not at all					✓	Easily	[illegible]
Quiet thought is possible	Not at all					✓	Easily	[illegible]

Figure 1:
Completed first page of Properties: Audit 8

As seen earlier (Table 1) the grammar looks at the research space's physical environment (place, sensory properties, affordances) and the creative behaviours that are supported within it (engaging with people, information and ideas, or disengaging from people and from the task). Each section of the grammar uses a semantic differential scale (Mehrabian & Russell, 1974) to assess elements from undesirable (0 score) to very desirable (4 score) features. In *properties* for example, colour ranges from 'monotonous' to 'cheerful', and from 'extremely bright' to 'calm'; natural light ranges from 'non-existent' to 'flooding the space', and the sun's glare from 'very strong' to 'non-existent'. In the behaviours section, the range captures the ease or difficulty of behaving in specific ways. 'Having informal or unscheduled work conversations' ranges from 'impossible' to 'very easy', and 'taking short walks' ranges from 'difficult' to 'many'. In the affordances section the range for each affordance is from 'none' to 'rich'. Fig. 1 shows a completed page of *properties* from Audit 8 with scoring and comments.

To date sixteen audits have been entered on the database. These are from ten universities (two from Georgia Tech, one from the University of New South Wales, three from the University of Washington Seattle, one from Edinburgh University, one from Kyoto University of Art and Design, one from Tama Art University (Tokyo), and one from the Fraunhofer Fokus Research Institute); two private companies (London and San Mateo, CA); two new media collaborative spaces (Betahaus, Berlin and CCC Berlin Hackerspace); and finally two artists' studios (Stag Studios, Edinburgh and Utrophia, London). The audited space is scored according to its observed capacity to support different aspects of creativity (see Fig. 1). For the purposes of this paper, the audits are anonymised.

The auditors (SPIRES travel scholars) were asked to identify one particular space in the research environment they were visiting, and use the grammar to assess its capacity to stimulate and support creative behaviours. Before travelling, they were briefed and encouraged to trial it in their own research environment. Each grammar came complete with instructions.

The audit is scored by taking the marks awarded to each category and showing them as a percentage of the highest possible score. A score of 80% or above indicates a HIGH support for creativity, between 60% and 80% indicates a MEDIUM support for creativity, and below 60% indicates a LOW support for creativity. Table 6 shows the marks given in Audit 6 (a single room in a new building) for properties, behaviours and affordances, and shows them as a percentage of the highest possible score.

Elements supporting user creativity	Highest possible score for support of user creativity		Score for Audit 6		
Properties	84	100%	59	(70%)	Medium
FBehaviours	60	100%	42	(70%)	Medium
Affordances	64	100%	40	(62%)	Low
Overall totals	**208**	**100%**	**141**	**(67%)**	**MEDIUM**

Table 6:
Score for Audit 6's support for research creativity

Audit 6's low score on affordances is given because the research room is particularly lacking in equipment that supports 'making thinking visible and accessible inside and between teams' and 'thinking visually together'. It is also low in affordances for 'experimenting, crafting, playing with ideas' and for 'thinking and writing solo'. All of these are remediable, as is its poor *properties* score for orderliness: "Other people's stuff in the way cluttering the floor".

Audited space 12 comes out ahead of all the others, setting a benchmark of good practice:

Elements supporting user creativity	Benchmark Audit 12	Database average score across all audits
Properties	84% High	45% Low
Behaviours	75% Medium	52% Low
Affordances	88% High	52% Low
Overall totals	**82% HIGH**	**50% LOW**

Table 7:
Audit 12 scores on support for user creativity

The two areas which brought the *behaviours* score into medium rather than high were i) the space did not support extended exercise, and ii) there were few opportunities to work solo without interruption. However, as Table 7 demonstrates, when looked at against the database average, Audit 12 sets a very high benchmark.

CONCLUSIONS

Csikszentmihalyi's (1996) assertion that there is no evidence linking creativity to 'delightful environments' is no longer sustainable. What is now clear, however, is that one size does not fit all – the research environment that supports my creativity may not support yours, and vice versa – and that to produce truly remarkable research the environment within which that research takes place should contain all the elements needed to support the widest possible number of creative footprints.

The work done by SPIRES work is significant in its potential to make a positive impact on people's research. The *Grammar of Creative Workplaces* can be used in two ways. Firstly, to assess the support given by a research environment to its researchers: because the audit identifies the extent to which each supportive element is present or lacking, it gives individual researchers, research teams and heads of research the tools to identify the gaps in their own space where creative footprints are not actively supported. Once the gaps are identified, they can be tackled; and this volume contains recipes and case studies that suggest possible beneficial changes to the research environment, and to individual and group creative processes. Secondly, the grammar audit is significant as contributing data to the SPIRES database. As more audits are added so the options for comparisons across disciplines and across countries expand. Audits from the travel scholars' 2013 visits are being added, extending the range of benchmarking.

The SPIRES work prompts directions for future research. There is a question over the grammar's objectivity/subjectivity and over inter-rater reliability, and SPIRES is in discussion with scholars in the USA on this topic. And finally, and intriguingly, one particular element, '*experiment, play, craft and try things out*', is singled out in the recipes and reported in the questionnaires as being important in shaping remarkable research. This factor would benefit from further examination through additional data analysis, an extended database and further research.

WORKING
WITH OTHERS

WORKING WITH OTHERS

> *"No social group - whether a family, a work group, or a school group - can survive without constant informal contact among its members." (Alexander et al, 1977: p618)*

Working with other researchers has always been central to great results, and the power of collaboration is increasingly recognised through co-authored papers and by the funding bodies. BITE authors are no exception and have written twenty recipes, three case studies and two papers from the sharp end exploring how working together might best be supported and enhanced. Three distinct themes emerge: the element of surprise or *serendipity* that so often emerges from working with others, the *affect* or emotion that is present in any kind of collaboration, and the *processes* of working together well.

Looking first at serendipity, where so many amazing ideas emerge and are sparked, there are several recipes for serendipitously encountering people, information and ideas. *Serendipity on the back of a napkin* says it all, and *Idea room* and *Creative spaces for interdisciplinary research*, among others, merge process, affect and serendipity. The case study on the Institute Gulbenkian of Science (or Instituto Gulbenkian de Ciência, IGC) in Portugal looks at how the buildings and the culture are designed for chance encounters and conversations, and SPIRES' sister project, SerenA, has inspired a full paper on serendipity.

Affect – or what the late fashion designer Jean Muir called *the messy bits* – is not often given the recognition it deserves. Our authors, however, building on the work done in the SPIRES Social Research Spaces seminar, are clear that positive affect or emotion is integral to working with others as well as to working solo. There are recipes for managing and acknowledging emotion, as in *Oh, I thought you meant...* and supporting others, as in *Research group as extended family* and *Sharing food*. There are recipes where process and affect are equally important as in *Can-do space* and *Yes we can - sometimes*. Each case study acknowledges the role that close social ties – liking one another – play in remarkable research.

And finally, there are process recipes for generating ideas, sharing ideas and checking out the validity of ideas. *Share what you made* and *Broadcast your mind*, for example, tap into the perspective put forward by Inger Mewburn (see her case study *The Alternative Academic: Online*) and by Martin Weller on the Pedagogy of Abundance (2011) where content is shared without restriction, and researchers find their work enriched because of it. *Research interest visualisation* discusses enabling software that puts people in touch with each other, and *Visualising the problem* suggests how a group of people might do just that face to face. The paper *How-What Space* shows how process and affect have been brought together to establish the common language so essential to great processes, positive affect and surprising serendipity.

Each theme also comes with its 'awful warning' recipe. To be taken with a bushel of salt, but with strong underlying implications: constructive processes can be sabotaged by *Death by form filling*; affect moves from positive to negative with *How to make your team hate each other and you*; and serendipity is killed outright by *Creativity crush*. As always with these anti-recipes or case studies, the message is clear: if you find you are nodding in recognition then it is time to tackle whatever is going wrong and get back on track with the antidote recipes.

#20

AUTHOR

Diana Bental

—

SERVE TO

Any researcher with an
affinity for the digital

COST

Low

TIME

SHARE WHAT YOU MADE

Improve your ideas by sharing them online
before publication

BACKGROUND —

Academics focus on publications as a way of sharing ideas, but we *make* things too, sometimes real working things, more often demonstrators and prototypes. It's often easier to share software or electronic versions of things - people can make as many copies as they like with little effort and no cost. In this way, people can interact with what you made: use it, comment on it, amend it, and extend it. Your product (or idea) will come back to you reshaped, in a new form, maybe almost unrecognisable. In a sense it doesn't matter what happens to your digital creation out there in the virtual world, as you still have your pristine original copy.

A good example of this type of digital remixing is the Scratch community at MIT. Scratch is a visual programming environment for children built on playful constructionist ideals. The designers of Scratch envisaged a creative cycle where children would imagine an idea for a program, create it using Scratch, play around with their program to refine it, share it with others in the online community, reflect on what they made and then start the whole cycle again (Resnick, 2007). Verbs like 'imagine', 'play' and 'share' might seem odd in an academic context but they commonly crop up in creativity theory. In fact, Resnick's creative cycle has similarities to the scientific publishing cycle where academics think of a theory, create a way to test it, analyse the results, publish the findings to a small set of journal reviewers, reflect on the reviewers' comments and refine their theories. The next stage in the scientific cycle involves replication and refinement by other academic groups.

Resnick's creative cycle
is more fun, though, and
involves less ego shredding!
Publishing and remixing in
the Scratch community is
much quicker than the
standard academic
publishing cycle, resulting
in immediate feedback.
It's free too. Open access
journals such as PLOS
enable authors to get
immediate feedback from
other academics once their
article has been published.
But why not try out new
ways of sharing ideas
digitally *before* you publish?

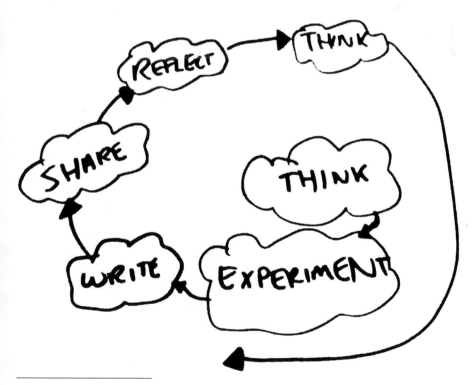

Creative cycle in academia,
adapted from Resnick, 2007

INGREDIENTS

- A digital artefact

- A virtual space to share in

- A community to share with

- An agreement or protocol
  on how to share - who
  owns it, what they can do
  with it

METHOD

1. Make it
2. Put it out there
3. Tell other people it's there
4. Collect comments, communicate
5. Look for things other people made
6. Make a new one - bigger, better, different

NOTES ON INGREDIENTS

You could try *GitHub* for sharing software, with anyone at all, *Dropbox* for sharing documents and images with groups of people, or *Google Docs* for joint authorship.

WARNINGS

In the electronic world there are many different ways of sharing and they can be complicated. You need to share using the same medium that other people in your field are using, and be willing to figure out how they work. Even when you're working on a joint project and wanting to share within the project, people on the same project will be used to different sharing mechanisms – give them time and support to learn new ones. You also need to be aware of legal implications of sharing – share what you made, not what other people own.

RELATED RECIPES

See also *Digital scholarship – start here*.

#21

AUTHOR

Derek Jones

—

SERVE TO

Anyone trying to get
ideas out of their head

COST

Free/low

TIME

BROADCAST YOUR IDEAS

Get your ideas out of your head and let
them grow

BACKGROUND —

When I have an idea in my head, I find that when I try and get it out it always looks very different 'on paper' than I thought it did. There is a simple reason for this – ideas in your head are complex and intangible things. When they come out, you are actually creating a slightly different thing – it changes as you communicate.

Understanding how you represent your ideas by externalising them as concepts is vital in creative research thinking. There are no explicit rules that apply to everyone except the overriding idea that what is in your head is rarely the same as the thing that appears in reality.

The other really important point is that by externalising your ideas you are actually acting on them – an essential aspect of creativity. If you don't act on your ideas then they're not much use (Fleming could easily have just put that Petri dish in the bin, you know).

Becoming familiar with what comes out of your head is also useful – it helps you control what comes out of your mouth.

66

*...it helps you control
what comes out of
your mouth.*

99

INGREDIENTS

**Some private space
(preferably sound-
deadened)**

**Notebook, sketchbook,
smartphone**

**Your computer and
access to the internet**

**A bit of time to give
things a try**

METHOD

1. Pretend to speak to other people when they are not
    actually there. Imagine that really critical friend you
    have and try presenting your idea to them in private
    before you do it in public. Or imagine you are being
    interviewed on a topic you are working on. By the way,
    it's no use pretending to speak – you actually have to
    vocalise this. Out loud. With hand gestures. Be passionate
    and be proud of your rhetoric.
2. As before, pretend to speak to other people – this time
    an audience of people. This is really useful when you are
    preparing a presentation, getting ready for your viva or
    simply if you want to practice pitching an idea. As before,
    you have to actually stand up and do this: talk out loud,
    pretend you are making eye contact with people and point
    to your presentation (if you have to). With care, you can
    try some of this while driving or running.
3. Carry a notebook or sketchbook with you at all times
    and make a point of *using* it. Many people who consider
    themselves to be un-creative are actually coming up with
    ideas all the time. The difference is that they are most
    likely not acting on them or dismissing them immediately
    out of hand. Avoid this and find a method of capturing
    ideas using your notebook that makes sense to you.

4. Have an online space where you publish your ideas and concepts as they emerge. Try tweeting or blogging your ideas as they come to you – this forces you to condense and communicate the idea in a particular format. It might not be ideal for your ideas and if this doesn't work for you, fine. Never force something that really doesn't work. But it can be useful to work out why – is it because you need to doodle your thoughts? Are words too limiting?

5. Try rich pictures. And I don't mean just to make nice-looking sketchbooks of the sort that have become quite fashionable lately. When we write, we are sometimes limited by words; we don't actually think using words specifically. So making use of graphical elements might help you explore your ideas in other ways (Laseau, 2001). Give it a try: you don't have to be artistic and the images only have to mean something to you. Once you get confident enough, show these to other people and see how much of them they can understand.

6. Try reading and answering academic blog posts. This can be great practice in responding to ideas in a creative but informed way. Do it properly too – don't just offer opinion: apply some critical thinking to your responses. Some digital scholars actively use blog answering as their principal 'online voice'. Or join Quora and try answering a few questions (www.quora.com). Again, do this properly – make it a piece of research and academic text.

7. For the especially extrovert, set up a tweeting whiteboard – give your whiteboard or sketchbook a Twitter or photo-sharing account (or even its own blog) and make your thoughts public (with thanks to Dr Graeme Earl, University of Southampton).

NOTES ON INGREDIENTS

A key step in any creative design process is to act – the idea is useless if it's kept in your head. Young referred to this as The Final Stage, or "...the cold, gray dawn of the morning after" (Young, 2003).

COOK'S TIPS

This recipe can be useful even if you are very comfortable with sharing your ideas. Try challenging yourself to broadcast in other ways and especially by arguing against yourself.

WARNINGS

Don't get involved in flame wars or irrational debates in online discussions – as Bertrand Russell said: "Never try to discourage thinking, for you are certain to succeed" (Russell, 1969).

RELATED RECIPES

See *Think with your hands* for other ways of thinking that don't simply rely on your brain alone.

#22

AUTHORS

Marian Dörk
Diana Bental

—

SERVE TO

Research groups

COST

Low, if you take turns

TIME

SHARING FOOD

The quickest way to your colleagues' hearts
is through their mouths

BACKGROUND —

Academic research is often an intangible practice. The laborious and lengthy processes of data analysis, programming, or paper writing can lead at times to a feeling of sensual and social deprivation. A supportive research environment is essential for people to be creative and productive.

This recipe proposes social food practices in order to literally nourish the relations with the people we share an office or lab space with. Instead of just going to the cafeteria or cafe together, food sharing can turn lunch and snack breaks into light-hearted opportunities for sharing and conversation.

This can have two key results: a sense of social cohesion in which people can share and create ideas, and those precious moments of relaxation in a work environment. Be aware that the food you choose says something about who you're including. Beer and pizza says young men. Tea and cake says middle-aged ladies. So vary what you provide to attract different people and avoid excluding those with particular religious or cultural backgrounds. Alcohol can be problematic for this reason.

This recipe is based on experiences in the Interactions Lab, University of Calgary, and Culture Lab, Newcastle University, and in the *Women in Computing* network.

When you bring food, you turn your hungry colleagues into good-natured collaborators.

INGREDIENTS

- A group of researchers willing to make food, try food, talk food

- An occasion, a goal to achieve, or no excuse at all

- Food prepared by one of the group

METHOD

1. The idea is very simple: bring in food for your lab mates. This food can be lovingly prepared by you or carefully selected from a store. Set out the food in a central area (maybe you have a lunch table?) then advertise the offering via your group's mailing list. For extra interaction with your lab mates you might want to walk around and personally offer food, especially small snacks such as chocolate or apple slices.

2. Sharing food should not be seen as an altruistic effort. Instead it is a tasty form of bribery that you can apply to get something from your colleagues. For example, consider the next time it's your turn to prepare a brainstorming at your weekly group meeting, present a paper in a reading group, or summarize your entire PhD research during a defence. When you bring food, you turn your hungry colleagues into good-natured collaborators.

3. It's not a new idea to bring food to a workplace. The common occasion is a birthday. If you really need reasons to justify bringing in food, there are plenty.

   a. A looming paper deadline may require higher sugar levels, so it might be a good idea to bring in a loaf of banana bread, muffins, or when things get desperate, doughnuts.

   b. When you have been travelling for conferences or vacation, the quickest way back into your colleagues' hearts is through their mouths. Bring some exotic candy or artisan chocolate, and fire off that email to the group's list with the longed-for subject: 'Chocolate on the lunch table'. Your colleagues will not only know that you're back, they will taste the sweet flavour of your return.

   However, sharing food with one's co-workers does not require an elaborate rationale. Feeling like baking some beautiful brownies or dishing out delicious dumplings should be enough of a reason.

WARNINGS

Consider your colleagues' dietary preferences and allergies. Your well-intentioned efforts might backfire, if a co-worker or, worse, supervisor has to leave the office due to a migraine.

RELATED RECIPES

See *Research group as extended family*.

#23

AUTHOR
Judy Robertson

SERVE TO
PhD supervisors

COST
Low

TIME
😕 😕 😕

NURTURING YOUR PHD STUDENTS

How to help PhD students succeed

BACKGROUND —

PhD students can be delicate flowers, but with a little light, water and attention they will flourish as independent researchers.

Nurturing PhD students is a core but unglamorous part of an academic job – academics don't get promoted by being good supervisors, but training new talent is essential. Don't underestimate how satisfying it can be when it works out well.

INGREDIENTS

- A PhD candidate

- An interesting PhD topic

- Patience

- Empathy

- Rigour

METHOD

1. *Select your PhD candidate carefully.* I have a preference for pragmatic, confident, easy-going students who I get on well with personally. However, it can be hard to tell what neuroses might manifest themselves during the PhD process. I would avoid candidates who want to get a PhD as a way of proving themselves to be clever, and favour those who seem to have a real love of the topic. I would probably avoid those who wish to continue their studies to delay having to get a job.

2. *Make your expectations clear at the start of the PhD.* Discuss with the student what they can expect of you, and what you expect of them in terms of regularity of meetings, working times, response times on written drafts, authorship and so on. Setting these ground rules early can avoid misunderstandings later.

   a. *Meeting times.* There will be periods of lower and higher intensity working during the PhD process, so it makes sense to be flexible about this. I like to start with regular weekly meetings while the student settles in, and gradually begin to offer them a choice about the time interval before the next meeting as I get a sense of their pace of working. There are times when the student would probably prefer to get on with a task rather than meet to talk about it, but you need good judgement to distinguish this case from occasions where they would rather *pretend* to be getting on with a task than meeting you to talk about why they are having trouble. At high intensity times, such as when they are just about to launch an experiment, begin data analysis or submit a paper, it's a good idea to budget more time for meetings and general help.

   b. *Working times.* My preference is for full-time students to work in the university during the working day, although I don't insist on 9-5. Mostly I recommend this so that students don't get isolated and also so that they develop regular working habits. Treating a PhD like a job can remove some of the stressful feelings of guilt and inadequacy which it often seems to evoke. Getting the pace of the work right is important: if you put in something like eight hours a day, five days a week, of focused work you can be reasonably sure that you are doing enough over the three years to get the work done. It avoids the situation where the student does nothing for ages, constantly feels guilty, then goes on a work binge to make up for it, producing lower quality work and tiring themselves out for the next task. Obviously you'll need to be more flexible with part-time students and those with other commitments, and this will require some negotiation.

c. *Response times on written drafts.* For your own peace of mind, let your students know a reasonable time period by which they can expect feedback on their drafts and try to stick to it. Most students don't mind if you tell them in advance that you have other commitments and will take longer to give feedback than usual. Occasionally students bring drafts to meetings hot off the printer, or email them a few hours beforehand. It's your job to teach them that if they want thoughtful feedback, they need to send their drafts to you well in advance. For the student who writes huge amounts of text, ask them to identify a particular aspect they want you to focus on – you don't need to provide the same level of detail in your feedback on each draft. Sometimes high-level structure is most important; at other times, feedback on the building of an academic point within a single paragraph will be instructive.

d. *Authorship.* There are different customs about the authorship of papers written by PhD students. It's a tricky ethical issue. You have invested your time in developing the student's skills, but the student has often carried out the work. My personal view is that I am uncomfortable to have my name as an author on a paper if I have not contributed to both the work and the writing. By this reasoning, simple proofreading would not qualify me for authorship, nor would discussions in supervision meetings. There are two sides to this. Fairness to the students is one aspect, but maintaining your academic reputation is also important. You don't want your students attaching your name to any old draft without your approval! See also the Vancouver Protocol for further discussion on the ethics of authorship.

3. *Get the balance right.* Your students will inevitably produce poor or off-track work at some point. Getting the balance right so that you can challenge this without losing empathy can be difficult; but your students won't thank you in the long run if you go easy on second-rate work. If you can help students to separate themselves from the work they are doing (see the *My work is not me* recipe) then you will be able to critique it together – as if it was a journal paper you were reviewing. The ability to leap from being partisan protector to objective observer is a wonderful gift!

4. *Fade away.* I don't mean unaccountably vanish! Students *hate* that (see the *Tina says: 'Push!'* recipe). Just gradually decrease each student's dependence on you. Your ultimate goal is to turn them into reliable and independent colleagues. For example, if you want to teach them how to review papers, you could discuss examples of reviews you have received on papers you have written, get them to review published papers using the reviewing form for that journal, and ask them to review papers you have been asked to review (in parallel, *not* instead of you!) until they reach the point that they can write constructive reviews on their own.

5. *Celebrate your students' successes.* Don't forget what it was like when you got your first paper published! Celebrate your students' milestones even if such occasions have become commonplace for you.

6. *Be there in difficult times.* Equally, don't forget what it was like when your first paper was rejected or when your experiment went horribly wrong. Help them to learn from their mistakes without blaming themselves.

7. *Know when to stop.* This is one of the most difficult tasks as a supervisor. You have a responsibility to tell the student if you don't think they are going to be able to get a PhD, and you need to do it early enough for them to cut their losses and escape unscathed. Many institutions have yearly progress reports; take these seriously. Consult with trusted colleagues to make each of these check points an active decision about whether to proceed rather than a form-filling exercise. In my view it is better for the student to find out at the end of their first year that they are unlikely to be able to get a PhD, rather than waiting until they have invested three years and become more emotionally entangled with it.

8. *Review your practices.* You might think everything is going well, but your student might be stewing with frustration. It is worth checking with them: 'Is there anything you would like us to do differently?' from time to time. 'Stop/start/ continue' is a good technique: 'What are we doing that isn't helpful, that we should stop?', 'What should we start doing that would be useful?' and 'What are we getting right that we should continue to do?'

WARNINGS

One director of studies, when asked how he was, replied: "Dreadful – I've just been allocated three new PhD students: three unplanned pregnancies!"

#24

AUTHOR
Judy Robertson

—

SERVE TO
Those who need it

COST
Low

TIME

HOW TO MAKE YOUR TEAM HATE EACH OTHER AND YOU

An awful warning of how relationships can sour in a research group

BACKGROUND —

When establishing a research group, it is important to set appropriate expectations. Your team members should know from the outset that they are there solely to further *your* career.
You also need to remember that the seemingly harmless PhD students of today will be competitors for your funding tomorrow: enabling them to succeed is not in your interest.

To this end, expend some effort to destroy camaraderie between group members in case they should feel an urge to help each other. A little time spent crushing egos today will pay off highly in the future.

INGREDIENTS

- Two nervous PhD students

- An ambitious post-doc

- A funding drought

- External pressures,
  such as the REF (Research
  Excellence Framework,
  UK) or tenure process (US)

METHOD

1. Keep your students busy with time-consuming tasks which will not further their research but will be useful for you (e.g. organising workshops or booking travel for you). If they dare to question this, explain it will develop their transferrable skills and Look Good on Their CV or Résumé. You'd be amazed at what students do for these reasons.

2. Hugely increase your own publication count by 'co-authoring'. That is, get the team members to write papers for you and insist on having your name on them. Try to avoid having multiple team members as co-authors on the same paper because a) it increases team members' publication counts and thus advances their careers and b) you want to avoid team members spending time together. Note: actually contributing to the paper yourself is strictly optional.

3. Introduce suspicion between team members by criticising their work, and either implying or actually creating the conditions of a zero-sum game. Team members should think that the success of any of their peers will lead to their own failure. The last thing you want is the team getting together behind your back to plot a rebellion.

4. Choose a favourite team member who you will praise, and a victim who you will regularly humiliate. Swap these roles randomly and frequently for optimum stress.

5. Deny team members access to resources (such as software or travel money) when possible. This will save you money, but also hamper their efforts and make their lives more difficult.

WARNINGS

On no account actually attempt this recipe.

RELATED RECIPES

See also *A recipe for mediocrity* and *Death by form filling*.

Do the opposite of everything in the *Nurturing your PhD students* recipe.

#25

AUTHOR
Negin Moghim

—

SERVE TO
A research group

COST
Low

TIME

RESEARCH GROUP AS EXTENDED FAMILY

How to foster creativity and goodwill in your research team

BACKGROUND —

Group creativity is an important aspect of creativity. This raises the issue of social pressure and how it affects our creative thinking. Amabile (1983; 1996) among others looks at the social psychology of creativity and how the culture of an organisation or team affects the creative performance of the people working in it. This approach is also supported by iterative models of creativity, where ideas are generated and developed in the interaction between individuals and their colleagues (Sawyer, 2003; Resnick, 2007). This iterative approach works best where each individual in the group learns to trust the others. As Wheatley & Kellner-Rogers say: "In healthy human systems people support one another with information and nurture one another with trust" (1996, p. 39).

Social responsibility – or ethics – for the whole is most effective when there is a balance between having a high sense of belonging thus unlocking access to an infinite source of productivity and creativity, and the dangers of groupthink (Janis, 1982). Where the group is strong enough and trust is high, it can tolerate – and indeed encourage – dissent. Work by Nemeth & Nemeth-Brown (2003) proposes dissent as a stimulus to creative thought which, even when wrong, helps people avoid a tendency to conform. The critical thing to achieve is a balance between intrinsic and extrinsic motivation in the group's individuals. Intrinsic motivation is a significantly greater enabler of creativity than extrinsic (Lepper & Greene, 1973), yet we consistently ignore this in management and organisational systems. Balancing the extrinsic (group strategic need) and the intrinsic (individual creative footprint) is vital if you wish to engender creative social groupings (Hennessey, 2003).

Hennessey's top five killers of creativity are: expected reward, expected evaluation, surveillance, time limits and competition.

An effective research group is like a family that can argue and disagree, but all within a strong circle of trust and responsibility that heightens a sense of belonging.

INGREDIENTS

- An open-access
  office space

- Group activity board

- Comfortable furniture

- Chillout area

- Flat (non-hierarchical)
  management

- Encouragement of
  informal meetings

- Individual responsibility
  for self and for sharing
  information

- A willingness to be part
  of the community

- Camaraderie towards
  other members of
  the group

METHOD

1. *Define the group and the respective workspace:*
   It is important to be clear about what group it is that
   you are part of. A medium-sized group, say up to 10
   people, works well for building good family relationships.
   Too small and you may end up with several groups in a
   single office space, potentially causing divisions in the
   workplace. Too large and the group may be scattered
   over several offices, be less well defined, and the
   individuals may associate less with other group members.

2. In an ideal world the group should be situated in
   a dedicated physical space as well as having a clear
   professional identity. But the world is far from ideal,
   and if your group is housed in several office spaces these
   should be as physically close as possible, with a designated
   common area where the entire group can come together.

3. *Keep group members involved*: Lots of possibilities here
   – from informal coffees with other group members to
   five-minute stand-up meetings every morning (information
   only, keep standing so it doesn't run over the five minutes,
   schedule longer conversations for later) to organising a
   weekly lunch. Such activities can heighten the sense of
   belonging. It also gives a chance for everyone to have a
   say in organising events and decision-making, regardless
   of their position in the group.

4. *Make group activity visible:* When group members
    are constantly aware of their direct influence and
    their active role in the group, motivation levels remain
    high. People are supported through information.
    Do this through a whiteboard, a designated wall, or an
    online forum. Make sure that everyone in the group can
    access and interact with the information (see the *Jump
    Associates: San Mateo* case study), and that people
    outside the group can see what is going on, and contribute
    ideas and information too.
5. *Make it informal:* If you truly want the group to gel and
    members to feel responsibility towards each other at both
    a personal and professional level, then treat it as a family.
    Encourage informal meetings where people can chat at
    one another's desks. Create an informal chilling area where
    group members can relax and hold conversations without
    having to sync their calendars. And above all, encourage
    a flat, empowering group management style.
6. *Make it comfortable:* This is not only an essential factor
    for building group dynamics, it is a necessity for every
    human-centric research space (Williams, 2013). A research
    group which works hard and responsibly towards a
    common end needs a comfortable work space. Comfort
    in itself is not a motivator, but is what Herzberg (1959)
    calls a hygiene factor, without which people cannot do
    good work (Brill, Margulis & Konar, 1984). When you are
    choosing the comfort factors - whether it is a coffee
    machine or the seating – include everyone in the choices
    and help them to really feel part of the group.
7. *Make it a celebration:* Celebrate success collectively – the
    small wins as well as the big ones. Winning is fun (Foy, 1994)
    and generates momentum for further successes. However,
    do not create an employee-of-the-month board or similar
    within the small group. We want the group members to
    feel responsible towards their peers through comradeship
    and sense of belonging, not for CV-enhancing and title-
    winning purposes. This form of encouragement is best
    carried out at the super-group level if at all.

WARNINGS

Not suitable for individualists
who are not looking to
change their ways.

Not suitable for temporary
groups, where members
are swapped in and out
via a hot-desk for a short
period of time.

#26

AUTHOR

Judy Robertson

—

SERVE TO

Those who need it

COST

Low

TIME

DEATH BY FORM FILLING

An awful warning of how time-consuming administration can divert time away from productive thought

BACKGROUND —

Clearly it is undesirable for researchers to be allowed to think. Researchers' desire for autonomy must be subdued, lest it interfere with important institutional traditions.

Keeping researchers busy with 'make work' is the ideal solution. It will fracture their time and concentration, and if all goes well, will lead to time-consuming faction wars between academics. That should keep them out of mischief.

INGREDIENTS

- A fleet of colour-coded spreadsheets
- Zealous administrators
- Many, many working groups
- Conflicting external pressures

METHOD

1. Require researchers to account for their time in minute increments, according to complicated categories. This will regularly distract them from productive thought, and hopefully cause them to waste further time in organising rebellions and discussing this affront to their academic liberty in very long meetings.
2. Monitor the quality of researchers' work according to arbitrary, ill-understood definitions. Refer to these as 'outputs' as if your employees are farm animals. Change the definitions at random, midway through the monitoring process. Set absurdly high standards, in order to reduce self-worth. The more time researchers spend in self-justification, the less time they have to indulge in solving research problems and other degenerate behaviour.
3. Form working groups on as many spurious topics as you can invent. Take care to make the working groups large (to make discussions difficult and actions hard). Be careful in forming the groups: members with long festering animosities are ideal for your purposes. Keep an index of the most garrulous faculty members and sprinkle them liberally in each group.
4. Require departments to restructure at least every five years. Use your judgement here: if relationships in the newly formed departments begin to become harmonious, force a restructuring early.
5. Each of the above stages requires an insanely complicated spreadsheet with judgemental colour coding and administrators paid according to how many errors they find in the form filling.

NOTES ON INGREDIENTS

Take with a pinch of salt.

WARNINGS

Researchers tend to be quite resilient so you may have to change your procedures every few months just to keep them on their toes.

Some spreadsheets can be extremely useful and help researchers move forward with their work significantly – be careful not to confuse these dangerous items with those that you are advocating.

RELATED RECIPES

See also *A recipe for mediocrity* and *Creativity crush*.

#27

AUTHOR

Alison Williams

SERVE TO

PhD students

COST

Free

TIME

TINA SAYS: 'PUSH!'

How to cope when your supervisor disappears

BACKGROUND —

My campus is very windy. One day, having failed miserably to get hold of my supervisor, I was returning to the bus when I saw a middle-aged woman struggling with a rumbustious toddler and a run-away pushchair. I grabbed the pushchair and helped settle the child, and started to chat. It turned out the child was her grandson and as well as looking after him full-time she had just completed her masters. As we parted she turned to me and said: "When it all gets difficult, just remember: 'Tina says: Push!'"

This recipe looks at one aspect of 'it all gets difficult' – what to do when your supervisor disappears. The recipe has two flavours, one if you are in the first half of your PhD, and the other if you are in the final/writing-up stage. You've emailed. You've phoned. You've texted. You've written a letter. You've even hung around outside your supervisor's office hoping that they have been simply hiding under the desk and will have to come out for lunch or a comfort break sometime. Nothing. So what do you do now?

INGREDIENTS

One or two fellow PhD students at the same stage or slightly ahead of you

Incurable optimism (or, failing that, dogged determination)

Productive anger

METHOD

1. *If you are abandoned in the first half of your PhD.*
    a. Set up an alternative critical support group. Get a couple of buddies who are at more or less the same stage of their PhDs as you are. If one of them is ahead of the other two, that's useful as well.
    b. Set up a weekly meeting – face-to-face or Skype. Try and keep it same day, same time, so that it becomes habitual.
    c. Each week, you look at one person's work. This means that the first person has to circulate a piece of writing to the others with enough time for them to read it critically and reflect on it, NOT five minutes before the Skype meeting is due to start.

d. Take it in turns to produce the piece of writing. This gives you two or three weeks to write something meaty towards your current chapter or your next seminar presentation.

e. You will learn to critique each other's writing, to add unexpected references, to draw your peers' attention to things they may have missed, and to ask the killer question: *'What do you mean by that?'*

2. *If you are abandoned in the last half of your PhD.*
By this stage in your PhD you will have passed the tipping point and overtaken your supervisor in knowledge of the subject. The top PhD emotion as identified by Thesis Whisperer (2011) is: 'Elation when you realise you know more than your supervisor about your topic and you feel brave enough to argue about it'.

a. Work with your buddies. Set up a group if you haven't already got one.

b. Hook into your emotions. Work by De Dreu, Baas & Nijstad (2008) has made strong links between mood and creativity. Mood tone, both positive and negative, impacts your creative behaviour and thus your creative output.
Their work looks at a 'dual pathway' to creativity, and you can harness both paths: a positive tone (optimism, the elation mentioned above) leads to cognitive flexibility and inclusiveness, and a negative tone (anger) leads to persistence and perseverance. At this stage in the game it might be the latter you need more. I had two supervisors, both of whom disappeared in my writing-up phase. One because she just couldn't read any more of my (multiple) drafts and insisted that the next thing she read would have to be my final draft. The other because he got very busy with other projects. I remembered 'Tina says push!' and got angry. And it worked.

COOK'S TIPS

It can be great to have buddies who don't know your subject. They can force you to write more clearly, and if they don't understand what you are trying to say, why do you assume your external examiner will?

It can work just as well with one buddy. In that case, swap writing every week or alternate weeks. This puts the pressure on, but come on, you can do it!

WARNINGS

You can allow yourself no longer than two minutes of grumbling at the start of each meeting. This is seriously hard work.

#28

AUTHOR

Anita McKeown

—

SERVE TO

An entire institution or organisation

COST

Low

TIME

YES WE CAN – SOMETIMES

Empower researchers for effective research

BACKGROUND —

A culture of empowerment is just that – it fully uses the power of its people.
To develop a culture of empowerment it is crucial to understand the position of people in the working environment, where the flow of power is, and what the constraints are.
The *Jump Associates: San Mateo* case study shows how the *Yes we can – sometimes* environment can be supported and encouraged through culture, through the design of the physical environment and through processes like the ones described below.

In an empowered culture, people have access to the information they need to make informed choices. They have the power to make personal decisions, and can generate a range of options for their choices. They have the skills (there is good training) and the knowledge for collective discussion and decision-making. They have permission – indeed the requirement – to be assertive and to challenge groupthink assumptions (Janis, 1982). Without dissent, even when it's wrong, creativity is inhibited and reduced (Nemeth & Nemeth-Brown, 2003) and the group's ideas become more conventional (Uzzi & Spiro, 2005).
And finally people have to have a real awareness of their ability to make beneficial changes. As Foy (1994, p. 12) says: "Winning is fun. Not-losing is not-fun."

> 66
>
> *...the consensus process is truly empowering.*
>
> 99

INGREDIENTS

Empowerment is a high-level ambition, and these are high-level ingredients, all essential for building a team of empowered individuals.

- *Trust:* **development of trust in skills, responsibility and communication**

- *Understanding:* **an understanding of the roles and responsibilities within the context or for the task in hand**

- *Accountability/ Responsibility:* **who are the people involved – job titles/tasks and responsibilities? Awareness of the limitations of the situation/context activity**

- *Communication especially listening:* **appropriate mechanisms (strategies/ tactics) to facilitate negotiation and communication of boundaries**

- *Respect:* **shared language and recognition of diverse languages and skillsets as valid.**

METHOD

1. Create a proactive working environment by asking questions:
   a. Is everyone's voice heard and listened to at every meeting?
   b. Can/does everyone in the team proactively identify and instigate changes that help you reach your goals?
   c. Do they get recognised and rewarded for this?
   d. Is information and knowledge generously and transparently shared between all levels/members of the team?

2. Develop or enhance a framework that encourages – and allows – teams and individuals to make significant contributions to the research and the research process. This can be done using:
   a. values and vision for guidance;
   b. collaborative goal setting wherever possible ;
   c. shared decision-making procedures;
   d. a skills audit of PIs (performance indicators) and researchers to help to identify strengths and areas for improvement (e.g. self-management, leadership and any additional research/business skills required in today's research environment).

3. Map the cultural terrain. Undertake an 'audit' of the current culture within the working environment. As Wheatley & Kellner-Rogers (1996) say: "A system needs access to itself. It needs to understand who it is, where it is, what it believes, what it knows. These needs are nourished by information."

4. Make visual maps of selected areas. Get everyone together with large sheets of paper, and negotiate and identify:
   a. where the possibilities for agency/empowerment are, and the limits ('– sometimes');
   b. challenges to conventional hierarchies when making decisions;
   c. where there is potential for misunderstanding or where communication paths may need to be changed.

5. Use consensus decision-making. Decision-making comes in different flavours:
   a. by decree: Top down: 'Because I say so...';
   b. by majority rule: Voting may not fully cover all the issues or empower people to propose or generate motions – it can limit choices for voting;
   c. by consensus: This type of group decision-making process seeks the consent of all participants and is used to describe both the decision and the process of reaching the decision.

6. Only the consensus process is truly empowering. It may take longer, but the decisions are fully accepted by everyone, and the work goes so much better thereafter (consensus.net/ocac2.html).

NOTES ON INGREDIENTS

The open communication that underpins a proactive, empowered working environment can be approached in different ways. It is good to have a structure that ensures that all voices are heard. Here are some suggestions for small and large groups.

Small-group approaches:

- *Sitting in a circle*. Create a circle with just chairs or sitting at a round table. This makes the group more egalitarian, and everyone can see everyone else's face. A rectangular table or rows of chairs can become hierarchical, especially when the most senior person in the group sits or stands at the top.

- *Talking Stick*. To get all the voices heard, use a talking stick. There are simple rules: the talking stick, or other object, is passed around the circle, and only the person holding it may speak (en.wikipedia.org/wiki/Talking_stick).

Large-group approaches:

- *Open Space Technology*. This conference, seminar, meeting is co-created by the participants as part of the process. People bring forward the issues they *really* want to talk about, and all the discussions are recorded. That way, everyone can see what was talked about and see any threads that they might want to follow up later (openspaceworld.com).

- *World Café Conversations*. Coming out of Peter Senge's Fifth Discipline, a World Café conversation makes sure all voices are heard. It is also a process that participants co-create, bringing forward their burning issues for discussion. The discussions are recorded visually as they happen, and the output is a series of images, words and diagrams that effectively map the territory and capture any decisions taken (theworldcafe.com).

- *The Way of Council*. Things don't have to be resolved: hearing people speaking from the heart can be enough in opening up possibilities and affirming positions, sharing and being heard (ojaifoundation.org).

WARNINGS

Each method step is best used at first with someone who is experienced in the technique.

RELATED RECIPES

See *Just describe* and *Research group as extended family*.

#29

AUTHOR

Dorothy Hardy

—

SERVE TO

An organisation with resources to support creative research

COST

High

TIME

CAN-DO SPACE

Facilitate the creativity of visiting researchers

BACKGROUND —

It can be difficult to get work completed, especially projects requiring a lot of machinery, technology and expertise. This is a solution based on my visit to Peters Studios (*Glasmalerei Peters Studios*), Paderborn, Germany.

This is a family-run firm which welcomes artists and people commissioning glass artwork from all over the world. It provides the technical expertise and machinery to make architectural glass artwork from small to large scale. The firm is a world leader in the use of solar cells in artistic architectural glass.

INGREDIENTS

- A place (real or virtual) with a welcoming, can-do attitude

- A lot of up-to-date machinery and/or digital technology and expertise that can be drawn on at short notice, as necessary

- Personnel with the skills to use the available technology and to teach others to use it

- In-house knowledge of the places and people where even more technology and expertise can be obtained

- A feeling that, although there are time constraints, there is still time for breaks, for creative play, and the possibilities for more time and space

- Space to be alone, within or away from the environment, either to get on with the work or to take breaks

METHOD

1. Right from the start, make sure the space is dedicated to welcoming newcomers. 'How can we help you?' demonstrates the *can-do* attitude. New people and ideas are supported.

2. Provide assistance to realise projects from concept to completion. Find out what the researcher would really like, so that the end product fits with their desires.

3. Ensure that it is fine to ask questions, including 'stupid' questions.

4. Find the right balance between having people to help when needed and allowing users the space to do their own work, and to ask for assistance as and when required.

5. Allocate one or two people to see the project through to completion. Assistance will be required from others, not just the originator of the problem.

6. Ensure that there is some reflection time. Especially once the project has been brought to a conclusion, make space to sit down (ideally with the researcher) and decide what to do differently next time and what to do next.

NOTES ON INGREDIENTS

Each space will need to be tailored to creation of a different type of project, such as glass design. There needs to be a strong, interactive hub of knowledge, showing how the different spaces connect.

COOK'S TIPS

- This recipe is particularly good when a project needs to be completed and time is short. Each space can be visited as necessary.

- Use food, accommodation (welcoming spaces to stay in), time and humour.

WARNINGS

This recipe is best for intense spells of work. It is possibly unwise for a researcher to work in one space all the time, so encourage them to move out of the space for other work, and to visit other spaces. This will help to avoid burn out.

AUTHOR'S NOTE

Many thanks to everyone at Peters Studios (www.peters-studios.com) for inspiration, support and workspace.

#30

AUTHOR
Alison Williams

—

SERVE TO
PhD researchers

COST
Low

TIME

OH, I THOUGHT YOU MEANT...

How to improve communication with your supervisor

BACKGROUND —

SPIRES (*Supporting People who Investigate Research Environments & Spaces*) held a seminar in April 2012 focusing on social research spaces, and in particular on the relationship between student and supervisor. In the feedback sheets, 16 out of the 17 comments said how useful it was to look at this topic, and of those 16, 15 focused on communication.

We shared stories about how we felt our supervisors didn't understand what it was we were trying to discuss; or answered a different question; or got cross with us for not getting to the point. There was a persistent theme of talking at cross-purposes, and another of students being nervous of our supervisors and ducking issues and being compliant; this even though we felt strongly about things – and had good data to back up our assertions. Throughout, there was a continuing theme of feeling that we just hadn't been properly *heard*.

At the seminar people had a chance to work with a role-play facilitator and Inger Mewburn (also known as *Thesis Whisperer*). Through this, working on our own issues and listening to our peers' problems, we learned lessons about the ingredients of this recipe: clarity, assertiveness, TA (*Transactional Analysis*) and how it can help the student-supervisor relationship.

INGREDIENTS

- Clarity

- Assertiveness

- TA (*Transactional Analysis*)
  Adult/Parent/Child model

METHOD

1. Workshop attendees identified the importance of *managing expectations – mine and my supervisor's* and the importance of *early and specific ground rules for the relationship*. Talk to your supervisor about what their expectations for the relationship are, and what yours are. What is the best way of communicating? Can I expect an answer to an email question within three days? Does my supervisor expect me to deal with minor stuff on my own and not bombard her/him with emails every day? If I'm not sure what I need, how is my supervisor expected to know it? If I don't know what my supervisor is expecting, how can I meet those expectations? Or negotiate those expectations in the context of other pressures?

2. We also discussed *the importance of reasonableness.* Remember that you are an adult (more about this shortly) and that your supervisor is too. Yes, they know more than you do about your subject (until you surpass them, that is!). Yes, they know more about how to get a PhD in your university. But they are people too with problems and issues and personalities just like you. So be reasonable.

3. Think through how to change things *constructively.* Whether those things are about your PhD or about how you work together. Remember: getting a PhD takes a lot of teamwork.

4. *Be braver and talk about what is bothering you.* Assertiveness is "behavior which enables a person to act in his own best interests, to stand up for himself without undue anxiety, to express his honest feeling comfortably, or to exercise his own rights without denying the rights of others" (Alberti & Emmons, 1974). If this is something you have difficulty with – if, for example, you get emotional rather than rational when asking for something – or don't ask at all – then there is a wide literature to consult. Personally, I found Susan Jeffers' book *Feel the Fear and Do It Anyway* (Jeffers, 1993) invaluable. Before I read it I had been complaining to a friend about how I was just a doormat. "No," she said, "You're not a doormat, you're a fitted carpet!" I got the book, and got my PhD – the rest is history.....

5. Your supervisor's response largely depends on the way you raise the problem. It is very important to be specific, to *know exactly what you want from your supervisor.* Remember it is OK to ask – they are there to help and to guide you through the PhD process. And they get brownie points when you pass. Hold that thought!

6. *Use TA in your supervisor/student communication*: Transactional Analysis (Berne, 1964) looks at how we relate to others based on ways of reacting that we absorbed as children. Some of these are useful. Especially at the start of your PhD journey, your supervisor may be a *Nurturing Parent* to your *Free Child* – it's supposed to be fun. But if I think of my supervisor as a scary *Controlling Parent*, my reaction to anything they say is likely to be as an *Adapted Child*: whiny or *Good Girl/Boy*. Watch out for, and challenge, words like *should, must, always, never*.

7. The good news is that we can change these reactions. The *Adult-Adult* relationship cuts across the parent/child dynamic. Aim to keep things simple: ask for clarification, say what you feel ('I'm feeling confused right now. Could we go over that point again so that I really understand what it is you mean?').

8. If the other person stays in parent or child position, you can still respond as an adult. It will make a huge difference to how you feel, and you will be less likely to get hooked into a response that you regret later. And sooner or later they will follow your example. Adult-to-adult communication between student and supervisor feels great and is immeasurably productive.

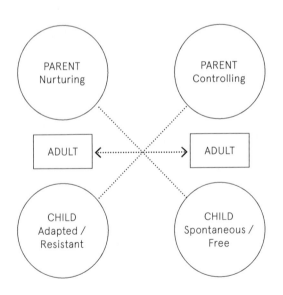

Source: Eric Berne (1964) Games People Play.

NOTE ON INGREDIENTS

See Solomon (2003) for an authoritative overview of TA.

#31

CREATIVITY CRUSH

An awful warning of how easy it is
to destroy group creativity using
minimum effort

AUTHOR

Derek Jones

SERVE TO:

Those who need it

COST/RESOURCE

Low

TIME

BACKGROUND

In this recipe, we consider
how to foster mediocrity
by wrecking the group
environment within which
researchers operate –
in particular, how to stifle
creativity by leveraging the
power of social factors.

INGREDIENTS

Goals, targets and other
quantitative objectives

Employee-of-the-month
schemes (based on
measures, not values)

A 'hands-on' office
manager, such as
David Brent

A joke book from the 1970s
to keep up morale

Posters to 'cheer people up'

Regular communications
to keep people focused
on the goals

METHOD

1. First of all realise this secret: creativity is really easy
   to kill - the smallest action can destroy it completely.
   This is easiest to do in a group situation by using a few
   social tricks, ensuring you snuff out the idea before
   it dares to become a concept.
2. Encourage a culture of extrinsic 'motivation':
   a. Set targets, not values – everyone likes a goal to
      work towards, such as increasing sales, output
      or other quantifiable objects. Ignore Meadows –
      the numbers matter more than the reason why
      we have the numbers (Meadows, 1998).
   b. Ensure that you measure performance in ways
      that allow non-subjective quantitative factors
      to emerge. Have a tick-box staff review process
      that is ignored except for reinforcement of
      specific elements, such as how much time
      was spent in the toilet.
   c. Don't measure output by quality – do it with
      numbers. If you suspect a researcher is holding
      on to that paper for reasons of quality, let them
      know that they are low on their target for the Pulp
      Author Frequent Publisher Staff Prize. That'll get
      them going.

d. In your regular newsletters (email, print, posters, intranet *and* podcast), ensure that everyone is reminded of the goals and targets. But don't forget to tell them how important they are. Contradictory messages like this really help destroy creativity and effective working in an insidious and excellent manner.

3. Try these in group creative sessions:
   a. Curl your upper lip at every suggestion made – don't say anything at all, just shake your head slightly and look disgusted. Doing this will have a far greater effect on the group than saying anything.
   b. Be impatient and stick to your deadline. Tap your fingers, and say 'come on people' or 'we need to solve this'.
   c. Set a goal. Start the meeting by saying 'we have to come up with a solution to X'. By pre-empting your group's creative outcomes, you take away any chance of divergent thinking – well done.
   d. Say 'I know, let's do some brainstorming'. There is a reason brainstorming doesn't work – it's because the individuals who think it does know less than they should about being creative.
   e. Remember, your team hasn't a clue about how to be creative – you have to tell them all about it. Why don't you read a few books on creativity and management and then just give it a go? Since you're in charge, it must mean you're better.
   f. Offer a nice reward – just ignore all the research that shows that superficial extrinsic motivation has a negative effect (Lepper & Greene, 1973).

4. Now that you have created the perfect social group space, do not allow your staff to engage in flexible working or working from home. Ensure that there are no other 'nice' places for them to use on the estate or that the use of these places is frowned upon when they return to their desks.

NOTES ON INGREDIENTS

Many of the ingredients and methods are based on Hennessey's top five creativity killers: expected reward, expected evaluation, surveillance, time limits, and competition (Hennessey, 2003).

Amabile and Kramer's work is well worth looking into if you are determined to do the job properly (e.g. Amabile & Kramer, 2011; 2012).

Sadly, the ingredients were also inspired by real life and direct experience.

Serve with a pinch of salt.

WARNINGS

Take care with some staff members – they might actually like such a regime. These people are after your job.

AUTHOR

Andrew MacVean

—

SERVE TO

Organisations or groups
wishing to improve
collaborative creativity

COST

Low

TIME

Quick

SERENDIPITY ON THE BACK OF A NAPKIN

Take advantage of good ideas from
chance encounters

BACKGROUND —

Encouraging serendipity
in the workplace is highly
desirable (Florida, 2002).
An unexpected exchange
of ideas can greatly enhance
the creative process.
By its nature serendipity
cannot be forced; however,
this recipe encourages
serendipitous exchanges
in a simple, low-cost way.
Does the pressure to
produce outputs limit
serendipitous encounters
within your institution?
Are you struggling to remove
these limitations to chance
encounters?

In this recipe, a culture of
serendipitous encounter is
encouraged and made more
probable. It uses an informal
dining environment situated
in a heavily populated area.
Supplying napkins is normal
procedure for tables in a
dining area: supplying pens
too encourages diners into
back-of a napkin thinking.
Key to this concept is the
idea of avoiding the
pressure to produce,
which can sometimes inhibit
spontaneous and creative
thinking (Amabile & Kramer,
2011). If no serendipitous
encounter occurs, the
napkins just clean up any
mess! Without the pressure
of formal outputs, problems
can be simplified, and
serendipitous thought
and encounters can be
informally recorded.

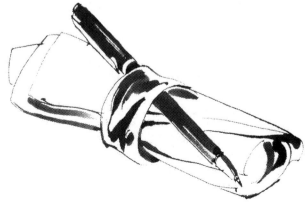

INGREDIENTS

- Set of railway carriage seats (if you can't get these, then any seating area arranged to facilitate face-to-face discussion will do)

- Napkin holders containing napkins and pens

- Alternatives to napkins are: whiteboard surface material, glass table top, scrap paper pile, small whiteboards

- Area of heavy footfall

METHOD

1. Find an area with heavy footfall with spare space for a few seats. This will afford the possibility of a maximum number of chance encounters.
2. Place your railway carriage seats near the area of heavy traffic. Seats should ideally be situated so that diners are not hidden from people walking through the area i.e. do not place the back of a seat facing a walkway.
3. Provide each place with a napkin holder, well stocked with both napkins and pens.

To encourage diners to use the area:

4. The seating design must be carefully considered. Seats should be comfortable and give good physical support.
5. Place the railway carriage seating in an area with additional benefits, e.g. access to toilets, to kitchen for food preparation, views to the outside world. Encourage people to use this space to eat away from their desks. This brings together diverse thought and skill sets. Consider banning technology in the railway carriages, so that people are not 'wired in'. This can encourage serendipitous conversations and a bit of low-tech sketching.

NOTES ON INGREDIENTS

See the *Jump Associates: San Mateo* case study for an example of this idea in action. The same use of railway carriage seating is made in the Glasgow Housing Association offices, Glasgow. In this instance, the seating is deliberately isolated from the busy footfall, so that conversations can be more private.

WARNINGS

Although closeness is important, there should be a balance between propinquity and privacy (Weeks & Fayard 2007; Fayard & Weeks 2011) depending on what is needed from the seating.

RELATED RECIPES

Make use of this recipe with *Attractor spaces*.

#33

AUTHORS

Meredith Bostwick-
Lorenzo Eiroa
Derek Jones

SERVE TO

Cross-disciplinary
researchers

COST

Low

TIME

'HOW MIGHT WE...' SPACE

Ask the right questions to generate creative answers

BACKGROUND

The 'How Might We...?' approach has been used by creative companies for decades, but the origins can be traced back to Min Basadur and his early days as creative manager at Procter & Gamble. His premise is that language can inhibit creativity instead of encouraging it: instead of asking 'How can we?' or 'How should we?' Basadur argues that companies who ask 'How might we...?' provide creative confidence (Ellspermann, Evans & Basadur, 2007; Berger, 2012).

'Might' acknowledges that some ideas may fail, while 'we' implies collaboration. At its heart, this is a framing process – a method that allows you to consider a problem in different ways. It primes your thinking and can help you with divergent thinking.

This recipe is intended as an idea generation process and it relies on people and space. If you need a structured process or output, have a look at *Just breathe* as an alternative.

INGREDIENTS

- Groups of researchers and thinkers

- A problem, research question or topic of interest to explore

- An unbiased facilitator (even better, a non-expert)

- Abundant writing surfaces (both horizontal and vertical)

- Room or space with suitable affordances: loose furniture, power/data, space to move and regroup

METHOD

1. A key to this recipe is the mix of behaviour, process and space. Locate a suitable space, preferably one that is open and flexible (see *Workshop space* and *Make do & mend space*). Take control of the space and do not let it dictate to you. Provide large sheets of paper or record items on a whiteboard. Find a good facilitator that will organise and record the session.

2. Identify a problem, research question or starting point. For expert thinkers, consider oblique starting points that seem tangential to the subject of interest or just pick a random subject!

3. Apply guidelines, such as Osborn's: defer judgement, combine and build on ideas, seek wild ideas, and go for quantity (Guilford, 1967).

4. Try the following starting points for divergent framing (in order of divergence):
    a. Ask 'How might we consider X?' Look for general topics and issues around the subject, record these and then consider each in turn in the same way.
    b. Say 'This is just a symptom'. Then ask 'What is the problem of the symptom?' See how far you can take this by iterating the question. Somewhere in this list of questions will be the 'sweet spot'.
    c. Ask 'How might we solve X differently?' Use this for radical idea generation but do not see these as solutions — only as starting points for further exploration.
5. Try to use other techniques to explore the issues raised (see *Visualising the problem*), such as drawing a target, where issues are 'closer' to the centre depending on relevance or some other factor.
6. The facilitator should record the session and ask the group probing questions, rather than offering information or directing the group towards a solution. Once the group or facilitator feels that enough divergence has been achieved, stop the session and take a break.
    Never push a session further than it 'wants' to go.

NOTES ON INGREDIENTS

Many creative organisations use this technique as a core activity in Design Thinking, for example, IDEO and Participle (see participle.net).

WARNINGS

Watch out for 'groupthink', where the ideas of a group coalesce to what is effectively a single idea (Janis, 1971). If this starts to emerge, end the session!

COOK'S TIPS

Wendy Newstetter, Director of Learning Sciences Research at Georgia Tech notes that facilitators do not need to be content experts or knowledgeable about each problem domain (Newstetter, 2006). In fact, being an expert in the problem area often makes facilitation difficult.

RELATED RECIPES

Try *Just breathe, Workshop space* and *Make do & mend space*.

#34

AUTHORS

**George Buchanan
Meredith Bostwick-
Lorenzo Eiroa**

—

SERVE TO

Research groups

NUMBER OF
SERVINGS

One or two per month

COST

Low

TIME

POPUP WHITESPACE HUBS

Spread ideas with regular cross-fertilising events

BACKGROUND —

Academics love to talk. Get the right people together in the right places and research ideas will start springing up like mushrooms. This emergent behaviour is in itself a 'space' where new ideas emerge naturally. The classic example is Bohmian Dialogue (Bohm, 2004). A shared cognitive space needs an appropriate physical space to act as a container.

This recipe presents one useful container space – 'popup whitespace'. Popup refers to the spontaneous conversational activities, and whitespace refers to a neutral environment (physical and intellectual). This combination creates a threshold space that exists only in-between and on the edge of something else, where others pass through: starting points and places of idea creation.

Director of the MIT Media Lab, Joichi Ito, describes the Media Lab as, "a place where we use undirected research to discover answers to questions that we haven't asked yet because you don't know to look there yet". Ito notes that "...novel, disruptive discoveries are found by searching in spaces where you don't know the answer, or even what you're looking for". What he terms, "white spaces" are the spaces where "we learn along the way" – those spaces which are "adjacent to areas where we have core skills and knowledge" (Ito, 2012).

INGREDIENTS

- Open reusable space

- A schedule of small-scale cross-fertilising events

- A willing and enthusiastic organiser

- White surfaces that absorb creative thought

- Flipcharts and pens

- Unfamiliar territory, interesting and challenging activities and processes, and interesting themes / starting points

METHOD

1. Identify an accessible but, most importantly, flexible and reusable space. Try to find places at the edge of a research group, department or even faculty. Think creatively about where these locations might be – they can range from rooms to simple wall spaces. They can even be outside your institution or exist online.

2. Populate this space with affordances (Gibson, 1977) to encourage open and divergent thinking. These can be as simple as providing flipchart paper and pens, whiteboards or napkins. Or you might consider providing digital working spaces.

3. Organise and run small-scale events that demonstrate cross-group themes in the community, and ensure these are publicised physically.

4. A key to these events is the starting point – make these open questions, interesting themes and give researchers the opportunity to pitch new ideas or thoughts. Think about cross-disciplinary connections for alternative starting points.

5. The other key is the activity – don't just have presentations; encourage the group to interact with the subject and have a few activities on hand to start things off. Avoid the traditional audience-facing-speaker seating layout – the 'speaker' should simply be presenting the starting point.

6. Start small and build around small, potential networks, before taking more risks. Recognise when it is working as a core group of interested individuals and when it's time to split the group up into smaller, more energetic versions.

7. At each event, provide refreshments (ideally fruit and water – hydrated brains work best!), and information pointers and resources (e.g. books, links to online repositories) that are relevant to the theme. If relevant to specific services, then host such information there before and after the event.

8. Remember to capture the event(s) - capturing discussions through participant documentation (sketchbooks, flipcharts, sticky notes) can be invaluable.

WARNINGS

If the events are too frequent, they will prove tiring, so ensure a steady, sustainable pace.

Recognise when the energy has gone out of the event or if a particular idea or person is taking over. This is an incubator space where starting points are the priority.

RELATED RECIPES

Goes well with 'How might we...' space.

#35

AUTHOR

Jeanne Narum

SERVE TO

Any researchers,
at any stage, wanting
to push the horizon

COST

Low (if you bring Lego
bricks from home)

TIME

SWEET SPOT

A process for imaginative horizon planning

BACKGROUND

In the summer of 2007, the
Project Kaleidoscope (PKAL)
community was introduced
to a 'Fanciful Horizon'
exercise by a team from
the Franklin W. Olin College
of Engineering. This exercise
was adapted from one used
in their introductory
engineering course;
it also reflects the planning
process that preceded the
opening of the college. This
recipe was developed with
assistance from Benjamin
Linder, Debbie Chachra,
and Mark Somerville.

The exercise is a structured,
collaborative approach for
identifying and shaping
out-of-the-box ideas that
can push an organisation or
research team towards a
horizon more fanciful and
creative, more transformative
than otherwise might be
imagined.

INGREDIENTS

- Lots and lots of Lego
(ideally from home) –
the more crazy and diverse
the Lego objects, the more
creative the process
becomes

- Various colours and sizes
of sticky notes, including
purple and yellow

- Large sheets of cheap
newsprint paper, flip chart
paper, and masking tape

METHOD

1. Determine your vision of...(whatever it is you are aiming for):
    a. Begin in self-organising groups of four; identify
        one person to keep the group on task, moving
        towards the fanciful horizon.
    b. Each person in the group generates approximately
        four ideas (single words or short phrases) that
        could describe the vision. These should be written
        on purple sticky notes. (5 mins)
    c. Each person reads their ideas to their group of
        four which collectively decides which are mundane,
        and which are fanciful vision, putting the purple
        sticky notes on the left half of the newsprint into
        boxes labelled 'mundane' and 'magical'. (7 mins)
    d. The group collectively reviews the ideas, considers if
        patterns are emerging, whether mundane visions can
        be tweaked to become more magical, whether magical
        visions can be revisited to become more realistic.
    e. Write your refined vision on a yellow sticky note,
        and place it in a box labelled 'sweet spot' on the
        left of the newsprint. (10 mins)

2. Develop magical strategies to realise your vision, repeating
    the earlier steps:
    a. Each person generates approximately four ideas
        (single words or short phrases) that could describe
        the specific strategies that a research group or
        community could take to achieve such a vision.
        These should be written on any of the other sticky
        note colours (not purple or yellow). (5 mins)
    b. The ideas are again shared, with collective
        consideration as to which are mundane, which
        magical, placing coloured sticky notes on the
        right half of the newsprint in boxes labelled
        'mundane' or 'magical'. (7 mins)
    c. Identify the least mundane, most magical, out-of-
        the-box strategy to realising your vision, and write
        your strategy in the 'sweet spot' box on the right
        of the newsprint using your colour choice. (5 mins)
    d. Build and share your vision and strategies:
    e. Combine into groups of eight; share 'vision' ideas
        in the 'sweet spot'; develop a common vision that
        can be described in one sentence. (5 mins)
    f. Using Lego from the communal box, build a model
        of your vision engaging the whole group of eight.
    g. Write on a large sticky note your collective vision
        and the one or two most magical strategies to
        realise that vision.
    h. Prepare a signed gallery sketch of your vision
        on a separate sheet of flip chart paper.
    i. Defend and clarify your vision and strategies
        to the assembled group – fun for all!

MAGICAL

THE SWEET SPOT

MUNDANE

#36

AUTHOR

Alison Williams

—

SERVE TO

Researchers at all
career stages

COST

Minimal

TIME

VISUALISING THE PROBLEM

Group problem solving through a visual
and kinaesthetic process

BACKGROUND —

People absorb and process information in three different ways: auditorily, visually and kinaesthetically; the majority (up to 75%) have a visual preference (Fleming, 2006; Fleming & Baume, 2006). It makes no sense to have people with a strong visual preference, and possibly a kinaesthetic secondary preference, sitting talking to each other processing everything in an auditory way. Information is poorly absorbed and links may be missed.

This recipe sets out how groups of people can work together to think together visually: on their feet, moving around, being able to *see* what each other are thinking as they work together. Letting the images spark new connections, seeing how the images suggest other things, realising where things are not working because the images make it very clear.

Georgia Tech's Department of Biomedical Engineering has a suite of rooms dedicated to problem-based learning (Newstetter, 2006). The rooms are small – approximately 6m by 8m (20 by 25 feet) – and the walls are covered from floor to ceiling in whiteboard material. Students at all levels use the rooms to work on complex problems set by the faculty. As they talk, they capture their thinking on the whiteboards, drawing graphs, diagrams, symbols and words. As the images build, so the ideas grow, are challenged, are changed, are built, and are critiqued. The level of learning and thinking is impressively high.

INGREDIENTS

The first set of ingredients gives alternatives for creating as large a blank white space as possible. The bigger the better!

- **Whiteboards (as large as you can get hold of)**

- **Talking walls (whiteboard covering floor to ceiling, wall to wall)**

- **Flipcharts**

- **Lining paper on the walls**

- **Glass walls or windows that can be written on**

- **Metal walls with magnetic blocks to hold papers in place**

- **Pin boards or noticeboards**

The next set of ingredients is about making the marks and images

- **Marker pens of different sizes and types – and *lots* of colours**

- **Sticky notes**

- **Coloured wool**

- **Drawing pins**

- **Masking tape or other adhesive tape**

METHOD

1. This is an iterative creative process, flowing from individual to group and back again several times. Here are some alternatives.

2. Make a diagram of the issue at hand. Map its progress. Invite others to critique it. Map the conversation as it emerges. Capture everything – there is nothing too trivial to contribute.

3. Gather solo thoughts on sticky notes (one thought per note) then put them up on the wall. Cluster them roughly, then more thoughtfully. You will need one or two or occasionally three iterations, depending on the group, the task, the focus etc. Invite people to add more, to ask questions, to draw links from one cluster to another.

4. Mind map the issue (Buzan 2002). One person draws the basic map with main branches, consulting the group about what is central or core to the issue under discussion. People are then invited to add more branches, twigs etc. To add words and pictures, icons and symbols, emoticons etc. Then, using one colour that has been kept back (ideally red), start making links/arrows between the different areas. See where the lines go – pay attention to where they cross over other groupings – there will be something to see/infer there. Pay attention to gaps in the map – something needs to emerge there. If you have a giant mind map spread out over a whole wall, you can use wool to show the links.

NOTES ON INGREDIENTS

If you can't write on the walls, use the windows. If you can't make images on the windows, use rolls of lining paper spread across the tables or over the floor. If you haven't got any paper, go to the beach and draw in the sand. If you haven't got a beach...look at the *Rebel space* recipe.

COOK'S TIPS

You may need a facilitator to help people to get started. Sometimes at the start of a session people need permission to make marks – and a gentle invitation to make or capture a point. Each person should have a marker pen or the means of making marks that has been agreed on: no 'holding the flipchart'. There should be empowerment of every individual: an expectation that everyone will contribute to the whole picture. Once curiosity takes over, any reticence about making marks/adding to the image will fade, self-empowerment will kick in and everyone will contribute.

WARNINGS

You have to give yourself permission to write on the walls, to stand up and get stuck in (see *Workshop space*, *Rebel space* and *Make do and mend*). It takes nerve to commandeer a wall or window, but remember: 'It is better to beg forgiveness than to ask permission!'

#37

AUTHORS

**Nicole Lotz
Derek Jones**

—

SERVE TO

**Large teams from
six upwards**

COST/RESOURCE

Low

JUST BREATHE

Breathe in and out for creative nirvana

BACKGROUND —

Applying divergent and convergent thinking to large teams can offer rich interactions and inspire creative thinking (Osborn, 1953; Guilford, 1967). Divergent thinking, in this context, is the process of generating multiple, different and original ideas in response to a problem. Convergent thinking is then used to apply an order to the ideas generated to converge on a few, or one.

The breathe metaphor can be used in creative sessions as a useful way of communicating this process. 'Breathing in' means diverging. Imagine taking a deep breath: you take in different ideas and everything around you. Now breathe out: and you are left with a few valuable ideas, discarding the remains back into nirvana.

Good breathing helps to avoid groupthink (Janis, 1971) which characterises a group that reaches consensus without thinking of alternatives.

INGREDIENTS

- Sticky notes, flipcharts, whiteboards and pens

- Some secluded places for small groups

- A large room with lots of wall space for posting and ordering ideas

METHOD

1. Post a problem statement to a large group of diverse people.
2. Breathe in (diverge)
   a. Discuss the problem in a large group for a few minutes (up to 10). This starts the divergent phase that generates multiple different ideas. Try to consider any relevant issues around the problem (see 'How might we...' space for some ideas on how to do this).
   b. Split into smaller subgroups to continue the breathing-in process for 30 minutes. This time, discuss some of the ideas in more detail, again, exploring as many issues as come out of the process as possible. At some point the converging or breathing out will begin naturally.
3. Breathe out (converge)
   a. Come back together into the large group and present all the ideas while putting sticky notes with the gist of the ideas and some detail on the wall. Others can make notes of similar ideas during the presentation.
   b. Discuss overlapping and outstanding ideas. End the convergence by trying to identify patterns in the ideas generated.
4. Now consider whether the original problem statement is still the right problem.
5. This should lead to another round of breathing in during which the subgroups take a converged idea and generate more ideas or alternative details. Use a sequence of divergence and convergence to work through the issues of any problem.
6. Don't diverge or converge too far – but make sure you go far enough. Somewhere in between these extremes lies the *Sweet spot*. On either side of this will be questions such as 'why didn't you consider...', so at the very least, you will be exposing yourself to these sooner rather than later.

NOTES ON INGREDIENTS

For a good primer on this, see Cougar (1994), the Creative Education Foundation (2013) and the IDEO toolkit for educators (Riverdale and IDEO, 2011). Remember that this is as much an acclimatisation activity as it is a problem-solving one – considering a topic is as much about exploring the context as it is the problem itself.

COOK'S TIPS

In very large teams breathing can be difficult, especially if the team is very diverse and the participants are not familiar with each other. In the divergent phase, some people in the group might speak up while others remain silent. Experiment with the subgroup arrangement to get a balanced team that allows inclusive team contributions to emerge.

WARNINGS

In the divergent phase, the details behind some ideas might get lost in a more superficial discussion and the team risks missing out on an informed process of ordering ideas. It can sometimes be useful to have one person dedicated to capturing the deeper levels and getting these out onto the wall so that everyone can see them.

#38

AUTHOR

Marian Dörk

—

SERVE TO

Early-stage researchers,
probably at the suggestion
of research directors at
organisation level

COST

Medium

TIME

RESEARCH INTEREST VISUALISATION

Use digital visualisation to identify
common research interests

BACKGROUND —

Effective research relies
on cross fertilisation of ideas
between different
researchers. Considering the
likelihood of researchers
with different backgrounds
working on similar or related
problems in a research
institution, it is unfortunate
how often they may cross
paths without knowing about
each other or their research.
Meeting around the
proverbial water cooler may
simply not be an option for
researchers in different
departments, based in
different buildings.

This recipe, developed through
conversations with Graeme
Earl, proposes a dynamic
technological visualisation
of the spatial and academic
dimensions of co-located
research activity. The
visualisation juxtaposes
researchers' changing interests
and locations on the campus.
It reveals commonalities among
people in their research topics,
problems, and methods,
prompting ad hoc brainstorming
meetings, coffee breaks, and
beer outings. Apart from
helping people find each
other, the visualisation can
also be used to stay aware of
the changing research
landscape – both digital and
physical – at a large institution.

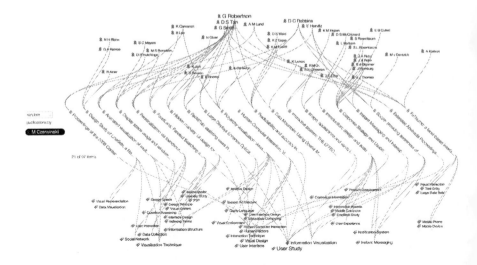

INGREDIENTS

Researchers willing to

- **Engage in interdisciplinary collaboration**

- **Share changing research interests and efforts**

- **Learn about colleagues' research**

- **Technology and software that will support this, e.g.**

  - **http://mariandoerk.de/ pivotpaths/**

  - **http://mariandoerk.de/ pivotpaths/ demo/#/1:0_361485**

  - **Inspires software – see Hensman (2012)**

METHOD

1. Researchers within an organisation are asked to electronically share their current research interests, methods, and problems in keywords and short phrases.
2. Researchers then view the visualisation, either in a shared screen in a common area or in the privacy of their own monitor, to see if they could find a research friend.
   a. The visualisation pairs up researchers that might want to consider having an informal chat together. This should be carried out with the lowest effort and expectation possible on behalf of the researchers. The invitations should be seen as primarily for interesting conversations and potentially for fruitful collaborations. By sharing one's own interests, the visualisation reveals those locations (offices, studios, or cafes) that have a high density of people with similar or complementary research interests.
   b. An interest map of a campus could help researchers to steer towards possible collaborators – or avoid them to have a proper break!
3. An alternative, less dynamic, approach could be based on recently submitted or published papers. While this could serve as a robust way to identify those with similar interests, it is by default always a bit out of date, as academic publications mainly represent research results, not research in progress.

COOK'S TIPS

To gather the necessary data (either weekly keywords or published articles), a beautifully designed visualisation could invite researchers to share their work in order to see their research effort in the context of their colleagues' efforts.

WARNINGS

University administrators should be careful not to turn this visualisation into a leader board or even the basis for evaluation, as this may impede staff relations and the desired collaborations.

#39

AUTHOR

Judy Robertson

—

SERVE TO

Groups of researchers
who wish to write together
for the first time

COST/RESOURCE

There are many free
solutions

TIME

Varies

VERSION CONTROL: MANAGING COLLABORATION ON ACADEMIC DOCUMENTS

Prevent tears and tantrums with some basic housekeeping

BACKGROUND —

One of the set-up costs on new collaborative projects is working out how to write together. Team members from different backgrounds will have different approaches to this, so to avoid stress, it is worth planning well in advance of a deadline how you are going

Which system you use depends on the purpose of the document you are writing, the mode of collaborative writing you choose, whether you are co-located and the technical skills of the co-authors.

INGREDIENTS

- A team of writers

- A sprinkling of different collaborative software tools to taste e.g. Google Docs, Dropbox, Microsoft Word

- One responsible and patient editor

METHOD

1. *Synchronous face-to-face collaborative writing.* If you're working in the same place with one other writer, it is possible to jointly write the document with one person dictating and the other typing. Make sure you swap roles from time to time. A similar practice called pair programming is used in the software industry to improve the quality of the software on the basis that two brains are better than one. I used this method to write a book with a close colleague and it was a very rewarding experience because we got to the point where we literally finished each other's sentences. Organise your drafts with a naming convention which includes the date and time on successive versions of the file. (Never name a file 'final' until the wretched thing is actually published.)

2. *Synchronous online collaborative writing.* If you can't be in the same place as your co-author(s), you can jointly work on the document in a tool which allows synchronous editing such as Google Docs (www.google.com/drive). Such tools generally enable more than one author to edit a document simultaneously, with a chat feature to support discussions about who is going to tackle which section. Google Docs has a clear time-stamped version history which enables you to roll back to previous versions of the document if something goes horribly wrong. For academic publication, often one author will need to take responsibility for formatting the document in the template supplied by the publishers. If the document is not for academic publication, group wikis can be useful as a way to document knowledge and decisions within the team. Wikis are a series of organically growing, related articles semantically linked together and jointly edited by a group. The best known example is Wikipedia, but you can set up your own wiki using software such as Media Wiki (www.mediawiki.org).

3. *Asynchronous collaborative writing.* Distributed teams often work on documents at different times. There are a number of ways of managing this. The most common relies on email, Microsoft Word, a frustrated co-ordinator and howls of rage. The co-ordinator delegates sections to others to write, receives the sections by email, and cuts and pastes (or merges them) into a single file. The problems really begin when the editing process kicks off because if you're not careful the co-ordinator gets multiple conflicting revisions from many authors and has to resolve them manually.

Microsoft Word's changes tracker and comments tool
can help with this to some extent, but it is still useful to
explicitly decide the order in which authors will edit the
document, and 'lock' the document to other authors
while someone else is editing. Version control software
enables actual locking of the files, but this can be
confusing for those without a technical background.
An email agreement and a big stick wielded by the
co-ordinator can achieve the same effect. Shared file
spaces such as Dropbox (www.dropbox.com) can also
be useful if you are managing a large set of interrelated
documents between authors, as emails back and forth
will not preserve folder structure. Dropbox maintains
file dates and indicates files which are conflicted (those
which two editors happened to save at the same time).
This book was edited using Dropbox and the editors
have not killed each other yet despite my tendency
to save files in the wrong folder.

4.   *Fancy flavours.* The technically inclined may be scornful
of such solutions. Mathematicians and their cronies love
LaTeX. This is fine if your collaborators do too, but if they
don't you'll have to generate pdfs and ask them to use a
pdf annotation tool to send comments. If you want to use
some kind of version control to maintain a history of the
document and enable you to retrieve previous versions
of your *LaTeX* files, you could try software such as GitHub
(github.com). For the true gourmet, with a passion for
scientific replication, I recommend *Sweave* (Leisch, 2002)
with *LaTeX* and *R.* This enables you to embed the statistical
commands you used to analyse your data or make graphs
in R within the source file of your report. The advantage
of this is that your analysis is always in sync with your
document so when you come to do revisions to an article
you don't have to scrabble around trying to remember
how on earth you got your results.

WARNINGS

Don't impose a complicated editing system on unwilling
colleagues and expect them to use it. It's hard enough
getting busy collaborators to write the text, so don't
put unnecessary hurdles in their way to give them an
excuse not to write.

#40

AUTHOR

Bruce M. Mackh

SERVE TO

Those interested in
implementing
interdisciplinary research
and instruction in and
through the arts

COST

Medium

TIME

CREATIVE SPACES FOR INTERDISCIPLINARY RESEARCH

Use the arts to explore familiar research
territory and expand research options

INGREDIENTS

Space: standard university
classroom with traditional
furnishings removed;
whiteboards and bulletin
boards are helpful; access
to water is advisable

Furnishings: tables and
chairs that can be moved
easily into different
configurations or stacked
and moved out of the way;
seating should be sufficient
for the number of students
enrolled in the class

People: a facilitator
enthusiastic about
challenging fixed
approaches through
innovative, collaborative,
creative methods
incorporating the arts
with STEM (science,
technology, engineering
and mathematics)
and humanities disciplines;
PhD students who want to
see how using the arts as
a way of exploring familiar
research territory can
expand and enhance their
research options.

Social: an administrative
team which supports the
idea of exploring in and
through the arts to kick-
start creative thinking,
innovation, entrepreneurship,
and a capacity for problem-
solving

Technology: (optional)
a wireless projection
system capable of linking to
individual laptop computers
for sharing work

Materials: a range of
theatrical props, musical
instruments, art supplies
and design objects e.g. hats,
scarves, wigs, and other
costume pieces, toys, canes,
maracas, triangles, rhythm
sticks, recorders, kazoos,
bells, finger cymbals,
penny-whistles, paper
goods, paints and paint
brushes, modelling clay,
wire, wood, paper, and
cardboard

BACKGROUND

In the work I've done as
the Mellon Research Project
Director at the University of
Michigan's ArtsEngine,
I've visited numerous US
research institutions where
arts integration is being
implemented in exciting
ways. This recipe is a
compilation of the
observations I've made
during these visits regarding
ideal spaces for creative
investigation, research,
and learning.

Similar art integration
projects have taken place
in the UK. For example,
Strathclyde University
challenges its PhD civil
engineering students'
preconceptions about the
use of materials, structural
form and environmental
context. SMARTlab
(University College Dublin)
challenges its PhD students
(in disciplines as diverse
as mathematics, computer
games, architecture, social
science) to rethink their
research topics and methods
through the lens of visual
arts, dance and movement,
or music/rhythm.

METHOD

1. *Space and furnishings*. Remove all traditional furnishings
   from the classroom and replace with sturdy, lightweight,
   durable tables and chairs that can be moved out of the
   way when necessary.
2. *Materials*. Create storage for required materials in a large
   closet or in labelled bins. Collect materials and put them
   in the storage area, renewing consumable materials as
   needed.
3. *People and Social*. In a research seminar/workshop,
   introduce an exemplar to be explored using creative,
   interdisciplinary, collaborative investigation in and through
   the arts. For example, in the Strathclyde civil engineering
   seminar, PhD students were introduced to a simple form
   of biomimicry through the example of Calatrava's fractal
   rainforest design for the atrium in a Toronto mall. They
   were then invited to make drawings of natural objects
   (flowers, twigs, feathers etc) and apply them to the
   problem of designing a water tower. One design, based on
   the pendant head of a snowdrop, introduced an innovative
   approach to water storage. Another, based on a sponge,
   spurred thinking about osmosis as a means of raising water
   up the tower.
4. *Cultivate a suitable environment*. Researchers to
   feel safe in taking risks, stretching beyond their personal
   comfort zones, and engaging with movement, voice,
   and materials. Invite additional personnel as needed,
   e.g. for experiencing idea-generating through synchronic
   interaction (Sawyer, 2003) invite a drama colleague to
   conduct a mini-seminar on theatrical improvisation.
   The facilitator's role is to ignite the spark, then make
   sure the blaze neither fades away or rages too far afield,
   remaining a productive, beneficial, exciting generator
   of new ideas.
5. Watch the fun begin!

WARNING

Embarking upon this kind of venture without adequate
financial support can result in the failure of the program.

#41

AUTHOR

**Meredith Bostwick-
Lorenzo Eiroa**

—

SERVE TO

**Cross-disciplinary
students, researchers
looking for a spark!**

COST

Low

TIME

IDEA ROOM

Dedicate a room to rigorous group
creativity

BACKGROUND —

In the times of Thomas
Edison, ideas came from
individuals. Today through
iterative creativity (Resnick,
2007) ideas are spawned
from group thinking and
collaboration as well as
from a combination of
individual and group
thinking or synchronic
interaction (Sawyer, 2003).

Entire workplaces have
become 'idea rooms'.
Groves & Knight (2010)
look inside what they call
the most creative spaces
in business: the research
environments in
organisations like Google,
Lego, Dreamworks
Animation and T-Mobile.
In academic institutions,
places like Georgia Tech's
Problem-Based Learning
suite and Stanford
University's Hasso Plattner
School of Design (d.School)
are leading the way.

In the idea room,
researchers engage in
an idea-logue or Bohmian
dialogue (Bohm, 2004).
This implies the collective
intelligence of the group
(dialogue means through
the word, not two people
talking), or of an individual
reflecting by themselves.

In an idea-logue an initial
idea morphs into a series
of overlapping ideas,
informing one another,
building momentum and
creating a richer, more
developed collective idea –
a larger idea or concept
which no longer can be
traced to a single individual,
but is now owned by the
larger collective.

An idea room is a physical
space and a process:
if the process is for visually
sharing and building ideas,
then the space needs to
be whiteboarded. If the
process is for talking in a
Bohmian dialogue, then
it's best to have comfortable
chairs in a circle.

The idea room can exist
within the cracks of an
institution or department
– on the edges, on the
borders of the primary
classroom, lab, or seminar
space. It can be physically
configured as an ante-room
or a place that clears the
mind, and allows for the
open exploration of
questions. It is equally
a place which eliminates
anxiety, tension, or
projected assumption
before approaching a
set of problems

INGREDIENTS

- Individuals

- A mentor or facilitator

- Small & medium round
  tables (to activate
  conversation; without
  hierarchy)

- No distractions
  (clear of clichés)

- Natural daylight
  (a nourishing environment)

- Whiteboard walls &
  surfaces (to map out
  cognitive processes)

- Sticky notes (to propose),
  pencils (to sketch), erasers
  (to reconsider)

- SMART boards (to capture
  diagrams and notes for
  future reference)

- A reflective atmosphere

- A variety of seating options
  and reconfigurable
  furnishings

METHOD

1. Agree the guidelines: How are we going to work together
   so that all voices are heard? These typically will be:
   a. No interrupting
   b. Respect all ideas; build on them rather than
      demolishing them
   c. Have fun
   d. Silence is good
   e. What is said here, stays here
      (unless otherwise agreed)
2. Start by checking-in. Go round the group so that
   each participant can say how they feel at that moment
   and what their intention is for the session.
3. Next, people engage in open discussion whether through
   Bohmian dialogue or making marks on the whiteboards/
   walls. (See notes on ingredients in *Yes we can – sometimes*).
   Anything that is agreed to be discussed later is put on a
   sticky note in a designated space so it doesn't get forgotten.

4. Concepts from problem-based learning can be useful in the idea room for researchers. For example, 'inquiry notebooks' and 'concept maps' can be used to collect data on how well the group is progressing in tackling a problem. Newstetter (2006) discusses how cognitive maps may be graphical representations that depict the understanding and structure of knowledge. The idea room then provides a space "to evaluate and map the depth and complexity of conceptual knowledge" (Newstetter, 2006).

    a. An inquiry notebook is a way of reflecting on your own process: ask yourself, and note your answers to, questions about your questions. Where did they come from? What was my thinking that prompted those questions? Are they limiting or expanding my enquiry? What resources did I use? How did I know about them? How have I gathered the pieces of data or information together? Is there a pattern forming and if so, what has been my thinking?

    b. A concept map is a visual representation of your thinking – Buzan's Mind Mapping (2010) is the most widely known and used method. For further information and ideas of different concept maps, consult the *Visualising the Problem* recipe.

COOK'S TIPS

The idea lab is not a banal space for problem-solving, but rather an incubator for ideas generation, 'problem-finding' questioning and critique.

RELATED RECIPES

This recipe goes well with the *Workshop space, Visualising the problem* and *Yes we can – sometimes* recipes.

WARNINGS

Proper utilization and scheduling is key for the idea room.

While creativity can be spontaneous, the idea room is a rigorous space which uses the routine practices of pre- and post-critical thinking to tap our creative processes, develop our cognitive skills and understanding of the underlying causes and effects of our own successes and failures.

THE ALTERNATIVE ACADEMIC

—

Online

—

AUTHOR

Inger Mewburn

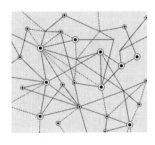

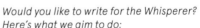

The Thesis Whisperer is a blog newspaper dedicated to the topic of doing a thesis. It is edited by Dr Inger Mewburn, director of research training at the Australian National University, and author of this case study.

THE BIRTH OF THE THESIS WHISPERER

I thought up the idea for the blog in the shower (as you do), inspired by a phone call from a student who asked: "Are you the thesis whisperer?" In retrospect the idea had been brewing for a while, ever since my brother-in-law remarked: "Your next job will come via the Internet, but only if people know what it is you do".

"Thesis Whisperer" was as close to a job description as I was likely to get, but I also liked the idea of this as a kind of teaching practice which could be described as research supervision without boundaries.

The first page I put up was my editorial guidelines (http://thesiswhisperer.com/about/) – this was a guide for myself, a way to inform new visitors what to expect, and a provocation to potential guest posters:

Would you like to write for the Whisperer? Here's what we aim to do:

We want to be concise. PhD students have to do a lot of reading so no posts will be longer than 1000 words

We want to learn from people's stories about doing a research degree – but we don't need to hear about your topic. There are enough journals out there for that.

We are not a 'how to' guide to doing a thesis, but we are happy to dish out practical tips and techniques that work for us.

We don't want to just talk about writing – successfully finishing a thesis or dissertation is about more than that. But we don't want to be sued, so we are going to always keep it nice.

We want to stimulate conversations so our posts will always be opinionated, hopefully without being obnoxious.

We want to hear your voice. Doing a thesis can take the fun out of anyone's writing. This is a place you can relax because there is no examiner watching.

We can't pay you. But we promise to never rip off your work and present it as our own. If you want to write for us it is because you have an urge to share your experience and help others so it may travel further than you think (note the licensing arrangements below).

Interested? Email inger.mewburn@anu.edu.au, preferably with a sample piece of less than 1000 words. If you want to suggest a post or ask a question – visit our feedback page.

Want to use our material? You are free to reproduce any posts from the Whisperer through the Creative Commons "Attribution-noncommercial-sharealike" licence. *Most of the photos on this site are copyright-free and sourced from* Morguefile.

Strangely, aside from updating my employment details (that new job did, in fact, come through the Internet) and adding a moderation policy for comments, I>ve never found it necessary to revisit these editorial guidelines.

WHAT IT IS AND WHAT IT DOES

Since the first post on 7 June 2010 ('*How is research writing different to driving a car?*') there have been a total of 246 published posts – over 250,000 words of original content. In the first three years or so of operation, there were nearly 1.5 million hits and 6,500 comments, which I'm sure is minuscule compared to some of the big fish in the blog pond, but personally satisfying. The Thesis Whisperer is proudly a niche blog. I think there is a real sense of community around it, a community which is truly global as there have been visitors from almost every country in the world.

What do people like about the blog? The list of top ten most-requested posts of all time gives us some indications:

1. How to write 1000 words a day (and not go batshit crazy).
2. Academic assholes and the circle of niceness.
3. How do I start my discussion chapter?
4. The Valley of Shit.
5. What to say when someone asks you: 'Should I do a PhD?'
6. Should you quit your PhD?
7. Developing your inner Yoda, er – scholar.
8. About the Thesis Whisperer.
9. Surviving a PhD – 10 Top Tips.
10. Turn your notes into writing using the Cornell method.
11. Publications in your PhD.

OK, there are 11 Top Ten Posts, but who's counting?

While the top post is about writing, many of the most popular are about academic cultures: "Academic assholes and the circle of niceness" even went viral after being picked up by the Times Higher Education and the Chronicle. Because I have used pictures of Yoda, leprechauns and dinosaurs to illustrate my blogs some people come to the site via those, but the majority are looking for guidance on writing (3,229), accessing the site by searching for *thesiswhisperer, phd whisperer, thesis whisperer blog,* and *PhD discussion* (2,480 total), and specific queries such as 'zotero vs endnote' (566) or the technique 'shut up and write' (490). Readers want support with the PhD process, the culture that surrounds it and the emotions that accompany it.

NEW MEDIA AND ACADEMIC MEASUREMENT

New media platforms such as blogs give us pause for thought about what it means to be an academic, specifically how academic performance should be measured.

Performance metrics – generating data about how well or badly the university performs on various activities – has become something of an obsession for governments of right and left-wing persuasions all around the world. Universities have whole units of people dedicated to monitoring performance and reporting back to government. Despite cries from academics that measuring student feedback is not a way to ensure quality teaching, or that counting research publications is no way to ensure research quality, there's no sign of this trend ending any time soon.

While there used to be some truth in the statement 'not everything that counts can be measured' these days, most of it can. Sadly, the systems we use inside universities to measure performance, not to put too fine a point on it, are crude. Scholarly journal citations are a thoroughly outdated form of measurement when compared with the real time monitoring available, for free, in software platforms such as Wordpress. There is, emerging, a whole set of other ways to measure academic activity, especially the vexed issue of 'impact'.

Perhaps the problem is not that we measure, but that we don't measure *enough*. This idea comes from Gabriel Tarde, a late 19th century economist. Scholarly conversations could be subjected to assessment regimes, including measures of esteem. Tarde's view of economics was overshadowed by Marx, but lately he's been making something of a comeback. He was interested in mesmerism, crowd behaviour and fashion –he was especially interested in influence and how it spreads. He had this theory about 'imitative rays'. Cities like London and Paris, he said, spread their influence out across the country with imitative rays like the sun and draw people to them, and change other urban centres to be more like them. Money – increased wealth – was but one way to 'measure' these systems of influence. Now we have real time measures of influence on social media in systems like 'Klout'.

So why do universities continue to use extremely crude techniques to measure performance when much more supple and powerful ones are available? My tiny 11-inch MacBook Air, less than the size of an A4 piece of paper, can perform incredible feats of number crunching. I have been using it to dabble in the emerging field of social network analysis, which concentrates on the connections, rather than the individuals. It seems to me that there is vast, untapped potential in this form of analysis. But it takes skill and investment in people for us to be able to make use of such methods. These new metrics don't always make sense. For instance, the most common search term used to find my blog is 'Yoda' – because I once included a picture of the little green man from the Star Wars movies in a post.

These new metrics require interpretive powers: you have to be able to find the story in them.

SOCIAL MEDIA IN ACADEMIA

And finally, why is it worth an academic's time to tweet and/or blog? The ThesisWhsperer blog is accessed by people from every country in the world bar four – a wide readership. My followers on Twitter operate as a huge network of collaborative resources – when I don't know something I just ask them, and vice versa. The site has many posts about becoming an alternative academic (top tip for blogging: be regular. It doesn't matter if you are going to post only once a year – people will say 'It's February! So-and-so's blog will be going up now'). The academic motto used to be 'publish or perish'. An alternative for the days of social media is 'be visible or vanish'. And as I say in a post (Mewburn, 2011):

> "Recently I read an article in Forbes magazine which claimed the Curriculum Vitae (CV), which we all use to describe ourselves when we apply for jobs, will be replaced with your 'digital footprint' in the next ten years. In other words, people will understand you and what you do via searching for you on Google."

Good blogging!

CASE STUDY

THE IMPORTANCE OF SOCIAL STRUCTURE SPACES

—

London
and Berlin

—

AUTHOR

Evgenij Belikov

In late 2012, SPIRES generously funded my travel to several physical spaces where creativity and research in the broad sense play important roles. My remit was to investigate each space in terms of the three SPIRES themes: the physical research environment, the technological research environment, and the social research environment. To investigate the physical environment I applied the Grammar of Creative Workplaces (Williams, 2013), and to capture technological and social aspects I interviewed people working in each space to using a questionnaire developed specifically by myself and SPIRES. I visited a large research lab, a co-working space, and a 'hackspace' in Berlin as well as an artist-run studio space in London.

FRAUNHOFER INSTITUTE FOR OPEN COMMUNICATION SYSTEMS – RESEARCH LAB, BERLIN

The research lab visited (*Fraunhofer-Institut für Offene Kommunikationssysteme*) is part of a large organisation which has over 50 such labs in different areas of applied sciences. It hosts around a hundred researchers organised into six departments and several smaller research groups of four to ten scientists and student research assistants. The lab is well known and works with academia, industry, and government to develop new concepts and products, filing numerous patents and publishing dozens of papers annually.

The physical space is up to a high standard. The large building has six floors, roughly one per department and provides many small offices for two to four scientists, a canteen with affordable food, a library that is rather small but has a good inter-library loan service, toilets and showers, different meeting and demo rooms, and opportunities for chance meetings. The rooms are equipped with modern computer workstations, whiteboards, comfortable chairs, and tables that are height-adjustable so researchers can switch between working while sitting or standing. From this point of view, the space is excellent. There is also a canal and a park nearby. However, most parts of the physical space are functional and there are no facilities specifically designed to foster creativity.

Technologically, the place is top-notch and provides a great opportunity for researchers with good ideas, since travel support and equipment are provided. The process of acquiring new equipment is simple if the need is well justified. There have been multiple spin-offs, some of which are successful, due to the commercialisation and patenting support offered by the institute.

On the social side, however, interviewees reported issues regarding the social climate, including difficulties in communicating across departments and research groups. This was seen as a product of being mostly focused on their own projects and not sharing much expertise. Deadlines were tight and the focus on applied research and commercialisation often prevented interesting ideas being further investigated in detail. Another issue seemed to be that strong market orientation led to rather frequent marketing-related changes of focus in the topic areas. However, the interviewed researchers liked the flat hierarchy in the institute and assessed the social climate in smaller groups as usually being better than that in larger groups or inter-group projects.

BETAHAUS – CO-WORKING SPACE, BERLIN

This co-working space is aimed mainly at freelance *'digital natives'*, web workers, online journalists, and graphic designers and offers over 100 workstations. The main idea is to enable short-term project-based collaboration in an open and fluid environment that would help potential collaborators find each other and facilitate the generation of new project ideas. Additionally, the space hosts several early-stage start-ups and a couple of more established design studios. Although not a research space in the classical sense, a lot of day-to-day creativity is required to participate in short-term projects, especially if they do not involve using standard solutions.

The physical space is suitable for its purpose. It is located in a converted five-storey industrial building and accommodates (in ascending floor order) a cosy cafe with free Wi-Fi and a shared workshop (including a 3D printer), small well-designed meeting rooms, and a larger presentation space, open plan offices in which individuals can rent a desk, small rooms for start-ups with semi-transparent walls, and some larger enclosed areas for more established studios. The support for affordances is rather basic, there are not many whiteboards, and some people brought their own chairs as those provided were deemed less comfortable. Moreover, the environment is rather noisy, but the opportunities to meet other people and to have unplanned encounters are valued by most people more than the physical affordances provided.

As most freelancers only need a laptop (which they bring in) and an Internet connection for work, the space appears to accommodate these needs. Although the technological space is rather basic, it is appropriate for the kind of web-based projects pursued by most of the workers. The core complexity of the technological space stems from the wide range of software used by individuals, including blogs, database-driven websites and web-services, CAD, Adobe InDesign and Photoshop.

The social space is deemed important; people enjoy chance meetings and casual exchanges of ideas during unplanned discussions in the cafe or while waiting for the printer to finish its job. Perhaps this is the main selling point of the space – networking opportunities – as many freelancers have found jobs because of such conversations or by using the noticeboard where people can offer work or advertise their skills. The administration regularly organises invited talks and so-called bar camps, to bring the informal atmosphere of a bar to what is essentially a knowledge-exchange and networking event.

The core issue that freelancers face is the lack of stability and reliability as jobs come in irregularly and sometimes they have to juggle multiple projects but then sometimes, as no projects are around, they give up their desks and work on their own projects in the cafe. The apparent harmony also depends on the success of the project and on-time delivery. Good quality work results in good reputation that guarantees more projects and allows some individuals to gain the stability and be selective about which task to embark upon.

One recommendation for the space would be the provision of quiet and individual spaces to retreat to and concentrate in, away from the general buzz of the rest of the space.

CHAOS COMPUTER CLUB – HACKSPACE, BERLIN

This 'hackspace' has a long tradition of successful hacks that were even able to influence policy-making in the past. This fringe space has a unique feel to it, mostly due to its history and the mix of individuals involved as members of the club. The core interest areas include freedom of information, surveillance, reverse engineering, security, privacy, and independently informing the public about the risks associated with new technologies.

The physical space is not very large, acting as club rooms, hosting a chill-out area, a workshop, a kitchen and what seems to be a server room. Access to the space is limited for non-members, but I was able to assess the central places and their affordances. Obviously, a high-bandwidth Internet connection was provided along some other services such as Jabber instant messaging.

The technological space is seemingly basic, but the expertise shared by the group members is immense and is often demonstrated by competing with governmental or research institutions. The group often challenges these bodies by disproving many of their claims, sometimes rather spectacularly. Some members, for example, are involved in the recently created Pirate Party which acquired some seats in Berlin's state parliament trying to inform and influence politicians on computer-related issues. Some very specialised equipment is available in the workshop, for example, microchip scanning equipment that allows security mechanisms to be broken.

Perhaps the most valuable asset of the club is its members with their diverse experience in computing in industry and academia. The social space appears to be highly valued by the members. The social structure is flat and based on mutual respect and sometimes resulting in a sort of teacher-student or mentoring relationship between members. Although most members are individuals that have strong opinions and are against conformism, there is a set of shared values that form the foundation and the motivation of many club activities. For instance, there is the classic 'Information wants to be free!' slogan. Moreover, most of the members are highly concerned with issues of security, privacy and trust, and constantly providing sanity checks for numerous governmental proposals. Although the physical space is not remarkable, it is an impressive example of the power of social space overcoming societal and technological issues.

UTROPHIA – ARTIST STUDIO SPACE IN LONDON

I also visited an artist-run studio space which hosted six resident artists who produced and distributed artworks, organised community events such as DIY workshops, and invited other artists to participate in exhibitions usually framed by parties and concerts. Unfortunately, the space was bought from the local council by an investor and had to close down despite a decade of engagement with local communities. At the time of writing, the artists were deciding on whether to look for a new space.

A former job-centre, the three-floor building was adapted by the artists to suit their needs. It accommodated six studios, one of which also acted as a shop, a large shared exhibition/workshop space, a storage room, a kitchen, and two accessible flat roof areas, one facing the busy main road, and one rather quiet and shaded on the opposite side of the house. The space seemed to fulfil most of the artists' needs although it had no proper hot water supply (this led to an improvised water tank being installed on the roof which worked well in summer). The artists generally valued having their private thinking and working spaces all of which were highly customised and individualised. This was the most chaotic of the places I visited.

The technological space was related to the diverse production processes involved (such as painting, sculpting, printing, recording, and film-making). The mix of the technologies was quite diverse including crafts and digital technology. I was struck by the confidence of many artists to try out new things and technologies, to mix and match things and engage with ideas playfully.

The social space was quite dynamic and based on close personal relationships. It was deemed important and was often quite emotionally charged as work and private social spaces overlapped to a large extent. Some artists were rather secretive about their ongoing projects for fear of others 'stealing' their ideas. On the other hand, most of the artists were curious about others' views and happy to discuss new ideas.

SOCIAL SPACE IS KEY

In summary, the most striking observation from my visits is that the social culture is invariably regarded as highly important by each of the disparate groups of researchers, digital freelancers, and artists. There is, however, little observed systematic effort made in improving this aspect of the environment. There is a reported need for an open and respectful feedback culture, where people can trust each other, share ideas and knowledge, and truly collaborate on immediate issues rather than, as sometimes reported, delegating work and avoiding responsibility.

High professional standards and integrity are key in areas involving scientific research, and strong personal relationships are crucial in self-organised groups, as in the Hackspace and Utrophia. Keeping task groups small, as can happen in the Fraunhofer Institute, and hierarchies flat (Hackspace) helps to improve communication and sharing. Frequent social activities, as seen in the Betahaus co-working space, help to build up connectedness within a team and joint successes reinforce this positive communal experience and seem to improve the group's creative output.

CASE STUDY

SERENDIPITOUS ENCOUNTERS

—

Portugal

—

AUTHOR

Maria João Grade Godinho

—

Figure 1

—

Figure 2

The Instituto Gulbenkian de Ciência, (IGC, Gulbenkian Institute of Science) is a scientific research institute in Portugal, considered to be one of the centres of excellence in life sciences in Europe (http://eu-life.eu/) (Fig. 1)

The excellence of IGC manifests itself in the calibre of its members, with its senior researchers being frequently distinguished with international prizes for the quality of their work, and young researchers considering IGC to be a top European place to do postdoctoral research. For a small and modest country such as Portugal, it is quite an achievement for IGC to be having such an outstanding impact in scientific research at an international level. I visited IGC to try to figure out the reasons for its success – how, I wondered, was this such a creative place?

The campus is situated in Oeiras, a small town near Lisbon, and includes landscaped gardens surrounding three buildings which host all the IGC personnel and their research facilities, as well as researchers from two other institutions currently occupying a section of one of the buildings (Fig. 1).

Given the outstanding quality of their scientific research, a close look at their laboratories appeared to be a reasonable approach in order to hunt for clues to their success. The laboratories appear just like others in any part of the world: they are very cramped and considerably messy (Fig. 2) – an amalgamation of various machines, equipment, tools and reagents, altogether forming a maze within which busy researchers go about their jobs. Perhaps the one difference in relation to other laboratories where I have worked is that most of the various research groups are located in vast common areas aligned along wide corridors, which are organised in sections with common equipment and interspersed by more exclusive sectors identified by the name of the principal investigator of a group. While observing the activities of the researchers, I realised that in order to do a job it is necessary to commute between spaces, and these trips often involve encounters with others and negotiation of the use of common resources. Not all laboratories are located in these open, shared areas but those in separated rooms often have big glass windows to the corridor, so there is still some degree of openness. Noticeably, some of those windows were being used as drawing boards by the occupants, with diagrams and writing all over them.

Figure 3

Figure 4

The IGC has two PhD programmes and a very active bioinformatics department which also offers courses to people from outside the institute. All these classes take place in ordinary classrooms, very much organised in a formal, traditional way, similar to the arrangement of their seminar rooms. The one oddity is the presence of a piano in one of the seminar rooms, which apparently gets used by those in need (and capable) of a little musical relaxation. Also, another seminar room accommodates a collection of the highest ranking scientific images entered in a science communication competition organised by the IGC, as one of their many activities to connect with the wider community. Other artworks which were produced by one of the two artists that were in residence at IGC are on display in the reception foyer of the main building (Fig. 3). Furthermore, one of the exterior walls of the campus has a mural of graffiti that was commissioned by IGC to commemorate its 50th anniversary.

The very quiet library occupies a section of one of the buildings, and although slightly dark and somewhat austere, it does have some brightly coloured sofas near a wall with enormous windows overlooking the gardens and the small stream that runs nearby. This setting gives the place a sense of peacefulness and tranquillity. There aren't many computers in the library nor is it well equipped with other technological devices, although there are computer rooms around the institute. Near the library there are a couple of private offices available for PhD students to occupy during the writing up of their dissertations, in quietness and isolation.

While wandering around observing the space and how people move about using it, I noticed that there were many chairs and sofas scattered around spaces in between places (Fig. 4). For example, in the main building, where most of the laboratories are situated, each floor has three main corridors that come together at gathering areas. These intersecting spaces contain common utilities such as printers and photocopiers, toilets and water coolers, as well as coffee and snack machines and also sofas and chairs.

Figure 5

Figure 6

These zones are incredibly busy, with people constantly moving to and from the adjacent areas, and act as the perfect hub for casual encounters and unplanned conversations with members of other teams. Similarly, many corridors have comfortable chairs and white boards scattered along them, some of which were displaying evidence of past meetings where ideas were discussed, judging by the diagrams and scribbles still on display (Fig. 5).

The busiest of these areas is the reception foyer, in the main building, where screens advertise the various seminars occurring each week and other activities involving researchers from IGC, with copies of their most recently published scientific research articles displayed on shelves, in addition to cabinets with flyers for events in other research institutions and for cultural activities happening in Oeiras or Lisbon.

The potential for casual encounters with researchers from other groups is further increased by the organisation of the campus: one ancillary building has all the seminar rooms along with the refectory and the cafe, while the main building houses all the laboratories and associated facilities as well as the reception and administration. The third building hosts the library, classrooms, the information technology and bioinformatics departments and also the researchers from other institutions, which are there as short or long-term guests.

This spatial arrangement literally forces people to move around, boosting the chances of serendipitous conversations with co-workers, as each person goes to a seminar, to the library or to have lunch. Moreover, the outside area between the main building and the refectory has been developed into an *al fresco* eating and drinking space, with tables and chairs where people can enjoy their meals or have meetings in a pleasant outdoor setting, which is far more relaxed than an office. The institute's own refectory, serves various options for lunch at very low cost, and has its own cafe operating during the afternoon - something of utmost importance in Portugal. As in many other European countries, the ceremonial drinking of coffee is a very important aspect of local culture. A peculiar but nevertheless very popular outdoor area, also considered as an important gathering place, is the designated smokers' corner, with benches for people to sit and relax while satisfying their nicotine addiction and socialising with other smokers. Given that there are beautiful gardens surrounding all the buildings (Fig. 6) the spaces outside truly become places to use and are explored by everyone, besides being used for public engagements and community activities.

Figure 7

Towards the end of my visit, while I was sitting quietly digesting all the information I had gathered in trying to understand what it was that made the IGC such a stimulating place, I just felt relaxed and comfortable, soothed by the friendly chattering of people passing by and pleased to be in such beautiful surroundings. So I wondered if that was the secret of what makes the IGC so special: all the little things it provides in order to enhance social encounters and promote conviviality among its workers. These aspects are manifested in several ways. First, in the spatial organisation of most research groups so that researchers mingle while sharing common areas and facilities. Second, in the various outreach activities organised by the institute, including teaching programmes and courses as well as residencies for artists and open days for the general public, all of which connect the IGC to the wider community. Third, the layout of the main building encourages encounters between people working in different areas, and the landscape of the campus, including not only the buildings but also outdoor areas, provide opportunities for people to communicate and exchange ideas with various others. All of this is apparent while it is ensured that there are quiet locations where it is possible to work in seclusion, away from all the buzz and activity.

I therefore propose that the secret of the IGC's success in promoting their researchers' creativity, and consequently achieving international research excellence, resides in providing them with a stimulating social environment and meeting their needs for comfort and pleasant surroundings. (Fig. 7)

HOW-WHAT SPACE

mapping epistemic gradients in interdisciplinary research

AUTHOR
Mike Fraser

INTRODUCTION

This chapter describes the importance of and some techniques for communicating epistemic gradients across research teams. These forms of communication help align the shape of research teams that enhance collaboration.

When forming research teams to address novel interdisciplinary challenges, there tends to be a focus on creative thinking around the problem area. In the PATINA project we have focused on understanding the relationships between personal and institutional approaches in order to design effective research. As a research team exploring research, we have continuously focused on the idea that we should practise what we preach. To some degree this has required tests to be placed that require any design the project produces to also apply to our own project – for example if we expect others to use a research technology, the PATINA team should also be able to adopt the technology. Beyond artefacts to enhance research, however, we have also continually revised and debated the processes of the project. We have reflected on the process of our research, including the ways in which we designed the project itself, which must reflect any research processes that we design for others. This chapter will specifically concentrate on the forms of communication within the team which enable research processes to be determined.

One topic that has emerged in PATINA is a distinctive focus on the underlying goals and beliefs of different research fields, and the ways in which differences in these belief systems, or *epistemes*, are communicated across the team. Drawing on a range of humanities and social science literatures, I suggest that understanding epistemic differences is often dismissed in interdisciplinary discourse as a 'meta-problem', an abstract description of research rather than a tangible property of it. I especially suggest that some areas of science and engineering that underpin technology development can claim indifference to episteme while also maintaining an implicit view of the value of diverse epistemic positions. Thus, interdisciplinary research that integrates technical, social and aesthetic design requires communication about shared epistemic positions as well as shared outcomes. In simple terms, I suggest a research process which goes beyond discussions of *objectives* (what should be achieve) and *personalities* (how well the team get on) to incorporate an explication of the *epistemic gradient* (the operational range of research belief systems) of the team. I suggest that conducting an analysis of epistemic gradients at the early stages of research design will be an important feature of understanding the methods that the team will agree and use, and establishing respect for one another's working practices independently of debates around the objectives of the work. I also describe a simple technique which research teams can use to support the work of uncovering epistemic gradients, for use during the authoring of new research proposals or at 'sandpit' type events.

RESEARCH EPISTEMES AND EPISTEMIC GRADIENTS

Foucault suggests in *The Order of Things* (1970) that an episteme is "the strategic apparatus which permits of separating out from among all the statements which are possible those that will be acceptable within ... a field of scientificity". The key aspect of this definition is the contrast of *possibility* with *acceptability*: a field of research is constituted by boundaries which define and are defined by the notion of acceptable statements, and not all possible statements of knowledge are also acceptable to a field of research. A particular field's episteme represents and informs the range of acceptable questions for members of the field to ask, and statements of fact that they can make. It is very likely that different research fields have different such boundaries – perhaps overlapping, perhaps not – of acceptable research statements and questions.

Contemporary with Foucault's work was the somewhat contrasting work of Latour and Woolgar (1979) whose careful anthropology of the science laboratory provided a nuanced description of the culture of science seen as a social culture derived from its lived work, rather than a culture formally following the scientific methods stated to be at work. Latour's actor-network theory that emerged from these studies has inspired numerous further studies of science laboratories, prominent among which are those of Knorr-Cetina (1999) which have used ethnographic observation to graduate the idea of scientific practice, treating each scientific setting as an opportunity to understand and compare the particular organisational characteristics of different scientific work, and unpacking the notion of science to reveal a diverse range of epistemes constituted in their particular cultures and interactions.

Heritage's work *Epistemics in Action* (2012) provides compelling examples of the ways that individuals produce and share requests and assertions in their interactions. He specifically describes how the epistemic status of the speaker and hearer influences the ways in which requests and assertions are heard and oriented to. Heritage introduces the powerful notion of an *epistemic gradient* to indicate the interactional expression of the range of potential epistemic configurations. His work indicates that everyday conversations about research derive from and create the phenomenal field boundaries of a disciplinary episteme. It suggests that practices which recognise epistemic differences are deeply entrenched in the ways we talk; but it also provides encouragement that if we design and configure research conversations then we have an opportunity to redefine the boundaries of our personal and shared epistemic gradients. Thus, conversations with one another across research disciplines that reflect explicitly on epistemic practices and cultures can influence a shared sense of the range of belief systems at play.

Heritage's work also provides an excellent challenge to the theoretical view adopted by some philosophers (e.g. Schmid, 2012) that epistemology is a notion independent of human action. His work not only provides an opposing viewpoint, but because that viewpoint is evidenced by examples of naturally-occurring conversation, it suggests that everyday interaction does strongly configure and draw on epistemic positions.

Heritage's work is thus an excellent example of how interpretive fields can address Flyvbjerg's (2001) challenge of how the humanities and social sciences can evidence their contribution towards the natural sciences. The importance of discussion around the relationships between epistemology and ontology so prominent in interpretive work becomes key in understanding the relationships between the arts and humanities, social sciences, engineering and science. Such debates and discussions feature so little in the discourse of the natural sciences, yet it is becoming clear that interdisciplinary collaboration beyond science and engineering requires the ontological discourse so typical of collaborations within science and engineering with an epistemic discourse so typical of debates in more interpretive fields.

Indeed, some commentators (e.g. Grasswick, 2010; de Vries, Lund & Baker, 2002) suggest that a lack of communication between scientific and non-scientific communities can erode trust to such a degree that the underpinning episteme itself becomes questioned independently of the practice of 'normal science'. Part of the problem is that there is typically a connection between research epistemology and research methods (Darlaston-Jones, 2007), so concerns arise in the quality of research when there is no communication that can support trust or understanding of the epistemic gradient between the communities or individuals involved.

To bring the issue back to a specific interdisciplinary example, in the PATINA project much of our work has been situated within the field of human-computer interaction. HCI has, for three decades, increasingly acted as a test bed for interdisciplinary collaboration, initially incorporating perspectives from psychology, but over time drawing on broader interpretive social sciences, humanities, art and design. Indeed, the epistemology that underpins the interdisciplinarity of HCI is a contested and debated part of the field's own discourse surrounding its development and boundaries (Brey, 2005; Harrison, Sengers & Tatar, 2011). Yet within this broad field, the level of discourse is limited in some subfields, and many core HCI research groups align with very specific epistemes that represent their own interdisciplinary mixture, for example HCI laboratories that align with quantitative experimental work drawing on traditions in cognitive psychology tend not to train their students in more interpretive techniques, nor in methods drawn from the arts which take very different views of the *a priori* requirements of evidence and inference (Chenail, 2008). In PATINA we have found that such differences become obstacles that manifest even in discussion between computer scientists, where differences in episteme influence issues such as the ways that technologies are used to innovate. In this area, as Adams, Fitzgerald and Priestnall (2013) suggest, influences from art and design draw people towards 'catwalk' technologies in which innovation is enabled by inspiring others, whereas influences from traditional computing gravitate towards 'prêt-à-porter' technologies in which innovation is enabled by high levels of scalability. It is only through communication, and researchers working hard as 'boundary creatures' (*ibid.*) that the underpinning belief systems that motivate such differences can be resolved.

Overall, there are two key features or properties that such communication within interdisciplinary teams should incorporate:

a. it must explore the relevance of both episteme and onteme – put simply, researchers must explore why and how they address problems in addition to what and when the goals of the project are to be achieved; they must discuss the reasons for the activities as well as their topic; and

b. discourse must happen early on in the project design, both in the context of the disciplinary research traditions at play, and explicit focus on their epistemic gradients, both in the abstract and with respect to existing and future projects.

In the following section we describe a first attempt to design a simple process which can be used to help researchers acquaint one another with their epistemes. This approach is designed to support initial phases of discourse around potential collaborations, and could be used in intensive face-to-face workshops such as 'sandpit' funding events, or as part of more distributed team formation such as the remote development of projects with unfamiliar partners.

HOW-WHAT SPACE

I wish to explore how discourse techniques can play a role in teams from different epistemic traditions. It is unlikely that even design polymaths will be able to cover the extent of specialist knowledge required to bridge the range of skills and knowledge across the spectrum, in addition to the motivations, phenomenological, anthropological and social scientific disciplinary underpinnings, that will be needed to imagine, share and build complex designs. As a result, design will often require teams of computer scientists, social scientists, and arts and humanities researchers to understand one another's practices.

In this section I outline a design space which is intended to help simplify communication and understanding of research across interdisciplinary teams. It is important that participants collectively have the full range of skills required, and can understand the unique contribution of one another's fields and how they differ from traditional forms of disciplinary boundary.

How-What Space is simply a diagram which maps the ontology of the discipline ('What') on the y-axis and the epistemology of the discipline ('How') on the x-axis. Each independent researcher in the team completes a How-What diagram, labels the axes, and marks their previous projects approximately onto the diagram. A discussion across the team then explores how each of their diagrams could be synthesised into a single diagram, on which the future planned project can be marked. In conducting this exercise a number of debates will arise about the process, and it is important these are resolved within the team rather than through the advice of this paper; this discourse is what is needed to share an understanding, but a few points to be aware of about this process are outlined below.

Firstly, the diagram explicitly places episteme and onteme as orthogonal issues; this is deliberate. Some disciplines will find it easier than others to differentiate and name/label their epistemic traditions than others; indeed some may claim their disciplines have no epistemic tradition at all. The justification of such statements forms part of the opening up of traditions and the raising of awareness around implicit unquestioned boundaries of validity, particularly within the natural sciences. Some debates may not be easy, especially in the abstract, which is why previous personal projects provide an excellent and less contentious starting point for understanding implicit positions than proposed collaborative work.

Secondly, the boundaries of the 'How' x-axis do not have to be abstract; indeed it is interesting to suggest that the labels be as tightly bound to the individual's research experience as possible. A possible extension is for each researcher to draw the wider boundaries of their understanding onto the diagram, as well as the narrower boundaries of the projects they have undertaken themselves.

Thirdly, the boundaries of the 'What' y-axis may also be tightly scoped, so that the perceived structure of the researcher's discipline can be revealed, and the place of their research within it. This could be linearised into the diagram in many forms. Explaining the ontic mapping onto the diagram also forms a key part of the individual's discourse with the wider team.

Finally, it needs to be made clear that there are no incorrect answers. In contrast to the previous section which motivates this approach, in this practical exercise the term *episteme* is used in a very broad way to indicate research belief systems and methods of different disciplines or subdisciplines, not precisely according to any particular definition. Definitions are not critical; here it is the discourse which the broad categories inspire that matters. In fact, some disciplines are so disengaged from their own epistemology that it may be counterproductive to aim for precise categorisation as part of this discussion. The exact labelling of the axes and the order and placement of disciplines within the space is a fine personal judgement which will be subject to significant disciplinary debate, but exactness is not the goal.

In my experience researchers can respond to traditions outside their epistemic scope very strongly, denying the legitimacy of the tradition as genuine research, for example (Chenail, 2008). The strength of this reaction can be particularly forceful in comparison to responses to work outside a researcher's ontological experience, especially if their disciplinary discourse is principally focused on developing research topics through uniform methods, to the exclusion of methodological debates. For this reason we have called the diagrams How-What rather than a grander title involving episteme-onteme, as the abstract philosophical debate about their meanings across multiple traditions would create an unnecessary and counterproductive barrier to communication focused on the team's knowledge and interests. Indeed it may be productive at first to draw diagrams of research methods rather than their underpinning theoretical or motivational systems.

In the diagram below (Fig. 1), I have illustrated a computer science example, which draws computing abstractions on the y-axis from the physical layer ('low abstraction') through to application software ('high abstraction'), and research methods from theoretical proof ('reductionist') to holistic design ('interpretivist') on the x-axis. The purpose of this diagram is to foster discussion and debate rather than to precisely categorise different disciplines against their computing abstractions of interest. In this example I have approximately placed according to my own world view some broad computing disciplines in relevant quadrants of the space – photonics, microelectronics, communications are all broadly in the bottom-left quadrant; AI (artificial intelligence) and software engineering are broadly in the top-left quadrant; ubiquitous computing, HCI and CSCW (computer-supported cooperative work) are in the top-right quadrant; and a recent project exploring the human legibility of low-level computing is in the bottom-right quadrant.

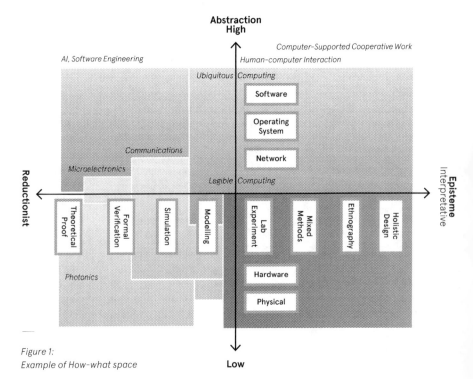

Figure 1:
Example of How-what space

This diagram can then be put to a number of different purposes. Firstly, we can identify a historical trajectory through the diagram to illustrate the development of computing design. The principal traversal has been from the bottom-left quadrant to the top-left quadrant, i.e. up the stack from hardware to software abstraction layers. HCI, ubiquitous computing and CSCW have then in different ways provided trajectories of work from the top-left to the top-right quadrant, moving from mathematical reductionist approaches through cognitivism somewhere in the middle to highly interpretivist approaches exemplified by areas such as ethnomethodology or holistic design. The ideas outlined in this paper in many ways represent the shift from the top- right quadrant to the bottom-right quadrant: a move back down through the stack under the influence of these interpretivist traditions. However, as well as helping to articulate this change in emphasis to an HCI audience who are highly aware of epistemology and research methods, I suggest a more valuable use of this diagram is to explain how new forms of HCI research can interact with physical, electrical and electronic engineering researchers who self-identify in the bottom-left quadrant. There is often misunderstanding within computer science and engineering about what HCI actually is or does as a discipline. The original incarnation of the field creating user models of software interfaces places HCI in the top-left quadrant of H-W space, whereas 'legible computing' places it in the bottom-right quadrant, wholly opposite in both technology and epistemology. This simple tool for communicating interests to collaborating microelectronics researchers, and even physicists and chemists can provide a valuable grounding to collaborations.

Secondly, disciplines unable or unused to articulating their own epistemic traditions, either through strong associations with science or through isolation from other areas, can identify their mutual interests and concerns in H-W space to identify potential differences in understanding of legible computing goals. Interdisciplinary teams often sit in rooms discussing ideas orthogonal to one another while believing they are discussing the same or similar ideas. I suggest that one way in which such communications turn out to be orthogonal is illustrated in this design space – scientists and engineers assume that methods and values are relatively unimportant and homogeneous; artists and social scientists assume that research methods and traditions are in the foreground of designing studies when they may in fact have been ignored altogether until too late when it is realised they directly clash with epistemic traditions of other members of the team. Overall, then I suggest scoping and articulating projects in H-W space will be an important way of precisely articulating an intellectual site for respecification which respects both the topic and the epistemic traditions necessary to explore collaborations.

CONCLUSION

This paper has described the importance and character of epistemic traditions and gradients in interdisciplinary collaboration. I have described How-What Space which enables simple communication across research teams, enabling discussion between scientists and engineers who may have limited holistic methods training on the one hand, with arts, humanities and social science researchers on the other hand who may have limited understanding of the means by which existing and imagined topics in science and engineering might function. I have also described how HCI as a field sits firmly at these crossroads and hopefully this paper goes some way to providing a design lexicon for communication required for a programme of redesigning projects across the interdisciplinary computing spectrum.

SERENDIPITY IN PRACTICE

A social state

AUTHOR
Mel Woods

INTRODUCTION

The term serendipity, "the faculty of making happy and unexpected discoveries by accident" [OED], was first coined in 1754 by writer Horace Walpole in a letter to his friend. The phenomenon he named was inspired by a Persian fairy tale 'The Three Princes of Serendip' in which the princes go on a journey making discoveries, links and associations, solving problems through their sagacity. In his 1954 lecture at the University of Lille, Pasteur described serendipity with an additional state of receptivity: "In the elusive role of serendipity and the field of observation, chance favours only the prepared mind" (Pasteur, 1954).

When the word serendipity was originally ascribed, understanding of the world informed by culture, education and religion was vastly different from today. We are once again in the middle of rapid development and expansion, but the technological transformations that have occurred in recent decades have profoundly altered daily life and society. The new information technologies have triggered economic and societal changes that have led to a radical reorganisation of work and production processes as well as of space and communication. What does unite an understanding of serendipity then and now, is the value of human agency in knowledge and discovery: in short human experience remains intrinsic.

This paper will discuss different approaches to serendipity and how we might harness it through the design of environments, tools or systems that facilitate chance encounters.

UNDERSTANDING SERENDIPITY: A DISCIPLINARY APPROACH

There have been many attempts to deconstruct and demystify serendipity, from the information science and human-computer interaction (HCI) disciplines (e.g.Van Andel 1994; André, Teevan & Dumais, 2009; Makri & Blandford, 2012). André et al summarise a number of definitions of serendipity that have been explored by researchers and argue that:

> ...rather than one understanding of serendipity, we have seen a kind of continuum of understandings from inadvertently finding something of personal interest, to the critical breakthrough of a domain expert making a key 'sagacious' insight between a perceived phenomena and an opportunity for a new invention. [sic] (André et al, 2009, p. 313)

Serendipity in practice has been well documented, particularly in the history of discovery and innovations in science, information and technology. There are many well-quoted examples of breakthroughs that have occurred as a result of fortunate accidental discoveries. The Post-it note, the microwave, penicillin and possibly the most famous example, Newton's discovery of gravity as a result of an apple falling on his head, are all attributed to the phenomenon.

In art, chance, or the spontaneous random event has played a vital role in the creative process for many artists and in art movements. The Surrealist and Dadaists sought to juxtapose objects in new and unexpected ways. Guy Debord (1956, 1967) and the Situationists developed theories of the dérive (or drift) with improvisation theory and the gap between intention and outcome seen as crucial to the meaning of serendipity and chance in art. Recent software for mobile devices such as *Serendipitor* and *Situationist* draw explicitly on these manifestos and theories from art movements in history. They rely on the user's insight and perception of value to create serendipitous encounters.

In the field of creativity, receptivity and curiosity in research and practice is actively encouraged. Being prepared, curious and open-minded about the world can provide a useful process to enable a leap of the imagination beyond rationality, to develop intuition and ideas of consciousness. This particular approach to discovery, and of unexpectedly finding knowledge, material possibility and acting on that to positive effect, can often be defined as serendipity.

Although many creative practitioners court serendipity and acknowledge the positive role it plays in their practice and everyday life, and many intuitively harness the process, few have attempted to formalise it, to pursue it as a method for creative practice. An exception, John Cage, was explicit in recording the methods he employed to create his work. This is evidenced by the concepts and framework of artworks themselves, using uncertainty, surprise, juxtaposition, rules space, randomness elements and chance as tools for the creative act (Kostelanetz, 2003).

DESIGNING FOR SERENDIPITY

While information scientists seek to define serendipity, computer scientists seek to 'engineer' it; the SerenA project aims to contribute to the 'design of effective research spaces' through an empirically based understanding of the term. The research aims to: 1) build an understanding of serendipity through empirical studies, specifically within information discovery and research; 2) create an understanding of how art and design methods and thinking support serendipity; 3) design and develop a system and devices to support and promote connections and information between people and ideas; and 4) implement and evaluate technologies with novel approaches in digital and physical spaces. The context of the project is to understand how serendipity sits alongside dramatic advances we experience in the way in which we discover information, how we search and research, and how archives are made available, while increasingly using digital information systems and communication networks.

In order to gain an empirical understanding of serendipity, a series of semi-structured interviews (Makri & Blandford, 2012), and a diary study (Sun, Sharples & Makri, 2011), focused initially on the experience of serendipity from the perspective of academic researchers, across a range of disciplines.

Makri's interviews resulted in a number of reflective 'stories of serendipity' (2012), from which an early process model was derived. This was iterated through a second round of interviews, this time with creative professionals, after it emerged that they were a group who appeared to experience serendipity more often than did other groups. The second stage interviews conducted on the nature of serendipity also found several actions and attitudes of mind that creative professionals pursued that can increase its likelihood. These include varying routines, being observant, making mental space, relaxing boundaries, drawing on previous experiences, looking for patterns and seizing opportunities.

A process model (Fig. 1) derived from these studies provides a foundation to consider whether serendipity can be designed through engineering systems and technology. An alternative approach can support the process of design for tools, spaces, interfaces and mindsets that could address one section of the model (e.g. designing to support 'making connections').

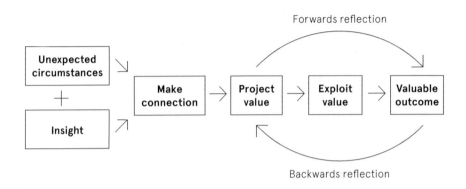

Figure 1:
Serendipity Process Model, 2012

At the same time Sun et al's diary study (2011) set out to enable participants to rapidly capture and record how serendipity happens on the fly in their everyday lives. This identified: 1) key elements to support understanding of serendipity; 2) the influential role of context in serendipitous experiences; 3) a framework of understanding how serendipity happens; and 4) the positive impacts of serendipity in people's information research.

The roles of context and environment in the design of technologies to support embodiment have been explored (e.g. Dix et al, 2000; Dourish, 2001; Schmidt, 2000). Through the diary study, Sun et al (2011) also found that context e.g. the state of the individual experiencing serendipity, temporal factors and most importantly here, their environment, played influential roles for people experiencing serendipity. Participants highlighted space, infrastructure, and features – for example, spaces where a lot of information could be found (such as libraries) – and constantly changing environments, where unfamiliarity focused people's ability to engage with new information, as well as spaces and features that promote relaxation.

DESIGN, ARCHITECTURE AND SOCIAL SPACE

In our discussion of serendipity, and the constituent elements of the process that come together to bring it about, the role of environment or space clearly contributes to the context. We could ask questions such as: Was the lab in which the microwave was discovered ordered or messy? Did taking a break in nature have a positive effect on Newton? Is the juxtaposition of images and ideas in the artist's studio or academic's desk a contributing factor? Might individual bespoke approaches to organising information, materials, space and light help creativity and serendipity?

One discipline that actively works with the affordances that might support serendipity and environment, is architecture. The design of buildings and spaces for social, learning and work environments no longer simply focuses on cost per square metre or person. These obsolete measurements that only address infrastructure do not take account of other factors, such as the value people feel when they are connected and the importance of informal interactions and their effects on generating great ideas. Individual buildings (and cities), that include flexible, open, and collaborative spaces for work, have a correlation with the variables of the outcomes of a space – engagement, productivity, efficiency measured according to the need and requirements of the organisation. Lindsay and Kasarda (2011) describe these innovative practices from small companies to cities and offers techniques for 'engineering serendipity'.

Within the SerenA project, an early investigation probed the influence of architecture on social interactions. A pilot study, *Mapping Ideas in Space* (Woods, 2010), was conducted at Dundee Contemporary Arts (DCA). The study used 'social architecture' to represent the social fabric of a building in the broadest possible terms, from the way people moved through the space to the knowledge and ideas that manifested within the space. The study attempted to identify and understand the relationship between the physical and ideas space of DCA, a contemporary art centre, a building that was designed by Richard Murphy Architects which is 'inclusive and enticing and encourages interaction between the public and many forms of visual arts' (Richard Murphy Architects, 2000).

The research incorporated theories of space syntax and data collection, with seven participants (of varying familiarity with DCA) who were instructed to freely explore the space, marking thoughts and ideas stimulated by the physical or ideas space of the building (Fig. 2) on a floor plan with supplied stickers.

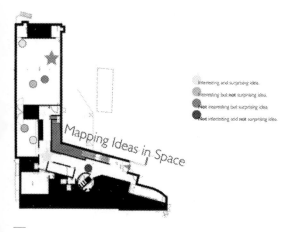

Figure 2:
Participant 1. Data Ideas Mapping in DCA

After completing the first exercise which identified categories for the thoughts as interesting and surprising (or not), participants were asked to retrace their steps, reflect on each idea and rank each idea in order of 'usefulness'. An exit questionnaire completed the study.

Findings from the study showed participants were stimulated by flow, space and light, and found those features stimulating, surprising and delightful. The majority commented in the exit questionnaire that the open cafe area had energy, and commented on the use of that communal space.

EMOTIONAL ENVIRONMENTS FOR SERENDIPITY

Van Andel (1994) states that 'designing for serendipity' is an oxymoron. However, although we cannot directly 'engineer' serendipity itself, we can as highlighted previously, attempt to create opportunities that can support it. So, how might the look, feel, sight and sound of an environment and its social constructs support serendipity? Potentially, designing for attitudes of mind, such as 'varying routines' or 'making mental space', could in turn increase the likelihood of the key features of serendipity.

Open-mindedness and designing for emotion (Norman, 2004) are critical aspects of a broader desire for design which is playful, creative or delightful; an experience which engages the user more fully, an experience which provokes 'ensoulment', a term coined by Nelson and Stolterman (2003) to describe an emotional response to a product which results in a deeply moving feeling of being significantly changed.

With designing for emotion in mind, two workshops were conducted, the first to explore 'Design for the Prepared Mind' to understand states of mind that support serendipity and the second 'Understanding Delight in Design: User Experience, Technologies and Tools' to consider the role of emotion and delight in products, services and spaces. In order to understand emotion and delight, a series of exercises were conducted from mapping the emotional space, ripping affordance design exemplars, and through using a paper-based framework (Fig. 3) to break down and explore the concept of delight.

Observations and plenary discussion from the workshops formed two main concepts. Firstly, that mindfulness such as having an open mind, views the uncertain elements in life, such as chance and chaos, as a potentially positive state. Furthermore, participants stated their own practical or mindful ways of harnessing uncertainty and followed reinforced pathways of action that resulted more often than not in positive outcomes.

In the second workshop, delight was perceived across many products, spaces and services. There were examples of delight (see Fig. 3) that could be appreciated by many but were only truly delightful for an individual; the affordances of these examples were complex and varied. However, consensus was reached over examples of true, deep, emotional delight (e.g. sharing a meal with close family or friends) that were so intrinsic to being human, that without those experiences, life would not be as enjoyable or worthwhile.

Figure 3:
Cards showing participant-generated delightful experiences, tools and spaces.

The second of these observations echoes De Botton's discussion in *The Architecture of Happiness* where he comments on the most genuine values of being human: beauty and well-being in the presence of architecture and the spaces and homes we build for ourselves. De Botton refers to "...the truth of the maxim that beauty lies between the extremities of order and complexity" (De Botton, 2006).

SERENDIPITY AFFECTING RESEARCH SPACES

So what lessons can we derive from seeking serendipity in the design of effective research spaces? Is it that it is more prevalent in the digital world? Is Google giving us too much of what we know we are looking for? Or do we seek out serendipity as our ability to recognise it has become stifled by the overwhelming burden of 24-hour digital culture?

Alternatively do we recognise that face-to-face contact, affect and being present, means we literally bump up against people, ideas, knowledge in an embodied state, and that certain spaces and social constructs support this? So we might amplify our affect and humanness to sharpen and support our natural instincts of curiosity and empathy through both the consistency of the pursuit and the tools at our disposal. We should design spaces that force us to vary our routine (by alternative wayfinding), be observant (by creating flexible dynamic spaces), making mental space (a relaxed and playful area), relaxing boundaries (creating social opportunities for knowledge exchange), drawing on previous experiences (having interdisciplinary teams and transfer of skills), looking for patterns (storytelling) and seizing opportunities.

As a valuable outcome from our research, we propose designing to support spaces with social agency, designing to surprise and delight the senses, and designing with flexibility and for uncertainty. In our attempt to explore and support serendipity, can we catch it? Probably not. It is on the move all the time, flexible, fleeting but we can certainly play with it and design spaces to support it.

WORKING
ENVIRONMENTS

WORKING ENVIRONMENTS

> "...when you build a thing you cannot merely build that thing in isolation, but must also repair the world around it, and within it..." (Alexander et al, 1977: p xiii)

This section explores the contexts within which research takes place and focuses on the physical elements and spaces we all use.

We start by looking at some of the digital tools that are now ubiquitous in our research environments, from personal devices in *Smart working with smartphones* and *Tidy your Desktop* right up to entire rooms and spaces in *High-end technology lab*. But sometimes, it's good to step and switch off – so *Off-grid creativity* provides a few tips on how to go about this.

Making use of objects in our environment is explored in *Lowbrow powwow*, which introduces the idea that the personalisation of space is important for effective working environments – a theme extended in detail in *Intimacy*. The ways in which we personalise our environment also have an effect on how that space is used. *Meat(ing) Place* considers this at the group level whilst *Get into the zone* looks at how this might apply at different scales.

Realising that you can affect your environment is an important step towards improving the environment itself. *Make do and mend*, *Work that space* and *Beam me up (or down)* all present practical tips on what you can do to improve your surroundings. If even the smallest change is difficult in your institution, *Rebel space* provides some interesting alternatives and other 'nomadic' environments are presented in *The bus as a research environment* and *A mobile thinking shrine*. Many of the reasons we need to adapt our environments are considered in *A recipe for mediocrity*, which, although ironic in character, highlights some serious issues that many readers might recognise in their own workplace.

The recipes end by looking at particular examples of physical environments, from the personal space in *Thinking den*, to an institutional version of it in *Bookable nomad space*. Ways to make additional use of existing space are provided in *Attractor spaces* and *Workshop space*. If you are intending to go to a very different environment then *Don't Panic!* will help you prepare for it and, finally, don't forget that your working environment does not have to be a be a building - try *Meeting in the great out of doors*.

In this section there are three case studies. *Harmony with nature: Kyoto* explores The Kyoto University of Art and Design and considers the elements in this institutional setting that contribute to its creative physical environment. *"I can't bear this space": Room 101* provides us with a salutary lesson in why our working environments matter, by presenting the reactions of users to a particular case study space and the direct, negative effect it has on creativity. Finally, *Jump Associates: San Mateo* takes a look at a creative physical environment and how it relates to the creative process in an observational study of Jump Associates San Mateo office in California.

The first of two papers at the end of this section, *Connecting design in virtual and physical spaces*, considers analogies between the virtual and physical, recognising that there is a significant common factor between these two types of space – people. In analysing some of the recipes in this book, the desirable attributes we find in physical space may be transferred to the virtual.

The section ends with a short position paper, *The spatial constructs of creative situations*, in which the reader is invited to consider space as something that is not simply static and physical. Space, it is argued, requires the embodiment of the physical, social and human – from this, creativity will naturally emerge.

#42

AUTHOR
Nick Pearce

SERVE TO
Researchers

COST/RESOURCE
Varies

TIME

SMART WORKING WITH SMARTPHONES

Embrace the tool of the digital scholar

BACKGROUND

Over the last 10 years I have found myself increasingly integrating my smartphone into my academic life. As scholarship has become increasingly digitized the mobile phone has become an integral tool of the digital scholar (Pearce et al, 2010; Weller, 2011a).

For good or bad, I am constantly connected to my emails and checking Twitter throughout the day. I respond to emails, find out about new research opportunities and publicise my own work frequently, wherever I happen to be located. This recipe is about making the most of smartphones.

INGREDIENTS

- One smartphone (possible flavours: Apple, Blackberry, Android, Windows)

METHOD

1. Purchase smartphone. You may want to select the platform before the handset. Considerations should include budget, specific features (such as a particularly good camera or larger screen) and interoperability with technologies you already own.
2. Synchronise work email and calendars. Despite all the recent developments in social media and apps, the working life of an academic researcher still revolves around the ubiquitous email. Having access to your inbox and calendar through your phone is still the most useful, and widely used, feature of a smartphone.
3. Download relevant apps.
   a. Twitter. If you are on Twitter you will want to download a Twitter client to enhance your use of the tool (e.g. notifications of Retweets, DirectMessages). There are many to choose from such as the Twitter app, Seesmic or TweetDeck.
   b. Blog. If you blog you will want to download an app to manage this on the go. For example, the WordPress app allows you to look at your stats, approve comments and of course write a blog post.

c. Web. All smartphones come with a built-in browser, but this is unlikely to be the best available or best suited to your needs. Have a play with the different smartphone browsers available (e.g. Opera, Firefox, Chrome). You may want to use the same browser that you use at work to better integrate your bookmarks for example.

4. Find apps specific to your discipline. There are various apps and resources related to your discipline which you may want to download. For examples see:
   a. http://libguides.mit.edu/content.php?pid=174869&sid=1481857
   b. http://connection.sagepub.com/blog/2013/03/26/top-smartphone-apps-for-a-smart-academic/

5. Get smart working! You may want to set your phone to silent...

NOTES ON INGREDIENTS

Battery life. As the capabilities and screen sizes of phones increase, the battery life inevitably struggles to keep up, and as you use your phone more the battery life will become even more of an issue. At the moment you can't really expect your phone's battery life to extend much beyond a working day. There are strategies for extending battery life such as making sure that Bluetooth, GPS and Wi-Fi are turned off when not being used. You can also get USB adapters so that you can charge your phone from your computer or your car.

Downtime. Although it is great to be connected and available throughout the day, there are issues with being overly connected. Everybody needs a break from time to time. Most phones can be set to only check emails between certain times, for example. You may want to turn your phone off for certain periods (e.g. when writing) or even just turn it over so as not to be distracted by notifications.

Limits. There are practical limits to what can be achieved solely on a smartphone. I sometimes find I have issues with the synchronisation between my phone's calendar and my work calendar, for example. Although most phones (and especially Windows phones) will allow you to open and maybe edit work documents this is far from ideal on the small screen and touch interface of most smartphones.

COOK'S TIPS

There is often no need to pay the inevitable premium to own the very latest phone. You can get a SIM-only contract and purchase nearly new phones (i.e. 6 – 12 months old) from eBay or similar.

RELATED RECIPES

See also *Digital scholarship - start here.*

#43

AUTHOR

Derek Jones

—

SERVE TO

Anyone using a digital research workflow

COST

Low

TIME

TIDY YOUR DESKTOP

Invest time in your digital workflow

BACKGROUND —

My personal research place varies considerably but most often there are two essential components: my laptop and myself – on a train, sitting in front of the telly, or even just standing at any horizontal surface that I can find. It is an intensely personal space and I have modified it many times to suit what I need it to do (even though I'm never quite happy with it).

My digital space is a really important part of my research, so if yours is too, why don't you give it a once-over?

It might sound really trivial to consider these tools that we all make use of each and every day of our research lives but there is a really important idea behind it – little things can be more annoying than big things.

INGREDIENTS

- **Your computer**

- **Access to the internet (plus some key resources – see notes on ingredients below)**

- **A bit of time to give things a try**

- **Something in your workflow that could be better**

METHOD

1. There are a couple of ways to make this recipe – if you want a quick snack then just browse the steps which interest you. If you want the full three-course sit-down meal then start with a plan.

2. Plan

    a. Sketch out your basic workflow and try to take into account those things that you do regularly. It is really important that you sketch these as objectives – instead of writing 'check twitter every five minutes' try writing 'maintain research network'. A good starting point is Unsworth's list: *Discovering, Annotating, Comparing, Referring, Sampling, Illustrating, Representing* (Unsworth, 2000).

    b. Once you have your list, go through each element and see what you do right now – this time, write down the specific things you do. Next to this, note down in red pen where you get annoyed, frustrated, slowed down. In green pen write down where you think it goes well, what you enjoy, what makes you feel like you are doing things.

3. For each of the red-pen items, create a focused search on those activities and tools. Then search for alternatives.
    a. For each green-pen item, think about sharing your good practice with the rest of the research community.
    b. Reflect
4. Make sure that this is actually something that you need to be doing. If, for example, you have a strange copy and paste process for getting citations into your writing think about automated ways of doing this.
    a. Make sure you are making the most of what you are using just now. For example, are you getting the most out of that word processor? It can be well worth spending time learning to use the basic tools.
    b. Search
    c. First of all, don't be shy about asking colleagues what they do. Chances are, they will either be happy to share, won't have a better solution or are anti-social individuals who are best avoided anyway.
5. Create a targeted and well structured search for the element you are focusing on – make use of what you have (hopefully) already learned about searching for information.
6. Make good use of social media and keep an eye out for users that are actually demonstrating tools or processes (avoid software adverts).
7. Assess. Make sure that the changes you make actually work and, in particular, that you are not just using the latest software for the sake of it.

NOTES ON INGREDIENTS

Some great resources are:
- blog.macademic.org
- lifehacker.com
- academicpkm.org
- organognosi.com
- chronicle.com/blogs/ profhacker

COOK'S TIP

Learn one new thing to do with your computer each week or month – the time it takes to do this is (usually) very quickly recovered by the results.

WARNINGS

Don't get sucked into organisation, management and workflow tools just for the sake of them. To date, the author has tried over 30 'to-do list' applications and still uses a pen and paper for this – for you, not everything will necessarily work better in a digital environment.

Lifehacker is a great example of hidden gems buried deep inside days of searching time – don't get sucked into searching for the sake of it.

#44

AUTHOR
Simon Biggs

—

SERVE TO
Researchers (all)

COST/RESOURCE
Low – middling

TIME

HIGH-END TECHNOLOGY LAB

Balancing the technological and the human

BACKGROUND —

This recipe will be of interest to any researchers looking at HCI (human-computer interaction). It is based on observations in a research laboratory at a major US research university, dedicated to researching multi-user 3D multimodal interaction between both local and remote inter-actors. It is reasonably large and has no windows. There are six researchers based in the lab but as many as twelve can work in it for short periods of time.

The focus of the space is virtual environment development, not in-lab collaboration.
The researchers are from PhD to post-doc to senior research scientist level.
The senior researcher runs the lab. It is not a teaching space.

...one of the most effective and convincing full immersion VR experiences this researcher has ever experienced.

INGREDIENTS

- A room isolated from the external environment

- An extensive array of high-end technologies, including several powerful computers, numerous ancillary systems, 3D magnetic and optical tracking systems, large-scale high-resolution displays (projection and LCD) and various items of furniture, as required for the experimental situation

- Attention and thought about the physical space

- Challenge to the standard scientific laboratory model

METHOD

Pay attention to:

1. *High technical calibration*. This is a space for undertaking research into collaborative virtual environments. It is extremely important, when developing such virtual environments, that instrumentation is precisely calibrated to ensure affordances and feedback for the users feels consistent and accurate. In this lab the result is one of the most effective and convincing full immersion VR (virtual reality) experiences this researcher has ever experienced.

2. *The physical space*. The physical space in which the research is being undertaken is of a quite different quality. To be fully effective, work environments need a degree of orderliness (Mahnke, 1996). This one is cluttered, with multiple experiments co-housed in the same zones of use which complicate the understanding and use of the space and the systems installed within it. All in all it is a bit chaotic which also raises health and safety concerns. But it is likely that no H&S officer has ever visited the lab; and having worked in numerous labs I can say that this one is not unusual.

3. Because of the work being undertaken the space needs to be isolated from outside factors, such as sunlight. Even so it could be a pleasant and even engaging space to work in if the same degree of attention was paid to the physical space as has been to the virtual. Consult the recipe *Beam me up (or down)* for ideas about working in artificial light.

REFLECTIONS

The standard scientific lab model has been so ingrained that the researchers who work within them probably never stop to consider how the space could be different and allow them both a more pleasant and effective environment in which to do their work.

I prefer a recipe that allows a space to be created where communication between researchers is maximised and the work can be done in a relaxed and informal manner without it feeling like an overly technical or officious space. How to create such a space and ensure it can meet the requirements of the technical nature of the research is most likely to do with the culture and attitude of the inhabitants of the lab.

Work on that and you will probably create a context that will allow for the resolution of the issues underlying the difficult character of the space.

RELATED RECIPES

See also: *Research group as extended family* and *Yes we can - sometimes*.

#45

AUTHOR
George Buchanan

—

SERVE TO
Research groups

COST
Low to medium

TIME

LOWBROW POWWOW

Nourish your intellectual community
by sharing books

BACKGROUND

Providing easy-to-read books on intellectual themes
can help trigger new insights into over-familiar problems.
It can also provide a great place to switch off a bit, divert
your thinking and let your mind wander in other areas.

INGREDIENTS

- A bookshelf

- A set of accessible materials in mixed research themes (e.g. popular science, history, psychology) of loose relationship to the research domain, for example:

  - Stephen J Gould
  - David Bohm
  - Gerald Edelman
  - Edward de Bono
  - Christopher Alexander
  - Synchronicity: Jaworski
  - Molecules of Emotion: Pert
  - The Quantum Self: Zohar
  - Science as Psychology: Osbeck et al
  - Psychotherapy isn't what you think: Bugental
  - Emotional Intelligence: Goleman
  - The Muse Within: Bjørkvold
  - Thinking, Fast and Slow: Kahneman
  - This will make you smarter: Brockman
  - Flourish: Seligman

METHOD

1. Select the books, looking for accessible work that takes a wide view of its own particular theme. Also choose a wide variety of topics, so that no one area is over-represented. If budget is limited, ask colleagues to donate books they have already read.
2. Mix together haphazardly and provide on a bookshelf in social spaces used by groups.
3. Encourage book swapping and for visitors and locals to leave or recommend books (c.f. 'the book exchange').

COOK'S TIPS

It's also worth trying other books too – to the creative mind, there is no subject that is dull and uninteresting (Young, 2003)!

OTHER FLAVOURS

Try serving with *Attractor spaces* or mixing with *Off-grid creativity* to create a proper lo-fi zone.

#46

AUTHOR

Anita McKeown

SERVE TO

**Researchers at any
stage of their career**

COST

Free

TIME

INTIMACY

A strategy for personalising your research
space and process

BACKGROUND

Do you know your own
research process? Have
you considered what spaces
help you to work best –
or perhaps you know what
doesn't work? Do you feel
confident to create the
spaces you need to facilitate
your preferred process? This
recipe will help you to study
and redesign your research
space.

This recipe is based on
permaculture processes.
Permaculture is more
commonly known as a
system or method for
growing food in a
sustainable and integrated
way, but essentially it is
a design toolkit for human
habitation. One benefit of
permaculture is the key
maxim: the solution is in
the problem. By keenly
observing a system in a
number of ways, creating
a deep audit, we are able
to see where problems
or obstacles to an efficient
system might be and thus
how we might create
interventions to address
the issues.

> " *By creating a deep
> audit, we are able to
> see where problems
> might be.* "

INGREDIENTS

- A means of recording observations – pen, paper, notebook (digital or otherwise), camera, audio, video

- The OBREDIM acronym (more on this in the Method section below!)

- Reflective time

- The possibility of implementing some of your findings

METHOD

1. *Preparation stage.* If using a shared space or working on a joint project, discuss this process with your team or manager. It may be that you can undertake the audit within the team or as a group; if you are wanting buy-in from colleagues, it is best to involve them from the start.

You are now ready to use OBREDIM.

2. *O is for Observation.* When did you last look at your working space, environment or process? Permaculture practice usually begins with an extensive period of observation. When it's a living system, growing plants, planning landscapes etc. at least a year is recommended, enabling a full annual cycle to be observed and documented. But a much shorter version can be equally useful when using its design principles. Your observations of yourself or your working space can be scaled up or down depending on what is appropriate.

3. Draw any flows of movement or patterns or shapes that you see. These don't have to be artists' drawings or sketches – they can be simple technical diagrams or maps of what you see. You can make notes, draw the flow, patterns or shapes, and keep diaries, log books or field notes. Try to represent what you observe and reflect on your observations – make use of the research skills you already have. Be curious, ask questions, consider why things happen the way they do. Observe how and when you work best, how the patterns of behaviour among your colleagues and the physical layout impact you. It may be useful to consider the history of your department, how it has changed and the direction it might move in the future. Above all, ask yourself 'what if?' What if things were done differently in your research ecosystem?

4. *B is for Boundaries.* Think about the edges and limits of your research project or space. Where do your responsibilities start and stop? How does your research fit into the bigger picture of your department? It is sensible to anticipate the limits to what can be done and the potential obstacles to your suggestions, changes or ideas, particularly with respect to procedural matters. It might help to think of precedents you could use in persuading your institution to take your ideas on board, or plan some adaptations if an aspect of your idea is blocked.

5. *R is for Resources.* What resources are available – short and long-term? Sometimes there are changes that can be made that are lighter, quicker and cheaper – look at what can be done short-term or temporarily as well as trying to implement long-term changes. Look for unused spaces and consider sharing resources with other departments.

6. *E is for Evaluation.* The evaluation of the first three steps
    can be useful before you proceed with making any design
    changes to your research space. Have you covered
    everything you can think of? Are there any gaps? Have you
    observed all the elements? Have you stayed inside the
    boundaries and responsibilities? Are there resources ready
    for you – or if not, what do you have to do to gather them?
7. *D is for Design.* Only once the first three stages are
    complete should design begin. This is often difficult when
    methodologies and resources have already been set, for
    example within funded research. However, an evaluation
    of the current state of play will enable some appropriate
    redesign where needed. The design phase based on the
    first three stages will enable you to identify and consider
    current and future inter-relationships that will be part of
    your research ecosystem. This holds whether you
    are looking at a physical space or a research project.
8. *I is for Implementation.* Building on the previous steps
    enables constant and relevant updating on milestones
    and timetables. This makes it much more likely that you
    will be able to transform your project or your audit/
    analysis outcomes into practical results and objectives.
9. *M is for Maintenance.* Once you have analysed your
    research ecosystem and planned for its future, you will
    need to acknowledge variables and activities that will
    keep your research space or process surviving healthily.
    Plan small tweaks if they are necessary to achieve the
    plan's full potential, but the hope is that if the overall
    design has been done well, things should continue with
    few or no major changes. However, you can't plan for the
    unpredictable things that so often happen with live events
    and human dynamics. So if this happens, run the sequence
    again in light of the new information and/or variables
    introduced to the process.

RELATED RECIPES

Try this with *Just describe.*

#47

AUTHOR

Serkan Ayan

SERVE TO

PhD students at their first conference abroad

COST

Free

TIME

DON'T PANIC!

Enjoy being a stranger in a strange land

BACKGROUND

People can feel strange, when you're a stranger. Especially when you find yourself somewhere with very little that is familiar. This recipe is my response to my initial anxiety at being in a different country (Japan) for a conference.

I hope it will give you a couple of ideas about how to enhance your overall experience, and not to feel so strange that it gets in the way of the main point of your trip which is, after all, to make your mark at an international conference. And enjoy and explore a completely new culture.

INGREDIENTS

- Yourself

- Technology

- Strange place

METHOD

There are three parts to this recipe: before the trip, during the trip, and after the trip.

1. Before:
    a. Learn something about the upcoming experience: use Google Maps, street views, and relevant websites.
2. During:
    a. Are you going with someone you know? On a cognitive level, you'll feel safer and adjust better to the new space
    b. If you are on your own, invent a routine. For example, use a small toy to put into photographs you take. I inserted a small cardboard cut-out of myself into each of my photos, and helped situate myself in the space. Take lots of photos and *smile*.
    c. Just observe. Try 'people watching': How do they act? How do they show respect? Greet each other? Use the *Just describe* recipe to help here.
    d. Find a Wi-Fi hotspot and bathe in the technological pool to update your information about where you are.
    e. Buy small gifts that are contextually relevant. Buy them, put them in your luggage and forget about them – you will use them later.
    f. Finally, once you are able to orientate yourself in the streets around, do something you wouldn't normally do. Surprise yourself!
3. After:
    a. Give your friends the small gifts you picked up on your trip.
    b. Mix the giving with stories to create a context for your friends.

NOTES ON INGREDIENTS

Cultural ethnographer Jan Chipchase writes about explorations of culture and geography and in particular ways in which you can approach the observation of other places - as well as yourself in those places (Chipchase, 2013).

WARNINGS

If you do go with someone you know, make sure you don't just hang out with them the whole time or you will miss huge opportunities for networking. Branch out on your own and then you can debrief with your companion over beers in the evening.

Technological availability outside the conference is a major issue – before you go, try to identify Wi-Fi availability.

#48

AUTHORS

George Buchanan
Derek Jones

SERVE TO

Organisations and departments, or in spaces between these entities

COST

Medium

TIME

MEAT(ING) PLACE

Don't overlook the benefits of simply chatting to other people

BACKGROUND ___

'Meatspace' is a term that refers to physical reality as opposed to virtual spaces such as online social media, phone conversations, and texting. Its predecessor might arguably be the phrase 'press the flesh'. Sitting down with other people and simply talking is perhaps one of the richest examples of human behaviour and, in a busy world, we can easily overlook the simple benefits we gain from just chatting with other people.

When we do this in the right spaces we are doing more than simply creating noise and exchanging information – we are engaging in the rich sorts of experiences described by Alexander (1979), Bachelard (1984), and Oldenburgh (1989). We are actually creating place in its simplest form – by using people.

It's vital to understand that *place* is the important thing here. Place is a rich concept that depends on many factors, from the psychological and sociological, to the physiological and even political (Najafi & Shariff, 2011). So use this recipe to get the basics right.

"Architects create space – people bring place..." (Clark and Maher, 2001).

INGREDIENTS

- A subdued seating area away from busy access zones, but visible to passers-by

- Comfortable seating and informal tables

- Coffee-table books, long reading materials and equivalent visual distractions

- Intriguing objects of aesthetic interest

- Nearby refreshments

METHOD

1. Find and choose your venue, ensuring that it is both visible to passers-by and creates good opportunities for random encounters with those seated there.
2. Choose an overall visual scheme for the site and select and install appropriate furniture.
3. Obtain the objects and reading material, gaining input from users of the space as to the appropriate form of materials, and interesting subjects. Avoid duplication of items already in personal spaces, as copies of available items will not encourage use of the area.
4. Place objects, information and refreshments to encourage the use of the space as a restful area in which concentrated work is not done.
5. Respond to feedback on the quality of the reading materials and objects – ensure that these are adjusted and changed over time – items which are over-familiar can lose their interest.

NOTES ON INGREDIENTS

A good example of these spaces can be found in the mezzanine chill-out areas of the Paul G. Allen Center building, University of Washington, Seattle.

COOK'S TIPS

Avoid hard chairs or an 'office' feel if at all possible. If that's not possible, soften the edges by personalising these artefacts with other objects.

Get advice and suggestions for the right aesthetic for the location from stakeholders. Keep an eye out for spaces like this in other buildings – when you see one, take a picture or make a note. What is it that attracted you to it?

WARNINGS

If the place isn't working, change it.

RELATED RECIPES

See *Attractor spaces, Lowbrow powwow* and *Serendipity on the back of a napkin* for ideas.

#49

AUTHORS

George Buchanan
Derek Jones

SERVE TO

**Larger groups/departments
in institutions**

COST

Medium – high

TIME

GET INTO THE ZONE

Create zones in buildings as cues to
guide behaviour

BACKGROUND

Differentiating spaces within buildings or other large spaces can be an incredibly simple but effective technique to guide behaviour. Buildings with poorly defined behaviour spaces can confuse users and be less effective places.

People are actually very sensitive to the social use of space. Understanding variations of public, semi-public and private space is important when creating place (Carr, 1992). Think of a building as a miniature city and you'll start to get this (Lynch, 1960).

For example, corridors are for the use of everyone (public); certain places are OK to sit and chat in (semi-public); some meeting spaces are OK to sit and chat for a purpose (semi-private); and some spaces are personal and off-limits to others (private). And that's before we even consider liminal places – the spaces between spaces...

The learning centre/library in the Saltire Centre, Glasgow Caledonian University, is zoned according to noise and activity levels. The ground floor is noisy, full of activity and contact, café space, buzzing. The floors as you go up the building are quieter and set out for ever smaller groups until on the top floor there is silence and solo work only. The noise levels are also signalled by colour – the scheme goes from hot to cool colours as the noise goes from loud to silence. Natural light floods the space everywhere.

The Paul G. Allen Center for Computer Science & Engineering building in the University of Washington, Seattle, has a chill-out zone on each mezzanine where people can be solo among others. This, along with a huge whiteboard in each space, supports engagement with people, ideas and information even when people are working on their own.

INGREDIENTS

- Buildings with multiple spaces, a single large space (such as a library) or a series of connected spaces with a single community (such as a department)

- A bit of design thinking and creativity

- Paint, graphics, furniture, objects and lights

- Selected contact spaces with extensive views, good natural light, spacious feel (long internal isovists and lines-of-sight, good ceiling height)

METHOD

1. Before you start, it's important to see how your place is currently being used. Get a plan, take a wander around and use the *Just describe* recipe. Try to see if there are already natural zones forming and then reinforce these. Identify areas where no particular activity is currently taking place – could these be used?

2. If you are working with a building or larger space then consider getting some professional help from an architect or interior designer. If your budget won't stretch to this, then take a walk to the design department in your institution or have a mini design ideas competition.

3. Separate the building, department or large space into different zones preserving highly connected areas for contact spaces. As a first pass, try these categories: private/solitary; semi-private/quiet; semi-public/shared; public/active.

4. Make use of colour, furniture, objects, graphics and lighting appropriate to each activity type. Think about creating mood boards for each category you decide to use. Your gut instinct will serve you well here – what does a private/solitary space *feel* like?

5. Provide key facilities appropriate to each category (e.g. coffee shop/machine, sandwich bar, Wi-Fi, power, data projector, monitor, conference phone) – it's important to support the activity too, not simply to provide the space.

6. Pay attention to the contact spaces. Ensure that each has a unique design and responds to the needs of groups that inhabit the nearby areas/zones.

COOK'S TIPS

Remember, design of these places does not stop once you have changed them – keep an eye on your changes to make sure they are working and don't be afraid to keep adapting.

Believe it or not, you can even zone a single small office. If you are into bonsai (and have excellent self-discipline) you can even zone your desk.

WARNINGS

Don't allow these spaces to become stagnant – if they are not working then change them. Similarly, don't use rules to modify behaviour – allow the behaviour to emerge and then let it self-monitor.

RELATED RECIPES

Use this recipe to find space for *Serendipity on the back of a napkin*, *Popup whitespace hubs*, or even *Can-do space*.

AUTHOR

Debbie Maxwell

SERVE TO

Researchers at all stages

NUMBER
OF SERVINGS

Groups of three or more

COST/RESOURCE

**The cheaper the better!
30 minutes preparation +
30 minutes set up**

50

MAKE DO & MEND SPACE

Don't accept what you are given -
make your space work for you

BACKGROUND

Sadly, we don't always have the luxury of designing our research spaces from scratch or with an unlimited budget. This recipe makes the best possible use of temporary, existing spaces for those all-important work-together meetings where energy levels need to be kept high and creativity fostered.

The essence of the recipe is 'make the space work for you'. Do not accept what you are given without question – realise that you can do things with your group spaces.

The recipe can be applied in a number of contexts: as a research activity with other researchers (e.g. research workshops); as a participatory or co-design process with end-users or external stakeholders; as an exploratory or learning event; in fact, any time you have to use a space that is usually governed by someone else, or by organisational guidelines.

INGREDIENTS

Temporary access to physical space with seating

Dedicated, enthusiastic facilitator

Willing collaborators to make use of the space

Range of stationery/craft materials (paper, pens, portable flipcharts, magic whiteboard etc)

Plentiful supply of tea, coffee and water, and (if budget allows) biscuits and fruit

METHOD

1. *Consider the use*:
    a. Is it to foster group discussion? In which case, configure seating to reflect this by arranging chairs in a circle. Remove any 'dead spaces' in the centre of the room and encourage equitable discussion by ensuring that there is no 'head of table' arrangement.
    b. Is it for smaller breakout conversations? In which case, set up groups of three chairs, each with (if possible) a flipchart. Use the corners of the room to avoid listening to other conversations while trying to concentrate on your own one. Set it up so that it is easy to take the chairs back into a central circle for debriefing/plenary discussion.
    c. Is it for presentations? In which case arrange the chairs in a horseshoe – it fosters equality and prevents people dozing off at the back or checking emails instead of concentrating.

2. *Own the space*:
    a. Personalising a space is an intrinsic part
        of supporting and demonstrating creativity –
        individual or group (Barrett & Barrett, 2010;
        McCoy, 2000; Williams, 2013).
    b. Use additional elements and items: flipcharts,
        large sticky notes, static whiteboard material,
        wallpaper – make use of whatever you have.
        Almost anything can be repurposed to make
        do and mend – see Harding (2010) for 100+ ways
        to reuse magazines! Bring flowers or plants into
        the space – people will smile!
    c. If you are stuck with tables and loose furniture
        you could push them against the walls and work
        in the centre of the room. Or arrange them at
        angles instead of square to the front. Or in
        clusters – or even on their sides.
3. *Consider documentation capture*:
    a. The documentation process can be designed
        to customise and take ownership of a space,
        through attaching completed artefacts to walls
        and windows, or using as tablecloths. Participant
        discussion, when captured as it unfolds, can build
        intra-group trust and improve communication
        astonishingly. The cafe conversation is a powerful
        example of this process (www.theworldcafe.com).
    b. If you are making audio or video recordings, you
        can minimise noise interference from multiple
        discussions by situating groups of chairs and
        tables as far away from each other as possible.
4. *Encourage temporary longevity*. For example, if you will
    be using the space for more than one consecutive day,
    try to leave material adorning the space. And leave a *large*
    notice for the cleaners/janitor to 'leave everything as it is'.
    If people put their paperwork on their chairs, the cleaners
    can vacuum the floor.

COOK'S TIPS

If possible, always visit
the space you'll be using
beforehand, so that you
can plan your activities
and layout accordingly.

WARNINGS

Be aware that walls
and windows may not be
available for use. Check
beforehand whether you will
be able to use just one kind
of sticker or none at all.

OTHER FLAVOURS

Try starting with *Just
describe* and have a look at
Work that space for other
ideas of how to make the
space work for you.

51

WORK THAT SPACE

Change your space; improve your thinking

AUTHORS

Siân Robinson Davies
Evgenij Belikov

SERVE TO

Everyone

COST

Low cost

TIME

BACKGROUND

We often take the arrangement of elements in our research space as fixed. Though we might rearrange the space when first moving in, after this first period we might not think again as to how our spatial needs change with our changing activities and environment, such as the changing of the seasons.

Some recipes in this book are based on the principle that changing spaces affects one's creativity and aim at moving away from your workplace to a new space to induce creativity. This complementary recipe suggests rearranging the elements of the workplace itself to achieve a similar effect and to better reflect the requirements arising from the current activity.

By changing your environment you are expressing agency in that space – that you can effect change in your own immediate environment. This can be quite important in generating hope for creative thinking (Rego et al, 2009).

Similarly, change in and of itself has a few beneficial side effects for your thinking – basically, it makes you think, which in turn makes you come up with new thoughts.

INGREDIENTS

Your work space

Furniture, fixtures and fittings, plants, personal items, equipment

METHOD

1. Having spent some time in the space, you will have an awareness of how you use it, how you move around it, and areas that are most comfortable. But the chances are that you will also be quite familiar with it too, meaning that you might not have thought about its potential for some time.
2. Think about other possible configurations of the elements in the space in relation to your current activity and the environment outside the workplace. If you share an office, approach your colleagues and introduce the idea to them. Jointly coming up with suggestions for change can improve the atmosphere in the shared space.

3. Implement the change and assess its effect.
4. After a while go back to step two and check whether new needs have emerged that would merit another rearrangement.
5. Here are a few examples to get you started:
     a. You might want to move a favourite chair near a window in summer to use optimal sunlight and allow for a view to the outside while thinking or reading, but move it away in winter due to draughts. What other seasonal changes would you like to make?
     b. Try arranging equipment and furniture according to activities so that things are within reach. You might even have different areas of your space dedicated to certain activities.
     c. At the very least, have a thinking space – a favourite seat, a space beside the window you like staring out from, or even somewhere away from your main workspace.
     d. If a particular piece of equipment or furniture is not being used for a period of time, it could be packed away or moved elsewhere to allow space for other activities that take priority. When this happens, try replacing it with an interesting alternative or make use of the space in another way.
     e. The position of people's desks might need to be rearranged as different collaborations emerge. The chairs in any communal area might need to be rearranged to accommodate the number of people using the space.

COOK'S TIPS

Keep the elements in the space mobile to make things easy to rearrange and keep the changes reversible so that you can return to a previous configuration.

Have a look at what other people do with their spaces.

WARNINGS

Remember that the aim of this recipe is to facilitate new ways of thinking, doing and researching. Don't use rearranging your space as displacement activity!

If the space is shared with other people make sure you communicate your idea before implementing the changes to avoid any conflicts.

#52

AUTHOR

Mel Woods

SERVE TO

**Individuals and groups
requiring alternative
research thinking spaces**

COST

High

TIME

REBEL SPACE

Transform work practices with walk-in
workplaces

BACKGROUND —

This recipe is for a place
within a town or city where
you can hot desk for the
afternoon, hold a meeting
or simply connect with
other people, a walk-in
workplace – space where
people can:

- escape isolation if they are
  working at home or need
  a break from their normal
  working environment;

- work at a distance to
  cut down on commuting;

- work individually or
  collectively in a different
  environment or community
  to encourage new thinking.

The place is transformative
through the people that
use it, through being open
to many possibilities, and
through carrying traces of
people and ideas that have
passed through. The design
encourages collaboration
and sharing of ideas.
It challenges our ideas of
a 'normal' office space.
It is rich in unexpected
affordances, ways of
engaging with information
and ideas by chance.

As an example, Fleet
Collective, based in Dundee,
is a community of artists,
designers and other others
who make use of shared
physical, social and digital
creative workspaces
(www.fleetcollective.com).

Other interesting
precedents are

- SMARTlab University
  College Dublin
  (smartlab-ie.com);

- British Library reading
  rooms (www.bl.uk/
  reshelp/inrrooms/
  readingrooms.html);

- SocietyM (www.citizenm.
  com/societym-glasgow/);

- Mallorca Waka
  (www.ablab.org).

See this book's Berlin
and London case studies.
Also have a look at Carlson
(2008), Berardi (2009) and
Levine (2011).

INGREDIENTS

- People, who are curious, open-minded, creative, transient, working, generous

- People who subscribe to the ethos of 'What I give out, I get back many times over'

- Mix of spaces (boardroom, co-working, relaxing, individual/private, learning, exhibition, cafe)

- Flexible and easily adaptable spaces. All the furniture (chairs of different kinds, tables, walls, partitions) can be reconfigured easily and quickly. All comfortable – the chairs, for example, are suitable for extended use

- Spaces that have the appropriate sensory properties conducive to creativity: comfort, light, sound, spaciousness, movement and aliveness

- Affordances: a rich mix of magazines and books, posters and papers; art works; screens with film, video, information; areas for sharing information, requesting collaboration and feedback, seeking new approaches; all the usual support systems of fast reliable Wi-Fi, kitchen, power etc

- Support from departmental administration to make use of these spaces or a sufficiently empowered group of people to create your own

METHOD

1. For formal or semi-formal approaches:
2. Find hot-desking office space in your town or city or look for meeting spaces offered for rent.
3. For individuals and intermittent use, have an agreement with the owners of the space for use according to your needs. For example, a research department might wish to allow individual researchers alternative spaces to work in or to encourage remote working.
4. For groups or departments, consider holding away days or regular idea-sharing meetings. Arrange these regularly and don't allow them to become stale by having the usual agenda items.
5. For informal group approaches (and to really get into the spirit of the recipe):
6. Create your own place by finding a suitable disused or under-used space, either in your institution or elsewhere in your town or city.
7. Establish a theme or idea for the space: this could be as simple as a shared workspace, a common theme (such as 'ideas space' or 'shut-up-and-write space'), or even an agenda or manifesto for the place.
8. Enable the space with affordances suggested in the list of ingredients, but don't over-design this – allow requirements to emerge. In fact, go one step further and encourage people to bring their own fixtures and fittings.
9. Encourage other departments, disciplines or even institutions to take part in the theme and the use of the space.

The place is transformative through the people that use it

COOK'S TIPS

Remember, for this recipe to work really well, it's the people that make the place – not just the physical things. Keep collectives small and focused. When they stop working, create another.

Be open as to sharing the availability of the space with people from other disciplines and walks of life if you wish to encourage different places of creative working.

Other sources of space worth looking into are business incubator units, empty retail spaces, local schools/colleges and local libraries.

For the really brave and forward thinking research administrator, research and business start-up incubators are very good neighbours – why not create your own open business model?

WARNINGS

Beware the administrative implications of this recipe – if it's going to be too much trouble, find another way.

#53

AUTHOR
Diana Bental

—

SERVE TO
Researcher of any level

COST
Low

TIME

BUS AS RESEARCH ENVIRONMENT

Think while you travel

BACKGROUND —

I have a half-hour journey to and from work and I can read papers on the bus – the bus as a research space. It is just long enough to read a paper and think about it, make notes and reflect. I do what I can fit into the time – reading a paper. I can't write – the bus movement is too 'shoogly' (Scottish vernacular term meaning shaky, unsteady). Reading and thinking in a half-hour bus journey is good. The No. 45 is a nice quiet journey; I can always depend on getting a seat. It's a nice environment.

This recipe works well with other forms of transport, too: trains, planes and even cars. Williams observes that "train journeys appear in each data set" (2013, p. 102) and quotes interviewees as getting ideas when:

"Driving – like when I take the train."

"On the train on the way home."

"Trains are great places for things to pop out of my unconsciousness."

"I can think well when I'm on a train [going] through countryside like between the Lake District and Glasgow."

And:

"The second kind of problem is open question problem, and it is more likely there are two or three possibilities to get to the goal but you do not know which one is better. When you do this, moving or driving is freeing my mind for dealing with the second kind of problem."

INGREDIENTS

- Academic paper
  to be read

- Notebook and pen
  (if you can)

- Laptop, tablet or
  smartphone

- Bus journey of
  30 minutes or more

METHOD

1. Find yourself a seat on the bus
2. Read the academic paper
3. Think about it
4. If you find you can't concentrate, perhaps because of background conversations, then simply stare out of the window and defocus your mind. Or put your earphones in and listen to whatever sounds help you concentrate.

NOTES ON INGREDIENTS

The movement associated with travel creates the conditions associated with disengagement from context and others, making creative and good thinking more likely (Williams, 2013). Poincaré famously had one of his ideas when stepping onto a bus.

Avoiding travel-sickness is essential if you are going to read while travelling. You might be unable to use this recipe on a bus, but happy to use it on a train or plane.

COOK'S TIPS

Spaces such as this should be special – try not to incorporate them into your work plan by saying things like 'I'll get that finished on the bus'. Allow this time to be slightly different.

WARNINGS

Don't miss your stop! Sometimes colleagues will join you on the bus and want to talk. Pre-empt this by saying firmly, and with a big smile: 'Hello! I'm afraid I'm going to be terribly rude and ignore you while I get this paper read.' Nine times out of ten this will be a relief to them as they too want to read or think.

RELATED RECIPES

Works well with *What to listen to while you work*. Try *Defocus your thinking* for a different flavour along the same lines.

#54

AUTHORS

**George Buchanan
Debbie Maxwell**

—

SERVE TO

Researchers on the move

COST

Low

TIME

Low

A MOBILE THINKING SHRINE

Create a portable familiar workspace
to help you concentrate on the move

BACKGROUND —

Anthony Trollop wrote his novels on the train while working for the Irish postal service. He had a wooden briefcase that turned into a small writing desk balanced on his knees.

You, too, may want to be able to think creatively and well wherever you are: travelling, hot-desking, at home, in your usual workplace. If you are somewhere familiar you may want to be able to change the state of the place, give it a new shape, reframe it into something unfamiliar. If you are somewhere unfamiliar then you may want to be able to shape it into somewhere that feels more familiar.

INGREDIENTS

- Personal items (physical or digital) which make you feel at home

- Pen and paper, tablet computer or laptop

- A ritual

METHOD

1. Choose where to work. Consider what is needed:
   a. *Services available*. Are they sufficient for what you need?
   b. *Light, space and pace/vibe*. Does the space have lots of natural light? Is it big enough with long lines-of-sight and high ceilings? Does it feel alive?
   c. *People and community*. Are the right people around for you to connect to when you need or want to? Is there a supportive community that you can rely on when you need help of any kind, or to get unstuck in your thinking, or to relax/take a break with?
   d. *Inspiration*. Can you easily find inspirational ideas here? Can you link in with inspirational people? Is there information around from which you can draw inspiration?

2. Shape (the) place. Consider what you need to do for:
    a. *Familiar places*. What can you do to make the familiar unfamiliar? How can you break familiar habits and approaches in a familiar space? Change the furniture around? Realign the desk so that your view is different? Take in a small bright object and place it in your line-of-sight to remind you that you have chosen to change the state of your space? What else?
    b. *Creating your own territory in a changing environment*. When she was thrown out of her family home for being gay, Jeannette Winterson camped in other people's homes, sleeping on sofas and in cupboards. With the first money she made through writing, she bought a miniature rug. This rug became her home - spread out wherever she ended up, and transforming it into her place of safety, of writing, of thinking. What might you do to create a thinking place wherever you are?
    c. *Equipment*. You may need a stack of paper and a pencil, a pen, a box of markers and a packet of felt-tip pens. You may need electronic affordances - a laptop and/or an iPad. If so, what kinds of connection, service or access do you need?
    d. *Personalising the space*. You may like to have your personal music, photos and your equivalent of Jeannette Winterson's rug. These may be digital, stored on a laptop, or physical in the form of a favourite pen.
3. Devising a settling down ritual. Come up with a short, low-effort task which you do every time you sit down in your mobile shrine, e.g. playing a particular song, or looking at an inspirational quote. Checking your email is not suggested as a suitable ritual task, as it can draw you into another project away from the one you intended to progress.
4. Staying in touch versus offline. Do you want to be connected to the digital world, or will it be more productive to go off-grid for a while? This depends on the task you are trying to achieve and the facilities in the space where you are working.
5. Tidying up. Sometimes creating a thinking shrine involves no more than tidying your space. When you come to the end of a project - large or small - tidying the project paperwork, materials and books may be the ritual needed to rethink the space, to make it unfamiliar, to create the emptiness needed for the unexpected to arrive.

RELATED RECIPES

See also *Bookable nomad space, Rebel space*, and *Bus as research environment*.

#55

AUTHOR

Derek Jones

—

SERVE TO

Individuals needing a digital break

COST

Free

TIME

Varies

OFF-GRID CREATIVITY

Switch off to switch back on again

BACKGROUND —

Even the diehard digital native can find it useful to take a break from being constantly connected. 'Always on' can have various effects that can influence creativity, whether these are increasing stress (Heilman, Nadeau & Beversdorf, 2003), breaking the flow (Csikszentmihalyi, 1996) or reducing divergent thinking (Guilford, 1967).

I have an addiction to social media but I still find it quite useful to take a break from all of them from time to time. One huge benefit I have found in doing this is that it allows me to 'reset' my use of social media. After a break, I find that I concentrate on the things I really find useful about it and trim back on those that are simply less useful habits.

Similarly, I also find it incredibly beneficial to simply 'switch off'. I didn't say it was easy – just beneficial...

INGREDIENTS

- **No computer**

- **No phone (smart or otherwise)**

- **No internet access**

- **Peace and quiet – preferably somewhere a bit remote**

METHOD

1. Have an email inbox policy. 'Inbox zero' is a state that very few people reach but having some means of dealing with email overload is vital. The big tip here is to use simple rules that are easy to apply (either automated or manual) and then *stick to them*! It is also important to have rules for *when* you do this – constant interruption breaks the flow.

2. Have a period of disconnection associated with particular activities, if possible on a daily basis. For example, make lunchtime a disconnected event and use the time to simply take a break – it does actually improve your productivity. If, like me, you find that's too much guilt, then at least consider carrying out a low-tech task: reading a printed paper, journal or book; making notes with pen and paper or just sketching out ideas using *Serendipity on the back of a napkin*.

3. Create (or find) a disconnected place in your institution – a place with no Wi-Fi, network access or even power. Use this as a *Thinking den* or try *Meetings in the great outdoors*.
4. Take a break from all social media for a week or two – no matter how addicted you are. When you restart using them, think about what you missed and didn't miss and try to work out whether you could rearrange or readjust. Do you need to use every network you are on? Could you trim your following/follower lists? Is what you get out of using these networks worth the time it takes?
5. Take a complete break from all electronic communication when you go on holiday. Leave your phone behind for your next break and try to find somewhere with little or no internet access. By all means have an emergency backup for contact but make sure this is an emergency-only procedure.
6. Try to mitigate the stress of returning from a break – turn your out-of-office-reply into a more proactive message. It is rumoured that some people use the following message: 'I am currently [*insert_status_here*]. All emails I receive during this period will be deleted automatically.'
7. Consider email bankruptcy. As a last resort, if the inbox is getting overburdening, delete it and publicly declare bankruptcy (declaring it publicly is important). Needless to say, this is an extreme measure.

NOTES ON INGREDIENTS

Making use of 'on' and 'off' periods can be useful in creative thinking; recognising when each is required can help. Generally, most people work more effectively when they break up their activities to avoid monotony and fatigue.

WARNINGS

Some of the suggestions in this recipe are a bit extreme. But some of the consequences of becoming overwhelmed by being constantly 'on' are also pretty severe...

RELATED RECIPES

Goes well with *How to love several projects at once* and *My work is not me*.

#56

AUTHORS

Judy Robertson
Derek Jones

—

SERVE TO

Decision makers

COST

High

TIME

A RECIPE FOR MEDIOCRITY

An awful warning about how poorly designed buildings can stifle creativity

BACKGROUND —

Do you want to stifle your researchers' creativity? Stunt their intellectual growth? Foster apathy where possible? Follow these few simple steps and mediocrity will be yours.

The principal aim of these ingredients is to remove agency from the users of a space – you don't want agency if you want a predictable, controlled environment (Bandura, 2000). This also avoids any possibility of interesting adaption of space to suit users' purposes or to enrich their relationships with a place (Brand, 1995).

We concur wholeheartedly with Tschumi's (1996) statement: "There is the violence that all individuals inflict on spaces by their very presence, by their intrusion into the controlled order of architecture. Entering a building [...] violates the balance of a precisely ordered geometry (do architectural photographs ever include runners, fighters, lovers?). [...] The body disturbs the purity of architectural order" (1994, p. 123).

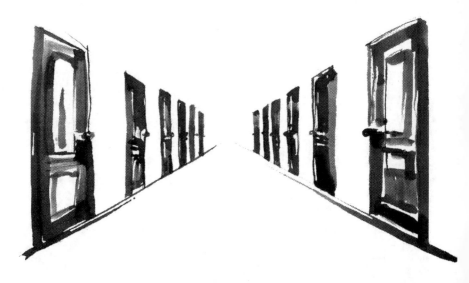

INGREDIENTS

- Inflexibility

- Tins of beige paint

- Breeze block walls

- Procedures in place
  of values

- A Building Management
  System (BMS)

METHOD

1. Paint all the walls in the institution the same colour, preferably beige. Refuse to change this under any circumstances.

2. Form a committee which must convene every time someone wants to pin paper on a wall.

3. Lock all windows and remove the keys, or if possible install windows which can't be opened. Ideally, of course, there should be no windows at all – it helps the concentration.

4. Automate all decisions about temperature or air quality, and if this is not possible then make sure that thermostats are controlled remotely by someone who doesn't work in the building. The aim is to prevent building inhabitants from working in conditions they find comfortable. We applaud the Scottish Enterprise building in Bothwell Street, Glasgow, (now, alas, defunct) where the temperature was quite properly controlled by the ambient temperature in Manchester much further south.

5. Decorate the walls with passive-aggressive notices spelling out exactly what people must or must not do to preserve the building in its pristine state.

6. Ensure that you forget that the whole purpose of buildings is for people to use them. This is easily done by separating the management of buildings from the users and ensuring that the management is only concerned with the fabric, not the purpose of the building.

7. Appoint building managers and administrators who love the building more than people, and can therefore be guaranteed to follow your policies rigorously. Impress upon them that their job is to protect the building from the infestation of people who are allegedly necessary for the university's core business.

8. Ensure that you have a fully automated Building Management System that 'cannot possibly go wrong'. That way, when people observe that the building is overheating you can ignore this feedback and rely on a system to provide you with the 'truth'.

NOTES ON INGREDIENTS

Serve with a pinch of salt.

WARNINGS

Be careful – if you aim for mediocrity, you might easily achieve dangerous levels of unhappiness. This might in turn lead to 'having to do something about it'.

So aim for it being not bad enough to do something about, but bad enough to have an effect.

#57

AUTHOR
Judy Robertson

—

SERVE TO
Research groups
and managers

COST
Low/medium

TIME

THINKING DEN

Convert an underused small space
into a thinking den for individuals

BACKGROUND —

Sometimes, you just need
a bit of time and space to
yourself to focus on
something. Researchers,
when reflecting on their
practice, often refer to
some means of focusing
the mind and there are
many ways to achieve this,
depending on your own
personal preferences
and situation.

This recipe encourages you
to make space for yourself
by getting together with
others to create a private
'thinking den' for just such
a necessary, convergent
thinking place.

INGREDIENTS

- An overstuffed building
- Some imagination
- A good wireless network
- Mobile office (laptop/ tablet, pen, paper, book)
- A small space which is currently un(der)used

METHOD

1. *Find a den* – You could set up a quiet space for your team members to get away from the hustle and bustle of the busy office. For focused productivity, quiet spaces with no distractions can be beneficial. The space needn't be big: a cosy den in a converted cleaning cupboard might be all you need, but do get rid of the mops first as comfort is a priority. The lighting should be good, and there should be a power socket for plugging in personal devices.

2. *Enable customisation* – The users of this space are likely to be transitory but they may make it their own for the short time they are there. Personalise your space by bringing your own items for inspiration (see *Mobile thinking shrine*).

3. *Shut off external distractions* – The whole point of the thinking pod is you're there to accomplish one focused task. Your thinking cannot be interrupted by colleagues. The phone cannot shatter your peace of mind. Email and social media get switched off at the door.

4. *Respect the den* – The den will work only if the people using it agree and respect some ground rules. For example, there should be a sign on the door indicating whether the den is occupied: if it is, tiptoe away quietly. Another could be not to hog the den – perhaps allow people to book it for a couple of hours at a time.

NOTES ON INGREDIENTS

The den does not have to be a physically isolated space – partial isolation can work too (but remember to respect the den).

COOK'S TIPS

There are other ways to develop a personal thinking space – some of these don't require a physical space. Use *Just describe* to work out what you have, then test a few methods to see what works for you.

Sometimes, all you need are earphones.

WARNINGS

Check with the health and safety people before you get too carried away. Sometimes what looks like dead space is required for a fire exit.

Be careful of a booking system – it can become tyrannical. As Émile Durkheim said, "When mores are sufficient, laws are unnecessary; when mores are insufficient, laws are unenforceable."

RELATED RECIPES

See also *Just describe*, *Mobile thinking shrine*, *Bookable nomad* space and *Rebel space*.

#58

AUTHOR

Meredith Bostwick-Lorenzo Eiroa

SERVE TO

Nomadic students,
vagabond researchers,
roaming interdisciplinary
teams

COST

Low-medium

TIME

BOOKABLE NOMAD SPACE

Make use of underused space by allowing the nomads in

BACKGROUND

We 21st century researchers are increasingly nomadic by nature. Similarly, many 'settled' researchers could benefit from a bit of wandering. Sadly, many spaces don't quite support our needs to roam – there's always something missing.

At the institutional and group levels, unused or underused spaces can be repurposed and adapted to encourage their use by providing the affordances required by the academic nomad. Add to this a few modifications to the furniture, a dash of advertising or branding and a booking system, and you will encourage activity in these spaces.

INGREDIENTS

- Nomadic individuals and/ or interdisciplinary teams

- Unused and underused spaces

- Clear signage, wayfinding and branding

- Abundant writing surfaces and whiteboards – ideally every wall should be covered in whiteboard

- Power supplies, data points and Wi-Fi

- Stackable seating and collapsible tables

- Scheduling capabilities (online booking system)

METHOD

1. *Identify the right space.* It is well worth checking the space you already have and how it is used – chances are you will have some underused space. You might also have spaces that could easily be adapted further. Use your creativity here and think about those in-between spaces in your building or campus (even those outdoors).

2. *Prepare your space.* Very often, all you need are the little things that might be missing. The best way to check this is to try the space yourself by working in it for an hour. What's missing? Power? Data? Furniture? Once you have this list, work out how you can provide these as simply as possible. If you are struggling to find these resources then remember that your nomads will also help if they know the opportunity is available.

3. *Advertise your space.* There's no point in creating this resource if you don't let people know about it. Make use of noticeboards and online group tools and let your group know that the resource is available. Give it a bit of identity using signage or consistent names for these spaces (you don't need much – word will spread).

4. *Book your space.* Giving each space its own real-time calendar – either online or a simple physical one. Provide additional information about these spaces online – even better, display images of the spaces or visual information on the affordances.
5. *Improve your space.* Now that it is working, how else can you improve it? What do the nomads want in there? Allow a feedback mechanism such as a small whiteboard or suggestion box to find out what is still missing. Be proactive in this too – try different things and ask 'did this work?' This should be an iterative and quick process.
6. *Share your space.* As an administrator or department head, you can list underutilized space for designated periods of time. Share this information to encourage cross-utilization of space and cross-disciplinary collaboration during off-peak hours, weekends, or other underutilized times during the day.

NOTES ON INGREDIENTS

This recipe comes from observation of other successful nomadic research spaces, such as Duke University's Link Rooms (http://link.duke.edu).

COOK'S TIPS

Bookable space can divide into a variety of sub-types: quiet study rooms, silent study rooms, large meeting rooms, seminar rooms, multimedia rooms, study pods, writing zones, idea places, etc. Think about making your nomad space serve a particular need like this and see what happens.

This recipe is best served with a host of complementary spaces, such as helpdesk services, access to printing and scanning facilities, cafes and vending areas.

Some expert nomads report that standing workspaces work better than sitting ones.

WARNINGS

Over-utilization is to be expected, along with outputs of massive collaboration.

Unassigned spaces may attract nomadic squatters and may spawn alternative learning communities.

RELATED RECIPES

This recipe goes well with *Attractor spaces, Relieving attention fatigue, Popup whitespace hubs*, and *A mobile thinking shrine*.

#59

AUTHOR

Alison Williams

SERVE TO

Those wishing to foster communication between colleagues

COST/RESOURCE

Low to high

TIME

ATTRACTOR SPACES

Create a welcoming space for researchers to connect with each other

BACKGROUND —

An attractor space does what it says – it attracts people to it. This is beneficial for creative thinking in two ways:

- Walking works for creativity as a quick break to disengage from the task at hand to refresh your mind (Beatty & Ball, 2011; Blanchette et al, 2005);
- Reducing the time you spend sitting down has additional health benefits.

A longer walk also works to incubate an idea in your intelligent unconscious (Wallas, 1926; Claxton, 1997).

Although the ancient Romans walked to think – *solvitur ambulando (it is solved by walking)* – just walking for the sake of it can feel strange. This can be especially true in a modern working environment, so it is good to have somewhere to go (Fayard & Weeks, 2007; Tett 2012).

Attractor spaces work well in situations like this: "Where are you off to?" – "To get a cup of coffee", "To pick up my printing", "To the George Lazenby Library".

...solvitur ambulando (it is solved by walking).

INGREDIENTS

- A medium-sized room,
  say 4.5m by 6m (15ft by
  20ft), painted in cheerful
  colours – somewhere
  that people like to go.
  The room should be easily
  accessible to everyone,
  and still be at least
  a one-minute walk from
  everywhere else

- Equipment that people
  need: photocopier,
  printer, stationery
  cupboard, water cooler,
  tea and coffee-making
  facilities, microwave, sink

- Information sources:
  noticeboard, screen,
  recent magazines and
  publications about all
  sorts of things

METHOD

1. Identify a shared resource that you and your colleagues
   make use of regularly (see the ingredients for a few
   examples). Try the coffee machine or water cooler.
2. Place this resource in the available room and treat
   the space like an information hub – not merely as a
   photocopying room. The function of this room is not
   just copying or making coffee, but exchanging information,
   making contacts, catching up via the grapevine.
3. If you already have a photocopier room, then turn
   it into an attractor space by adding extra ingredients
   (e.g. kettle, microwave, stationery cupboard, etc).
4. Augment the room by providing information sources.
   Noticeboards can be good but they need to be 'owned'
   by someone. The owner keeps the content interesting
   and up to date and empowers other people to use them
   (they are not just management megaphones).

5. Providing magazines and books on subjects relating to your work is very useful. Magazines sitting beside kettles and photocopiers get more thumb-throughs than some academic papers.
6. If you provide magazines and books, this officially allows you to name your space as a library – pick a suitably influential figure and name it after that person. The more important the name, the less likely management are to interfere with it.
7. If you don't have a separate room available to you, have a look at how the resource is deployed right now – could you make that space better? More commodious and welcoming to people? Do those boxes of photocopy paper need to be there?

NOTES ON INGREDIENTS

Don't be limited by the objects listed – this recipe can be very effective when you make use of spare spaces or even just spare surfaces.

You may just want to walk. In the military (all branches) the classic cover is 'walking briskly while carrying a piece of paper'. A clipboard is great – or a stack of papers that you are taking – ostensibly – to the photocopier.

COOK'S TIPS

The attractor space has additional benefits:

Other people are drawn to it, so there is an increased chance of serendipitous conversations. 'Water-cooler conversations', 'smokers' corner chat' are phrases in common use (Tett, 2012).

It keeps noisy machinery out of the lab or office where it distracts people.

It is a great place to put information that people read while they are waiting for the kettle to boil or for their photocopies.

External versions of this can work well too – have you visited the smokers' kennel recently?

WARNINGS

Don't make it too attractive – or no one will want to leave.

Remember that chatting is *not* time-wasting – it's building trust and increasing communication.

RELATED RECIPES

This recipe is worth considering with *Meetings in the great outdoors*.

#60

AUTHORS

Evgenij Belikov
Derek Jones

SERVE TO

Individuals and groups
wanting to improve their
working environment

COST/RESOURCE

Medium

TIME

BEAM ME UP
(OR DOWN)

See the light, and then change it

BACKGROUND

It might seem obvious,
but we have evolved to rely
on a single light source 150
million kilometres away –
this should be your starting
point. Of course, this light
source is not how we
actually 'receive' the final
light: it is filtered in
our upper atmosphere,
diffused through the lower
atmosphere, interacts with
objects and reflects off
others (Rea, 2003).

Light makes things visible,
highlights or draws attention
to elements in the physical
space and is implicitly
required by almost all of
the other recipes presented
in this book. The effects of
light on systems in the
human body are significant
(Wurtman, 1975), affecting
cognitive performance
(Chellappa et al., 2011),
growth and developmental
performance (Hathaway,
1992) and even influencing
the way we walk through
buildings (Taylor & Socov,
1974).

Basically, the effect of
light is pretty complex but
fundamental to our very
existence. This complexity
can't possibly be wrapped
up into a single recipe so
think of this as a starting
point for something you
probably take for granted
every day.

INGREDIENTS

- Your working environment

- Task lighting

- If possible, the building maintenance team in your institution

METHOD

1. *Start by understanding the lighting in your own environment.* Try to *Just describe* your workspace paying particular attention to the light quality – then look at the sources themselves. Start with natural light and then consider artificial sources. Think about: location and number; intensity (brightness, contrast, glare, dark spots); colour and temperature (warm, cold); and quality (what does the light feel like?). Try to record what you find that you think would be worth changing.

2. *Make the most of natural light.* Simply put, we have evolved in natural light and we need it for many of our basic physiological and psychological needs.

   a. Try to make the most of existing natural light sources by replanning workspaces to take advantage of the 'space within space' created by windows, rooflights and secondary light sources. Make use of the double affordance of windows – light and view. Power sockets are NOT more important than people!

   b. Secondary lighting (light that comes from internal windows and glazing, for example) can be used where direct external light is unavailable. If privacy is required then consider partial screening with blinds or translucent film. If you feel rebellious, apply tracing paper with sticky tack – make it look interesting by experimenting with patterns or layering torn strips.

   c. Look at how you are using existing windows – if that pile of books is blocking light, get a set of bookshelves! Slatted blinds let in light but try opening them fully to see what the effect is. And plants can have a wonderful filtering effect on incoming light (as can many other artefacts).

3. *Bounce your light around.* Remember, the effect of light is not just the source itself – the reflection of light internally can have significant effects (positive and negative). Check your surfaces and experiment with different materials on surfaces close to natural light sources. If you have issues with direct natural glare, redirect this rather than blocking it by using horizontal elements to bounce light onto the ceiling. Make use of lampshades or screens to generate interesting patterns on surfaces.

4. *Experiment with task lighting.* It's OK to bring in your own light sources to work (but remember that any electrical fittings should be safe and checked on a regular basis). Personal light fittings can help you meet your own lighting needs and allow you to personalise your space at the same time. If you work in a shared environment, club together to try a few different lamp types and see what works for you. Try small spotlights for focused tasks and (if you can) give a daylight bulb a go – they are more expensive but they can make a significant difference. Larger standard lamps might also be worth trying – try uplighting or reflecting artificial light off other surfaces.

5. *Switch the lights off.* Some people might find that a slightly darker environment feels better (see *The Creative Footprint*) but this often depends on the type of work you are carrying

out (don't forget that your monitor is a light source too). If you go for darkness then remember to get a top-up of natural light (see below). Or think about augmenting your lowered lighting levels with task lighting.

6. *Fluorescent hell*. If you work in an environment that uses nothing other than ceiling-mounted fluorescent fittings, then think about switching these off or reducing the number that you have on (see below). Augment your lighting levels with task lighting. If this is not an option, consider fitting diffusers to reduce the 'hotspots' of high-energy light. Paper makes a wonderful DIY diffuser material but take care to avoid fire risk.

7. *Lighting is dynamic*. Natural light depends on weather conditions, locations, and time of day and artificial light can be used to adapt to variations of natural light too. Dynamic lighting can also be used to guide or enforce switching from one activity to another or to change focus when one part of the space becomes gradually darker and the other is made lighter. Try changing your artificial light during the day to see what works for you – make use of task lighting and vary your lighting levels during the day.

8. *For decision makers* and those commissioning new buildings, make light a priority in your brief – not simply a functional requirement. Some of the worst lighting design comes from simply asking for uniform lux levels to enable task-based activity. Yes, general lighting levels are important but, if you are even slightly concerned about productivity and the quality of output from people in your institution, then realise the importance of physiological, cognitive and psychological effects of good lighting design. Engage a designer that understands this and think about the life-cycle cost of the asset you are procuring (not just the capital cost).

NOTES ON INGREDIENTS

Key considerations are the position, direction, distribution, wavelength (colour) and intensity of light, along with dynamicity. Light is very versatile not only as an enabler but also as an enhancer of *atmospheric effects*. As an enabler, artificial light allows us to work in physical spaces and at times in which no natural light is available. As an enhancer, light can be used to amplify or to counter environmental effects.

COOK'S TIPS

If you don't have access to natural light, remember to get a top-up of this regularly – preferably on a daily basis.

WARNINGS

Remember that responses to lighting are subjective – not everyone will feel the same way about the type of light 'mood' they like to work with.

RELATED RECIPES

Try a lava lamp in the *Thinking den* to do some *Defocused thinking*.

Try *Meeting in the great outdoors* or make use of *Attractor spaces* to get outside.

And don't forget an *Off-grid creativity* break.

#61

AUTHOR

**Meredith Bostwick-
Lorenzo Eiroa**

—

SERVE TO

**Tinkerers and creative
researchers**

COST

Low

TIME

😒 😒

WORKSHOP SPACE

Use unfinished spaces to tinker,
play and think

BACKGROUND —

Unfinished space has the
potential to be creative
because it gives 'permission'
to users to use it in ways
that finished spaces do not.
Workshop space waits to
be defined – an undecorated
room, machine shop, hangar,
or warehouse space – left
rough around the edges.

Its unfinished quality
encourages a dynamic fun
space in which to tinker, fail,
and figure things out. It is a
space where experimenting
is allowed (and expected).
It is a space where it is OK
to be messy.

Workshop space can
function like a 'popup
whitespace' and can form
itself on-demand when
there is a critical mass and
the need to solve a problem.

INGREDIENTS

- Creative individuals, especially 'free radicals' (Marshall, 2013)

- Lofted, raw, garage-type space

- A variety of tools, equipment and instrumentation

- High-performance hardware and software (an array of digital design tools)

- 'Idea closets' (smaller areas for quiet thinking and small-group collaboration)

- Access to spare parts, leftovers, junk and componentry

- Gadgets, robotics, building blocks, circuits, assemblies and prototypes

- Adjustable tables with open shelving

- Large-format layout surfaces – both vertical and horizontal

- Transparent storage units and magnetic surfaces for tool accessibility

- Abundant power, services and utilities as required

METHOD

1. Find a space that is unfinished, unused or that no one else seems to care about. To encourage 'big thinking' try to find larger spaces (double-height or lofted space) or an area which provides the physical space needed to work around larger prototypes and projects. It can be worth trying to get your institution to support the creation of such a space, but if you can't, try the *Rebel space* recipe.

2. Populate this space with affordances suitable for tinkering, making and playing. See the list of ingredients above for examples.

3. The active component of this *Workshop space* recipe is physical activity. Create a quantity of low-resolution prototypes that can be developed and tested quickly. Ideas are often assimilated through scrap, junk, rubbish, spare parts, and pieces from older, failed prototypes. Physically manipulate your prototypes to experiment with different ideas. A prototype is a physical sketch; it should be malleable, configurable, and editable. This should be a physical process where moving can encourage different thinking.

4. This physical workshop approach is not limited to physical products or models – ideas and concepts can be modelled too. Think about ways you can represent your thinking physically, for example:
   a. Ideas arranged spatially on surfaces or in 3D.
   b. Processes physically modelled using stakeholders and contexts.
   c. Detailed research explorations that use the physical space to represent scale and detail.
   d. Try taking a user trip or 'bodystorming' (Witthoft & Geehr, 2010) to physically act out scenarios or events.

5. Another approach is to break down, disassemble, and reassemble objects through experimentation. Start with something that is 'complete' and see what makes it tick – it can be surprising how many other ways there might be of doing something.

6. This is a cyclical process of quick, iterative physical thinking so make sure you record work in progress as well as completed ideas and prototypes. Try using *Broadcast Your Ideas*.

66

*Unfinished space has
the potential to be
creative because it
gives 'permission'.*

99

NOTES ON INGREDIENTS

John Marshall coined
the term 'free radical' to
describe those individuals
who have the intrinsic
power to change physical
environments and
institutional cultures for
learning (Marshall, 2013).
Marshall describes free
radicals as "...people with
certain aptitudes and skills
– flexibility, comfort with
ambiguity, self-direction and
the ability to manage change
– who are willing, energetic
and perhaps foolhardy
enough to knock down
walls and build bridges
to other areas".

Good examples of *workshop
spaces* are the Culture Lab,
Newcastle University;
Mixed Reality Laboratory,
Nottingham University; and
Google's Campus London.

COOK'S TIPS

The acoustics in unfinished
spaces can be terrible
so use soft furnishings in
places to help with this,
for example, zone areas
(idea closets) for quiet
collaboration.

WARNINGS

When left unsupervised
(be it an idea or a prototype),
another tinkerer may
suggest an alternative
approach to solving the
problem.

RELATED RECIPES

This recipe goes well with
*Popup whitespace hubs,
Broadcast your ideas* and
Rebel space recipes –
in fact, any recipe that
needs adaptable space.

#62

AUTHORS

Judy Robertson
Alison Williams

SERVE TO

Any group of people
needing to have a chat

COST

Low

TIME

MEETINGS IN THE GREAT OUTDOORS

Meet outside to get a new point of view

BACKGROUND

If you need to work with other team members, but you don't want to disturb your colleagues in the office, why not take your work outside?

Changing the environment gives a new point of view. Moving a regular meeting to the garden, park or forest can help the group to establish new ways of thinking.

There is considerable research into the beneficial effects of *biophilia*, the psychological attraction to life, aliveness or living systems (Fromm, 1964). It is also known and studied as naturalness (Ulrich, 1984; 1993; Barrett & Barrett, 2010) and as connection with the outside context (Kelly, 2001; Roessler, 1980; Wyon & Nilsson, 1980).

INGREDIENTS

- **A group of researchers who want to exchange ideas**

- **A climate with low rainfall**

- **Outdoor natural space**

- **Ways of recording: tablet, large drawing pad, pencils/felt-tip pens, voice recorder**

METHOD

1. To be truly disruptive, go outdoors with a group of IT or philosophy colleagues – anyone whose usual preference is to be in an enclosed interior cave. Native Americans will go on a 'medicine walk' where they consider a question and look in nature for metaphors and stimulus. This is a form of biomimicry, in which nature's elements of process, systems and models inspire new approaches to problems.

2. Use biomimicry to reframe your ideas, and biophilia to renew your spirits and thinking. Although Csikszentmihalyi says: "Unfortunately there is no evidence – and probably there never will be – to prove that a delightful setting induces creativity" (1996, p. 135) he still recommends heading for the hills whenever you can.

3. *Meetings on the move.* Seeing as you've disrupted the normal (Fromm, 1964) meeting dynamic by moving out of doors, why not take it a step further by introducing walking meetings? Beatty & Ball (2011) examine the beneficial effects that walking can have on creativity. The ancient Romans talked of '*solvitur ambulando*' (it is solved by walking). Blanchette et al. (2005) have researched the positive sustained impact of aerobic exercise on creative potential. Interviewees in Williams' study are conscious of the effect that walking has on their creative processes: "and [then] I come back to my desk and I might then feel better about the work and have moved on" (2013, p. 372).

NOTES ON INGREDIENTS

The SPIRES travel scholars have observed examples of how changing the environment gives a new point of view on campuses in Seattle, in Sydney, and in Tokyo and Kyoto where the attraction of being outdoors in inspiring landscape or in quiet natural corners can open up thinking.

Although it might be thought to be particularly inspiring for artists or botanists, these spaces are too close to their usual area of study to necessarily spur creative perspectives.

COOK'S TIPS

If you are cursed with a rainy climate, you could try colonising a corner of a waiting area or landing. Standing-up meetings can be an effective way to save time!

Create indoor destination points or attractors so that the walking has a point. 'Let's get a coffee' and take the longest way between the two points, rather than the shortest.

WARNINGS

Obviously be careful about confidential meetings if you think someone else is hiding behind the rhododendrons.

RELATED RECIPES

See also *Relieving attention fatigue, Off-grid creativity,* and *Attractor spaces.*

HARMONY WITH NATURE

—

Kyoto

—

AUTHOR

Negin Mohim

The Kyoto University of Art and Design (KUAD) is one of Japan's few private art institutions. Its predecessor was established in 1934. The university has hosted many national and international art exhibitions. What particularly stands out in this case study is the theme of large open spaces, accommodating the activity of several groups at once throughout various parts of the complex.

SETTING

The university is situated in the north of the beautiful historic city of Kyoto in western Japan and is easily accessible by regular buses or cycling, which is a very popular form of commute in a city like Kyoto. The main entrance is accessible from the main street in the area of Sakyo-ku with several convenience stores (of pivotal importance in modern Japanese life-styles) and Japanese fast-food chains nearby. The grand exterior of the university can certainly not go unnoticed. As well as the central building, there are several tall modern buildings surrounding the main building. They are seemingly disconnected from one another, but in fact these clusters of buildings are connected through several quirky paths running through the woods, linking the roof top of one building to the ground floor of another.

CHILL OUT AREAS

The internal space of the main building is airy, wide, with very high ceilings, modern, flooded with light, and well ventilated. It was very quiet when I visited even though a large number of students were working just outside the main entrance. The cafeteria, which seemed to be the 'go to' area for refreshments and informal chit-chat/group work, is stretched out across the right hand side of the main hallway. The cafeteria is further divided into three sub-areas: a large sitting area just by the entrance; a second sitting area by the cafeteria serving counter; and a third sitting area on a very large roofed balcony which overlooks the beautiful city of Kyoto. Students were using the space individually or in groups for discussions, meetings, informal chit-chat and refreshments. At the left of the hall is the information desk providing university leaflets and guides. The cafeteria is just across from the main exhibition area, from which students emerge to chill out for a few minutes or just grab some refreshments.

BIG WIDE EMPTY

Excellent use of wide open spaces, both indoors and outdoors, is clearly observable at KUAD.

Close to the main entrance there is a roofed, once bare, open space which is used as a working area. Art students in colour-coordinated work suits form groups of 5-10 and work on projects there. There is an energetic and exciting buzz in the air which is hardly noticed from few steps away. There are several instances of outdoor spaces being used as group work areas, such as this, in other sections of the university.

Through the main entrance and towards the end of the hallway is another wide space: the main exhibition area which is flooded with light from wide windows at the top of the space. The ceiling is very high, making allowance for the noise coming from several groups of 5-10 working in this one area. The natural light and tall ceilings are a recurring theme which I observed during my visit: tall ceilings, quirky empty spaces, floods of natural light, students working in groups. This space is further divided into smaller subspaces with two smaller open-space working areas to the right and another level above this sub-area accommodating offices and other rooms. Apart from student work projects and a very tall peculiar robot in the far background of the space, the room is free of any clutter. This makes sense as it is used by students to create crafts and will eventually be cleared for exhibitions.

SURROUNDED BY NATURE

The buildings are clustered in a mountain setting, and the surrounding natural landscape merges with the hard exterior of the modern buildings. The staircase from the exhibition space leads to the roof of the main building, from where you can see the woods which were previously hidden. This, and a panoramic view of the entire city of Kyoto, creates an excellent backdrop for the users of this space.

There are several access routes between the buildings, several of which are unusual pathways and bridges through the woods. There is plenty of signage around the open spaces guiding visitors through the paths, but if you don't know Japanese they are not of much use as they are all in Kanji.

Another striking modern building, situated on a wooden platform overlooking the entire city of Kyoto, is used for seminars and meetings. Behind the building, there are steps which take you into the mountains where individual students explore the surroundings or just simply relax under the shadow of a tree to escape the sun. Something about the harmonized sound of the crickets, the beautiful green surroundings, the modern roof garden and the beautiful view of the city makes it a nice escape from the buzz in the exhibition area. This theme is continued in another hidden gem on the top floor of the canteen building: an 'infinite roof garden'. The roof garden like many others is very quiet and sparse, with only a few individuals in sight, which makes it another ideal place to escape to for relaxation.

SUMMARY

One building – 'the cube' – was particularly pointed out by a couple of Japanese students as their favourite space. This building houses art exhibitions as well as classrooms and offices. At first sight it went against the observations made so far about the importance of modern design and links to nature: the building is very old, in the shape of a cube, made of classical red brick inside and out, with pipes and bits of rusty metal running through the interior. However, although it is very old, its rustic 'construction site' feel brings it into line with modern trends in design and architecture, and you can see clearly why it is a hit with the University's trendy art students.

Apart, therefore, from the observation that modernity is a core part of the look and feel of Kyoto University of Art and Design, the two key reflections prompted by this case study are: i) the excellent multi-use of indoor and outdoor open spaces for group activities; and ii) the integration of modern buildings with the natural landscape.

At an institute where art and creativity are at the forefront of its definition, work, play and relaxing have been made easy through the clever use of space and the clear contrasts and divisions between differently purposed spaces.

I CAN'T BEAR THIS SPACE

—

Room 101

—

AUTHOR
Alison Williams

What is it about the single-room research environment that elicited 'I can't bear this space' from a visiting researcher? Why did she find the space impossible to stay in for any longer than 45 minutes? Why was she unable to perceive what was actually in the room? And how do the people who work there day-to-day use and respond to the space?

In 2011 SPIRES part-funded me as a travel scholar to attend a creativity conference in the US and to carry out part of my research into the impact of physical space on creativity in the workplace. While there, I tested an early version of my visuospatial *Grammar of Creative Workplaces* (Williams 2013) through three audits of very different research environments. These were carried out in one of the US's leading science and technology research universities, with a 400-acre city-centre campus and 20,000 undergraduate and graduate students.

This case study examines one of the research environments audited and reflects on the impact that it had on the people visiting it (including myself), compared and contrasted with the impact on the researchers working in it. I discuss these two reactions, and finish with suggestions for dealing with similar research environments. All quotations are taken from the interview transcripts.

THE RESEARCH PROCESS

The method I used to test my visuospatial grammar compared two data sets: the first was gathered from an audit of the research environment, using the prototype grammar, and carried out by an independent assessor. The second set of data was collected from two semi-structured interviews with users of the space, conducted by myself as researcher. As an adjunct to this I also included reflective notes from my research journal.

I conducted the first test of the grammar in a Health Institute (HI), a 1980s modernist building. The workplace studied was a single room (for the sake of anonymity, let's call it Room 101) shared by seven graduate students. The audit was carried out when the space was occupied by three of them. The assessment took one hour, including walking round the second floor of the HI building to note ancillary spaces. Each interview focused on the impact the users perceived the space had on their creativity.

THE RESEARCH ENVIRONMENT: ROOM 101

The first floor of the HI research building interior, where the research room is situated, is almost entirely without natural light. The corridors are built on an internal square, with rooms going off to both sides also without windows, except to the corridor. The only windows observed on the floor were those of the head of department's corner office, the unmanned reception area beside the lift, and a corridor of further cubicles facing away from a long window.

The colour scheme in Room 101 at the centre of this case study is brown, ivory and beige, with white acoustic tiles on the ceiling and a grey carpet on the floor. The room is lit from the ceiling by florescent tubes with diffusers. There are no windows in the room, either to the rest of the building, or to the exterior. There is a single small pane of glass in the door that leads to the corridor.

Figure 1

The room is set out in cubicles for the seven graduate students (Fig. 1). The cubicles have high beige-coloured sides and brown cupboards above the desk areas. Two of the cubicles accommodate two researchers, and the other three are single. There is a door to one side of the room leading to a library/meeting room (also without windows) and another at the far end leading to a senior researcher's room.

ASSESSOR AND RESEARCHER RESPONSES TO ROOM 101

The independent assessor (IA), reader in creative practice at a UK university, found it stressful being in the building, and in particular being in Room 101. Notes from my research journal (RJ) demonstrate different aspects of this discomfort:

> IA finds it difficult to orientate herself in this building. Has to ask one of the grad students to help her. Is there also a question of lack of confidence? Needing an incumbent to negotiate the space? (RJ, 7 November 2011)

> Later: Went around the space with IA [a second time] and realised the extent to which her state of mind interfered with the assessment. Her visceral antipathy to the space [expressed in such terms as: "I can't bear this space"], and her unease at being a stranger in there, shut down her looking and she didn't see the only cubicle in which there were signs of life and imagination – where the place had been populated. (RJ, 7 November 2011)

The IA was not the only person affected by the room – I was too. The cubicle referred to above (RJ, 7 November 2011) was not the only one that had been personalized. Again from my research journal:

> Later: going round the next day [...] I realised [...] that I too had missed a whole cubicle at the end which is just crammed with papers, notes, pictures, life – also partial viewing based on embarrassed restriction – not wanting to [intrude] into places that are semi-private. (RJ, 8 November 2011)

Figure 2

Fig. 2 shows the densely populated and personalised cubicle, in sharp contrast to the others in the room which are almost completely devoid of objects (Fig. 1 above). Although it was in the corner furthest from the door, the cubicle was in plain sight. However, the assessor's antipathy to the room, and my wish not to intrude on people's work prevented both of us from seeing it on the first visit to the room. It was only on a subsequent visit to the room that I noticed it.

The IA's response to Room 101 and mine were initially affective ones. Using the grammar enabled the IA to distance herself to some degree from the affect, and to observe the space more closely. I discuss the degree of objectivity/subjectivity later in this paper. For now, I introduce the categories of sensory properties that support creative behaviours in a workplace – commercial or research.

CATEGORIES OF SENSORY PROPERTIES STIMULATING AND SUSTAINING CREATIVITY

In physical space there are six main categories of sensory properties that are central to stimulating, supporting and sustaining creative behaviours in the workplace (Williams 2013).

In total, 13 different senses emerged from my primary research and were supported by the literature as: the five classical Aristotelian senses of taste, smell, touch, sight and sound; the neurological senses of temperature, spaciousness, and movement/proprioception, and the Steinerian (1916) senses of speech, thinking, life, and the 'I' (Williams, 2013).

OVERALL CATEGORIES	SENSORY PROPERTIES SUB-CATEGORIES	ROOM 101'S AUDITED ABILITY TO STIMULATE AND SUSTAIN CREATIVITY
COMFORT	Taste/area for food and drink	Low
	Smell/fresh air/air quality	Low
	Touch/comfortable furniture	Medium
	Temperature (warmth/cold)	High
SIGHT	Sight/views	Low
	Natural light	Low
	Good artificial light (daylight bulbs)	Low
	Colour: cheerful/calm	Low
SOUND	Sound/quiet buzz	Medium
	Appropriate sound level	High
SPACIOUSNESS	Spaciousness/	Low
	Internal line-of-sight/isovists	Low
	Orderliness	Medium
MOVEMENT	Movement /proprioception (kinaesthetic sense)	Low
ALIVENESS	Speech/conversation	Low/medium
	Thinking/quiet reflection	High
	Life (feeling alive)	Medium
	The I/ego/personalising/ individualising the space	Medium

Table 1:
Sensory categories for the
properties of physical space, and
measures for Room 101

In the 18 sensory sub-categories of the properties that stimulate and sustain creativity, Room 101 scored *low* on ten of them, *medium* on five, *low/medium* on one, and *high* on two of them. Taking each category in turn:

COMFORT

1. Taste: although there was an area along the corridor for food preparation and eating, it was very small, and could accommodate only two people at a time.
2. Smell: Room 101's air quality was low. IA: "Very dry, de-energising".
3. Touch: The chairs were: "Comfortable but not too relaxing" (IA) and "I quite like this chair [...] It is comfortable to sit for a long time" (Interviewee 1), but the quality of carpet and cubicle walls was low. Interviewee 1 suggested: "We could have more soft pillows – different colour, that would be good decoration. Also you could sit there".
4. Temperature: The temperature was even, despite differing external temperatures. IA: "Good for working at desk".

SIGHT

5. Views: There were no views. "Window would be nice; it is one of the important elements" and "I would like to have windows so that the space can connect to the exterior" (Interviewees 1 and 2).
6. Light (natural and artificial): There was no natural light, and the artificial light was harsh and not able to be controlled by the researchers using the room.
7. Colour: The colours were dull and made the room appear smaller than it was. As interviewee 1 said: "I want a warm colour, so if we can have a colourful wall – I think the colour is important for me. So it's not just one colour".

SOUND / SPACIOUSNESS / MOVEMENT

8. Sound levels in Room 101 were low, almost silent: IA: "Very quiet – intimidating".
9. Spaciousness: Because the room was so small there was no feeling of spaciousness, and Interviewee 2 spoke of wanting to open it up: "[I would like to] lower down the cubicle walls to like [gestures at 45cm (18 inches)] [...] so no longer this high [120cm (4ft)]". Although the individual cubicles were orderly (apart from the one in Fig.3), there were flip chart pads and boxes cluttering the few otherwise empty corners, and posters crammed above the cupboards.
10. Movement: Movement was possible in the corridors, for example when interviewee 2 wanted to think, he would "just walk around the floor [of the building] two or three times and then go back".

ALIVENESS

11. Speech: While the IA perceived the room as "not conducive for chatter", Interviewee 1 said: "Easy to have a chat with my colleagues" and went on to say: "Most of our projects are not alone so we have to work with our colleagues and it's an open space. So people can just come to my desk and we can just discuss the project on my laptop and then we can work for a while over my desk, and we could just drag another empty chair and sit together and have a longer chat or discussion. Also we can come back to our own cubicle and do our own work". Interviewee 2, however, agreed with the IA: "If I want to have discussion – if I want to have some talk with some people [...] I feel like I am restricted to the cubicle".

12. Thinking: Both users and the IA were in agreement regarding the sensory property sub-category of *thinking*. The IA noted that: "The workstations could be private quiet places as they are individual cubicles – it is very quiet. [...] potentially good space for quiet reflection" and "Yes, quiet independent study space". The interviewees agreed: "[Getting an idea] happens when I am alone... immersed in my own thinking" and "It's [easier to] concentrate to write a paper in a small cubicle".

13. Life: The IA and interviewees had divergent views regarding the sensory property sub-category of *life*. The IA spoke of: "No life, no laughter, no fun" while interviewee 1, on the other hand, spoke about how: "The space [of my colleague in the end cubicle] is not that boring – sometimes there is a surprise over there, and it's like a stimulus".

14. The 'I' (personalisation): The IA noted: "Very little personal possession of the space, few artefacts", missing the two populated cubicles as noted above. The interviewees, on the other hand, had a different perspective: "People's working space – they like to make it work for them because information around them so that they can find it just by [...] scanning" and "Sometimes [my colleague in populated cubicle] will use some cute notepad or a cute drawing".

The main area of agreement between the IA and the researchers was that Room 101 was a place to do concentrated work. The IA saw "potentially good space for quiet reflection" and the interviewees concurred: "The cubicle works for me, if I want to have private space to work", "when you want to concentrate on your work you have some walls to separate you from others" and "sometimes I find out it's more concentrate to write a paper in a small cubicle because you don't have some other interruption from outside world – you just see the wall and the monitor and so...I think that is a good way for me to concentrate".

Here is something positive that visitors and users could agree on.

DISCUSSION

As a child, I never understood the saying 'It's an ill wind that blows nobody any good'. But the idea that there is something good in all situations, however dire they may appear to be at first, fits this context very well. The room, as a place for stimulating and supporting creative research, benchmarks the worst environment I have studied in this or any other research I have done. Here the users agreed: when asked where and how they get their ideas, both interviewees talked about being elsewhere: "Driving – like when I take the train, or when I am walking" and "It happens when I am alone. So if I am immersed in my own thinking, or when I walk down the street. I think in those moments I [have] a conversation with myself and [...] those ah-ha moments". The room had a singularly low assessment score of nearly every creativity-supporting sensory property, borne out by the IA's and my own strong dislike of it.

But even the most inimical space can have its uses. As Meades (2012) says: "There is no such thing as a boring place" going on to propose his version of Proust's "The real voyage of discovery lies not in seeking new landscapes but in having new eyes". Neither interviewee liked the room; they particularly missed natural light and views, and neither used it for the idea-generating phase of their individual creative processes. They wished for a brighter, pleasanter space and in this they agreed with the IA. But neither expressed the visceral antipathy to the space that the IA did. Instead the users of Room 101 were pragmatic; they used the room because "it is easier to concentrate in the workspace instead of at home [where there are] a lot of distractions". It was an alternative working environment to a cramped, noisy home. Instead of accepting the limitations they did what they could to personalise the space, either filling their cubicle with books, papers and sticky notes, or pulling their chair up to a colleague's desk and working together on a laptop.

It is worth reflecting on how both the IA's perception and mine shut down on entering the room. To what extent did the sensory deprivation of the room create that degree of stress in us as visitors, and what might be the long-term effect on the research work of the people using it daily? This is beyond the scope of this case study, but suggests enquiry into existing and possible future research.

LEARNING

The Grammar of Creative Workplaces (Williams, 2013) sets out three aspects of physical space for stimulating and supporting creativity: the sensory properties of the space, the creative behaviours that can take place within it, and the affordances that support those activities. Although Room 101 is not, and probably never will be, used as a space for creative thinking, it is suited to concentrated work. The sensory properties identified as supporting creativity also support other aspects of work: among others, for example, the different aspects of *comfort* support motivation, productivity and morale (Brill, Margulis & Konar, 1984; Milton, Glencross & Walters 2000; Wargocki *et al.*, 2000); and natural light beneficially impacts learning (Barrett, Barrett & Davies, 2013; Heschong Mahone Group, 1999).

There are possibilities for change in all three aspects of Room 101, particularly sensory properties. For example, while nothing can be done to add windows with views to the outside, bringing in natural elements – plants, a poster of the countryside – can support people's biophilia, i.e. their affinity with the natural environment, (Fromm, 1964; Kaplan, Talbot & Kaplan, 1988; Ulrich 1984, 1993) through the introduction of naturalism (Barrett & Barrett, 2010). Painting the walls white, and introducing colour on one wall, or through coloured chair covers or cushions, impacts mood (Franz, 2004; Ceylan, Dul & Aytac 2008; Barrett, 2010; Dul & Ceylan 2011); daylight bulbs in the cubicles for task lighting would make a tremendous difference not just to the quality of light, but also to the effect on researchers' mood, physical wellbeing and performance (see recipe *Beam me up or down*). The list goes on, and the recipes in this book cover much of it.

A key aspect here is agency: who is responsible for recognising that changes are needed and would be beneficial? Interviewee 1 said: "We haven't seen faculty that often". Is making changes something that faculty should initiate? The head of department's room has all the prerequisites of a stimulating and supportive environment with big windows, lots of books, interesting objects, and play elements, but none of this appears to have communicated itself to the researchers. Instead they are working in a room that could have been designed especially to demonstrate the ideas of *A recipe for mediocrity*. Do the researchers themselves feel they can make changes to it? Do they perceive that changes would contribute to their research performance and motivation levels?

Room 101 will never win a 'research environment of the year award', but much could be done, both by the researchers themselves and by faculty, to initiate changes that would enhance and support the quality of research and life within it.

JUMP ASSOCIATES

—

San Mateo

—

AUTHOR

Andrew MacVean

Jump Associates is a "fifty-person hybrid strategy firm focused on growth" (www.jumpassociates.com), with the aim of creating new businesses, or reinvigorating existing ones. Their work focuses on helping businesses solve a new class of problem, the type of ambiguous questions that "keep great leaders up at night and send the common consultant running for the hills" (Jump Associates, n.d.). Importantly, Jump Associates pride themselves on their working environment, having designed a unique social and physical space, which helps them in producing their creative breakthrough results.

This case study focuses on their flagship office, located in San Mateo, California.

PHYSICAL SPACE

At Jump, the importance of the physical space is well realised. As they describe on their website (Jump Associates, n.d.), "We're strongly affected by our surroundings. A great environment can lift us up, make us better at what we do, and inspire great thinking. Conversely, a lousy place can leave us depressed, tired and dying to go home. That's why we've worked very hard to make JumpSpace one of the most visually engaging, lively and generative places you'll ever visit."

The Jump office in San Mateo was recently built from the ground up. The existing space was completely gutted, after which co-founder Dev Patnaik worked with architect Michael Fazio to design the ideal space to encourage creative thinking and problem solving. To do so, Dev considered the informal network of interaction amongst employees, designing a space that would foster and nurse connections, which he believes underpins all good work (Businessweek, n.d.).

The Jump employees, or Jumpsters, enjoy an intimate connection between the work they are tasked with doing, and the physical space with which they are provided. In this section, a number of the physical spaces located within the Jump Associates San Mateo office are explored and discussed.

OVERVIEW

The Jump Associates office consists of a number of distinct spaces, each designed to foster or encourage a particular type of working practice. However, before exploring each of these individually, it is important to consider the space as a whole. While each individual space has been carefully considered, 'the whole is greater than the sum of its parts', with each individual space working with the rest of the environment in order to contribute towards the physical space on offer.

NEIGHBOURHOODS

Each Jumpster has a 'home' desk. While a lot of a Jumpsters' time will be spent working collaboratively in the dedicated project spaces, it is important that they also have a place to call home when they need to catch up on individual tasks. Home desks are organised into neighbourhoods, where a number of home desks are colocated in an open plan fashion. The neighbourhoods are home to a random assortment of Jumpsters, with allocations to neighbourhoods always changing. This rotation ensures that all employees get the chance to get to know one another, fostering collaboration and knowledge exchange irrespective of which projects the employees are directly assigned to.

TRAIN CAR CAFE

One particularly prominent example of a creative working space is the 'train car café' (Fig. 1). Taking inspiration from the mantra that the 'best ideas are written on the back of a napkin', Jump has tried to encourage this type of serendipitous process by creating a space that encourages this type of problem solving. The train car cafe has high-backed seats for the feeling of privacy, while also being situated within an area of high foot traffic, so that fellow Jumpsters can pop in with words of advice. Whether whole projects are undertaken in the space, or it is used for brainstorming over lunch, the train car cafe is the perfect example of how collaboration and out of the box thinking can be facilitated through the physical design of a space.

PROJECT SPACES

The project spaces are where the majority of a Jumpster's time is spent. These are dedicated spaces where Jumpsters from all over the company will come together to work collaboratively on a single project. As Jumpsters begin to work, these spaces quickly morph to suit the particular needs of the project, with the most important aspect of the project space being its flexibility. While the spaces contain all the basic key affordances of a collaborative project space (customisable table designs, floor to ceiling whiteboard walls, lots of art supplies, etc) it is some of the more unique design decisions that make the Jump project spaces particularly well suited to creative work. Most notably, the cube like space is not designed to have an entry door, but rather a rotatable wall. The beauty of this is that Jumpsters working within the space can use this rotatable wall to share their work with other members of the company who will naturally pass the room as they navigate the Jump offices. This is particularly useful when feedback from other Jumpsters is sought. The wall is rotated to highlight work to the rest of the office, while hard work continues on the other side of the wall from within the project space.

ZEN ROOM

Even in a demanding work environment, it is important to have dedicated space for employees to unwind and recharge their batteries; what Jump calls a Zen space. Jump offers various Zen spaces designed to facilitate different behaviours. Some spaces are designed for comfort and silence, so that Jumpsters can remain productive while enjoying some relaxation. Other spaces are dedicated sleeping zones, for power naps designed to recharge the batteries. As important as the physical spaces, Jump fosters a culture where using such spaces is not seen as a distraction from work, but rather as essential to the success of the company.

SOCIAL PRACTICE

In parallel to the physical environment Jump Associates have a very particular cultural environment. They have implemented various social practices, with the goal of optimising creative thinking while maintaining a comfortable and friendly working environment, despite the high-octane stresses of the industry in which they work.

Within this section a number of these practices are discussed and explored.

SCRUM

Every morning, the Jumpsters meet for what they term a 'scrum'. As the Wall Street Journal states, a Jump scrum is a "a short get-together where [Jumpsters are] briefed on company news, do yoga-like exercises and then play a quick brain-rousing game that forces them to think on their feet" (Spors, 2008).

The scrum serves the practical purpose of updating employees on important work-related news (Fig. 2). However, unlike a detached corporate newsletter, the scrum serves to energise the Jumpsters, breaking the ice every morning, and encouraging discussion across the entire workforce.

NO ZINGERS

While derogatory remarks may be common in other work places, Jump Associates has an explicit 'No Zinger' policy, which translates as a ban on Jumpsters making demeaning or hurtful comments towards other employees.

SHOUT OUT

Another practice ingrained in the social culture at Jump is known as a 'shout out'. Every Friday, at the end of the working week, Jump holds a shout out, where members of the team are recognised for going 'above and beyond' their regular call of duty. This may be the unsolicited helping of a colleague, or performing better than expected within a project (Fig. 3).

Rather than formalised work incentives such as bonuses, this more personalised reward encourages the sharing of achievements throughout the workforce. By hosting regular shout outs, achievements both big and small are recognised as important to the company, and good work does not go unappreciated.

SERENDIPITOUS EXCHANGE

As discussed in the description of the physical space, Jumpsters have a 'home' desk which is organised within a neighbourhood of other desks clustered around the office space. When working on a project, Jumpsters will find themselves generally located within one of the project spaces, where multiple employees will work together on their set project.

SUMMARY

Jump fosters a remarkable culture where hard work and success comes *because of,* not at the cost of, a relaxing and enjoyable work environment. This case study has presented just some of the many ways in which collaboration, serendipitous exchange, and creative thinking are encouraged within the workplace.

Essential to the success of Jump is a flexible, varied and inspiring physical environment populated with the affordances and properties that support creative thinking and collaborative behaviour. And additionally, Jump is characterised by a culture which encourages all the Jumpsters to use all elements of their workspace to suit their needs: individual, project group and organisational. The two elements – physical environment and social practice – work together to create an exceptional organisation.

NOTE

Images shown in this case study are the copyright of Jump Associates. Reproduced by kind permission.

CONNECTING DESIGN IN VIRTUAL AND PHYSICAL SPACES

AUTHOR

Jim Hensman

INTRODUCTION AND SCOPE

How can virtual spaces and environments be designed to stimulate and support creativity and remarkable research? In *A Grammar of Creative Workplaces*, Williams (2013) expresses the hope that this visuospatial grammar 'may have applications beyond the real and into the virtual world'.

Creating a grammar of creative virtua l workplaces is a major endeavour and beyond the scope of this paper. However, this volume and the broad community involved in its creation provide a unique opportunity to consider some of the approaches and elements that could contribute towards that objective. This paper therefore considers what could be applied from the recipes themselves, predominantly based in physical rather than virtual environments, to the virtual area. In addition, insights are sought into how the physical, virtual, social and other aspects of spaces relate to each other more generally.

The paper first looks at terminology and how the problem can be framed. It then looks at methodologies that deal with different aspects of spaces and how they relate to each other, before analysing selected recipes. Four of these are reviewed in detail before returning to draw conclusions about methodology and process at the end.

DEFINING THE PROBLEM

Virtual spaces and environments

What is meant by a virtual environment or space? I consider a virtual space in a general sense as anything that doesn't form part of a user's physical surroundings. This can include, for example, an operating system, such as Microsoft Windows, a framework such as a virtual research environment (VRE) (Carusi & Reimer, 2010), and individual tools, for example Second Life and others using virtual worlds. Again I adopt a flexible viewpoint. Although each of these connected spaces is of interest, I concentrate on the properties that are common to them and on the composite space as a whole.

Creativity, remarkable research and other objectives

In *A Grammar of Creative Workplaces*, Williams (2013) analyses behaviours and outputs in the context of different creative processes (individual and group) to identify and codify the elements of physical workplaces that stimulate and support creativity. This requires, as well as direct observations, an analysis of indirect correspondences and associations with creativity. Analogous issues can arise when considering virtual environments. For example, in the VRE study referenced earlier, and in a later internal study from JISC (Procter, Poschen and Wilson, 2013), neither refers to the words 'creative' or 'creativity', despite these concepts being of core importance to VREs. These concepts may need to be identified indirectly, through intermediary factors or intervening variables. Although models exist which tackle this issue of indirect correspondences to creativity (Franck, 1984), for the purposes of this paper a simpler approach is adopted. Because I am considering recipes that are related to and prompted by the need to support creativity and remarkable research, the recipes themselves and their context dictate the scope and help identify relevant factors in virtual spaces.

METHODOLOGY

The starting point suggested in investigating creative virtual spaces is to look at connections and parallels with other types of space. To provide some guidelines for this, I examine some of the existing literature on creative virtual environments and then on work which has associated virtual environments and spaces with other types of space. I then propose a methodological framework to analyse the recipes.

Factors impacting upon creative virtual environments

Literature recognising factors important for creative virtual environments includes Malhotra's (2000) study of nine virtual teams. 'Connection' was identified as a key factor, divided into "...task connection (made up of dedication/commitment and goal clarity); and interpersonal connection (made up of information sharing, trust and personal bond)" (Malhotra, 2000, p. 102).

Nemiro, Beyerlein, Bradley & Beyerlein (2008) deal with principles that include but are not limited to virtual environments, such as a common vision and purpose, and mechanisms for feedback. They also warn that the process of creativity may be more difficult to achieve through technology-mediated communication.

In a further study (Aragon, Poon & Aragon, 2009) which compared two quite different creative communities, a group of scientists and a group of children, it was how people used the technology – such as repurposing existing tools, augmentation (adding new features) and behaviour adaptation – rather than the technology itself that was noted as particularly significant. Generic factors such as these add weight to the usefulness of looking for and at commonalities across different types of space.

Connecting different types of space

Existing research which explicitly considers different types of space and their connections and commonalities is surprisingly sparse. In a rare analysis which looks at physical and virtual spaces together (Fayard & Weeks, 2011), three factors were seen as critical to both: proximity, privacy and permission. For example, proximity guidelines for physical space included: "Position common areas in central locations or near restrooms, stairwells, or elevators to tap existing office traffic" while the equivalent for virtual space stated: "Make shared spaces easily accessible (no more than one click away)".

The interface between the physical and the virtual from the standpoint of the user, such as the field of human-computer interaction (HCI), also bears scrutiny. Research in this field and related ones such as computer-supported cooperative work (CSCW) identifies and investigates various factors that cross the boundaries between different types of space. The concept of attention for example is defined as "the collection of processes that allow us to dedicate our limited information processing capacity to the purposeful (cognitive) manipulation of a subset of available information" (Sears & Jacko, 2007).

Attention and its associated factors, such as distraction, are valuable concepts both when looking at the coming together and interaction of different types of space in real-world situations, and in parallels between what takes place in different spaces.

As a key example of these parallels, the Inspires project (Innovative Networks Supporting People Who Investigate Research Environments and Spaces) explored common concepts that bridge different types of space. Developing cross-disciplinary links within and beyond the SPIRES community, Inspires combined automatic and manual techniques to determine semantic relatedness and generate ontologies. Several conceptual connections across different types of spaces were found including:

1.   General concepts: e.g. *interaction, usability, accessibility, adaptivity/adaptability, communication, engagement and motivation.*
2.   Application areas with related physical and virtual counterparts: e.g. *physical and digital libraries/archives, physical and virtual learning/research spaces, physical and online meetings.*
3.   Methodologies and techniques that could be used in different types of space: e.g. *actor-network theory, human behaviour simulation, evaluation techniques.*

Complex factors

The factors identified so far relate mainly to individual and static categories. However, this can be simplistic and the literature also identifies particular changes, juxtapositions of differences or even opposites as being key. The *engage/disengage* model of creative behaviour (Williams, 2013) is a complex and iterative sequence of different types of creative behaviours, as is the ability to shift between divergent and convergent thinking (Carroll & Ganoe, 2008) in the creative process. These examples suggest that temporal and dynamic factors should be included in the recipe analysis and more sophisticated categories and structures to represent them may be needed. Furthermore, the detailed context of a situation can often be crucial and particular aspects of it may critically alter success factors. Thus, for instance, a study of 44 R&D teams concluded that the level of complexity of a problem determined whether personal and synchronous or less personal and asynchronous modes of communication were most effective in finding creative solutions (Kratzer, Leenders, & Van Engelen, 2006).

An integrated approach to spaces

The previous discussion indicates that a number of factors and attributes can be identified that are common to and link different types of space (physical and virtual), which can then be manifested in different but analogous ways in each. From a conceptual viewpoint it is also valuable to look at spaces and their relationship in flexible and different ways. For example, a virtual environment can be understood from the standpoint of physical space as a unit of affordance (Gibson, 1977), i.e. a tool or piece of equipment for sharing visual information in the same way as a whiteboard (Williams, 2013). Taken from the standpoint of virtual space, the physical environment and its properties constitute a setting whose sensory input can in turn influence the user/inhabitant of the virtual space. Each of these viewpoints has validity in context and can provide different insights into our area of interest. A multifaceted and integrated approach to spaces is therefore an important one to keep at the centre of the analysis.

Additionally, social or collaborative spaces, as well as process and cognitive spaces are not distinct from physical or virtual spaces, and in one sense are part of them, defining a particular way of looking at the concept of space as a whole. The many other concepts relating to social spaces, for instance workplace relations (Amabile, 1983, 1996; Amabile & Kramer, 2011; Wheatley & Kellner-Rogers, 1996), are beyond the scope of this paper.

A framework for analysis

Although a number of potentially useful features connecting different types of spaces are suggested above, I propose a more structured framework of analysis: pattern language. Patterns and pattern languages were part of a formalism devised by the architect Christopher Alexander (Alexander et al, 1977), as a means of representing and sharing the essential elements of good practice in architecture and subsequently used in a wide variety of areas including software development and computer programming. Although the recipe field book uses a more flexible format, representing them through a pattern-based formalism provides a useful framework. Patterns are represented as a combination of a problem or need (seen as the conjunction of a number of contending forces which have to be resolved), the context in which this occurs, and an associated solution. The context can also link to other patterns for which it may form part of the solution, as well as others which it may make use of, creating a network structure which can define a type of language. The structure both of an individual pattern and the language as a whole facilitates finding connections between different patterns, as well as identifying possibilities for generalisation. The value here is to suggest principles that transcend specific requirements and types of space.

Using a pattern-based approach suggests a possible technique for looking at how recipes for physical spaces may be reflected in the virtual area. If patterns for physical spaces, for instance, are represented as a kind of language, then their equivalent in the virtual area can be considered a translation into another language. As with natural languages, this cannot be done meaningfully word for word, but requires the structure of the language in the form of syntax and semantics to be taken into account, which the pattern format and structure of connected patterns facilitate.

The pattern approach also suggests a way of tackling the problem mentioned earlier of how factors that indirectly contribute to creative spaces could be integrated into the analysis. These dependent sub-patterns, relating to correct lighting or usability for example, can be integrated with the high-level creativity patterns in context, specifying different but interdependent features of the environment.

ANALYSING THE RECIPES

Four representative recipes are now examined, and a basic principle or pattern proposed. This permits an insight into how an equivalent virtual space might be designed, and sets out the methodological principle that informs the connecting design between physical and virtual spaces.

#49 Get into the zone

This recipe highlights the importance of delineating physical spaces into different categories – public, semi-public, private and so on – to support different types of creative behaviours. Its implementation is discussed and the contact spaces between zones and their importance considered. This principle of delineation is also important in virtual space, but made more complex because of a number of factors including intrinsic difficulty in delineation. In virtual space an individual's role and identity can assume many forms, even sometimes within one part of it. Research (Zhao, Grasmuck & Martin, 2008) shows, for instance, that not only does how identity is projected in Facebook differ in general from other social networks and other types of social presence, but individuals often maintain multiple identities within it.

The delineation of types of virtual space and the transition between them can also be of crucial significance. In a typical workflow, access to the data can usually be limited to its author, or to a specified group, or public access can be made available. How easily and flexibly this can be done, for instance in drafting a document, making it available for group commenting and editing, and then publishing it publicly, can make a substantial difference to the efficiency and success of the process as a whole. In the development of web-based services, it is only relatively recently that systems can be said to have dealt with this problem adequately, as with systems like Google Docs.

The transitions between the types of contact space in the physical environment are especially important in the *#49 Get into the zone* recipe. Fayard & Weeks's (2011) observations of equivalent factors in physical and virtual spaces that facilitated creativity also describe ways of creating privacy. For physical space, one guideline suggested was: "Create alcoves or other peripheral areas that facilitate private conversations in public spaces" (Fayard & Weeks, 2011). This translated into an equivalent for virtual space as: "Create ways for people to move easily from group interactions to one-on-one conversations" (Fayard & Weeks, 2011).

Intuitively we convert the concept of an alcove in physical space that provides a way of moving easily from a group interaction to a more intimate one, to its virtual equivalent. This example is particularly useful because there is a well-known close equivalent from Alexander's architectural pattern language (1977) entitled 'alcoves'. This pattern proposes alcoves as a solution to the problem represented by the contending forces of a family wanting to be together in a room, while also wanting to be able to carry out different activities without disturbing each other or being disturbed. There is a general principle underlying all three instances which is reflected in different ways in the particular context of each. Thus the basic principle or pattern is:

Provide private space easily accessible from more communal space.

In the two physical examples this is for different reasons, family-based in one case and workplace-related in the other. In the virtual case the implementation will of course be different, but most of the terminology is interchangeable and even the concept of a 'virtual alcove' is a useful metaphor. The underlying reasons in all three examples relate to concepts such as interaction, communication and privacy - all concepts that cross the physical–virtual divide.

#32 Serendipity on the back of a napkin; #48 Meating place; #59 Attractor spaces

These three recipes describe different aspects of providing easily accessible meeting and discussion facilities that encourage interaction, as in the 'water cooler effect'. Identifying the essential elements in the 'language' that is used in these recipes allows us to understand more precisely what would be required in a virtual equivalent. The basic principle or pattern is:

Provide informal and comfortable solo space from which the individual can overhear others' conversations, and choose whether or not to step into the group space to intervene or participate without appearing intrusive.

This is a challenge to implement in virtual space, but having a pattern – a structured representation of the problem – allows related experience to be identified and drawn on.

The transposition between physical and virtual features is not as simple as it might appear at first sight and there is a considerable body of literature, as well as debate, about significant similarities and differences between effective physical spaces and their virtual-world equivalents in different contexts (for example, Bartle, 2003). In many cases the requirements described in the recipes above have been met in virtual world environments through direct equivalents of what exists in physical environments. Examples include water coolers in Second Life that actually dispense 'water'; meeting areas set around a camp fire, or in a beautiful setting, or on a beach. Work on virtual spaces for learning, which this author was involved with as part of the Planet project (*Pattern Language Network for Web 2.0 in Learning*), derived a pattern entitled '*Spaces for Lurking*'. This identified a general problem, where individuals needed a way to get a feel for what was going on in some activity before they felt confident enough to take part. Although arising from a quite different context, particularly in group learning sessions, key parts of this problem and its solution – which involved devising acceptable ways of observing group activity without actively taking part – are relevant to this requirement. Having a fire as a focus turns out to be one effective solution to this issue; it is acceptable to congregate socially around a fire without having to take part in conversation. This works indoors too: in one project with which this author was involved, an indoor fire was used as a focus for virtual world meetings, providing seamless access to social networking facilities such as Facebook. The physical world analogy is thus combined with a virtual one, both within the virtual world environment.

Finally, I examine how physical and virtual spaces and facilities can be used together. The very first webcam, based at Cambridge University, was used to let people know remotely whether there was coffee available in a pot in a central area – the Trojan room – an example of using a facility in virtual space to help optimise a facility in physical space. Virtual space facilities of many different kinds can be used in similar ways. The recipe *#38 Research interest visualisation* suggests potentially fruitful connections between researchers; it also indicates how it might be used to facilitate informal get-togethers in the type of physical location described by the three recipes above. If integrated with an application like Foursquare, it can take into account whether individuals are in the vicinity of the meeting location.

CONCLUSIONS

The exercise of translating between recipes for different types of space was more straightforward than expected. Even in recipes specific to a particular type of space, the more general elements of their translation to other spaces were either explicitly mentioned in the recipe or intuitively easy to derive from it. In many of the '*working solo*' and '*working together*' recipes these elements were present in a generic form. Some of the 'translations' between physical and virtual space corresponded with design rules and concepts arising from the wider literature, thus providing independent verification. Many recipes provided valuable pointers to how desirable attributes in virtual space could be achieved. Further investigative and experimental work remains to be done here, as it also does on other factors emerging from previous research, not reflected in the recipes. These include the importance of more complex temporal and oppositional factors, such as divergence/convergence in creative thinking and the familiar/unfamiliar dichotomy of the *#54 A mobile thinking shrine* recipe. Some of the outcomes, however, that could be dependent on more detailed contextual features, and which could be expected on more detailed further investigation, did not arise. Recipes also did not explicitly deal with examples of application areas that had close counterparts in different types of space, or with common research methodologies. Although these were identified in earlier SPIRES work, the SPIRES community did not bring them forward as recipes.

Connecting and integrating the recipes

In order to ensure effective use of existing recipes, and others that could be derived from them and supplement them, an integrated approach is suggested. This would employ the type of space most appropriate in any given case, and also allow different spaces to work together, interacting to create powerful composite solutions. A final aspect of this integration of different spaces relates to the possibilities arising from immersive spaces that blur the boundaries between the physical and the virtual space. Pederson (2003), argues that the traditional user interface mode of thinking which counterposes the physical and the virtual, needs to be superseded by a "...physical-virtual design perspective, abstracting away the user interface".

It is suggested that the modes of analysis and thinking introduced in this paper could provide useful ways of guiding future developments. One example from the Inspires project illustrates this. As part of the project, immersive visualisations were developed that could be used during physical events to connect and generate ideas, using information both from the discussions taking place and also from the profile of the participants. One of the demonstrations used a large screen with 3D life-sized images that users could interact with. Although feedback obtained through interviews and questionnaires was very favourable, it was also apparent that a crucial ingredient had been missing and had detracted from its perceived impact. Because the lighting had been optimised to highlight the on-screen display, participants could not see each other very well, which had adversely affected the physical discussion and interaction. A solution to this was later developed and demonstrated. This could be considered a pattern or recipe for the particular immersive context, but it also drew on aspects of patterns or recipes relevant to physical and virtual spaces separately – relating to lighting levels and space configuration, for instance, and thus creating a network structure of patterns. Integrating recipes from different types of space could thus provide important guidelines for work in a complex area like this.

FUTURE WORK

This paper suggests possibilities for creative virtual space design, and indicates the value of some of the methodologies and techniques that could be used for this and for creating a framework for a unified and integrated approach to space design. As mentioned at the start, the scope of this paper was necessarily limited. The recipes in this volume have been an important basis for looking at this area, but the existing literature has to be more comprehensively explored as well as experimental work designed and carried out if this is to be taken further. Particular consideration needs to be given to the framework defined in *A Grammar of Creative Workplaces* (Williams, 2013). Many of the affordances and other elements supporting creativity analysed there could directly be used to identify possibilities in virtual space and a number of the methodologies used could provide important components for a unified approach across different spaces. It is hoped that work like this, together with the community involved in the creation of the recipe field book, could be the basis in the future of the important research in this area that is required.

THE SPATIAL AND SOCIAL CONSTRUCTS OF CREATIVE SITUATIONS

AUTHORS
Meredith Bostwick-Lorenzo Eiroa
Derek Jones

INTRODUCTION

This paper presents an alternative way of considering space in terms of situated activity. We suggest that the activity and human response to space are embodied in the situations we experience. This embodied interaction with space we argue to be an essentially creative act, providing a conception of space that we term the 'creative situation'.

Four characteristics of such creative situations are presented. These are followed by six descriptions of active creative situations with instances of these drawn from the recipes, case studies and papers in this book. These descriptions are a starting point, rather than a complete framework, and are an alternative way of viewing and reconsidering our understanding of space.

CREATIVE SITUATIONS

The Situationists

> They wander through the sectors of New Babylon seeking new experiences, as yet unknown ambiences. Without the passivity of tourists, but fully aware of the power they possess to act upon the world, to transform it, recreate it. They dispose of a whole arsenal of technical implements for doing this, thanks to which they can make the desired changes without delay. (Constant, 1974)

The Situationists were the 'free-radicals' of urbanism – free artists and professional amateurs. They promised that their theories of the urban environment and architecture would one day revolutionise everyday life and "...release the ordinary citizen into a world of experiment, anarchy and play" (Sadler, 1999). Sadler, author of *The Situationist City*, notes their open self-criticism allowed them to always "play the radical card" – no matter how intelligent or useful the contributions of other urbanists outside of the movement might have been.

Sadler recognises that the Situationists almost certainly drew their inspiration for creating and experiencing a situation from Sartre. Sartre argued that life is ultimately a series of given situations which affect an individual and which must in turn be negotiated by that individual. Situationism suggested it was possible for individuals to process or manage such negotiations as an act of self-empowerment.

The Situationists theorised a city of situations that overlap, patch, collide, criss-cross, cluster, and punctuate a city by surprise. In the city, the past, present and future all overlap in a messy configuration (Alloway, 1959), hence all of the divergent factors of a city cannot be fully understood, far less controlled or ordered. This recognition of the complex interplay between elements, interactions and people provides a more dynamic way of viewing and understanding the city.

Activity and creativity

From this starting point, space in the city is more than simply the distance between walls. By making use of and interacting with the city, space itself is perceived and used as something greater than the sum of the parts – it has a dynamic property and potential. This free development of space is analogous to Tschumi's *event space*, in contrast to a predetermined or normative understanding of space. For Tschumi, there is no space without event: "[my] relentless affirmation: that there is no architecture without program, without action, without event" (Tschumi, 1996).

The essential ingredient here is the 'active' component and even apparently passive use of space is in some way active when considered from the point of view of the user. Our starting point is a conception of space that relies on the mediation of people and context. This mediation is active, particularly in terms of creativity, and is not the preserve of the specialist. The overlap, confluence and interaction of these active mediations provide the richness of form, activity and narrative in physical environments.

Following on from this conception of space, it is argued that creativity and the creative act are a natural consequence of certain types of space, or that these types of space actually emerge with the creative act itself. In fact, it is proposed that the inter-dependency of the space and the activity are such that there can be no *a priori* cause and effect. In other words, both the space and activity are necessary together, something recognised by Alexander, who defines his city unit as emerging "...both from the forces which hold its own elements together, and from the dynamic coherence of the larger living system..." (Alexander, 1965).

This embodied view of mind and space is important in architecture (see Wilson (2002) for a good review of current cognitive embodied theories of mind). If we accept that creativity is Mayer's summary of 'novelty and usefulness' (Mayer, 1999), then the emergence of the type of space we present here is necessarily a creative act. Space, by this view, we term a 'creative situation'.

Cities and research spaces

Events at the city scale are also applicable at other scales. Consider the conception of the *polis* provided by Kitto, where the socio-political organisation of the city takes primacy over the scale, size or shape of the city itself (Kitto, 1996). Indeed, some of the city states he discusses are equivalent in terms of population to some university campuses. The boundaries between city, town, neighbourhood, street or building frontage are certainly not fixed by scale. Lynch's (1960) five types of elements: paths, edges, districts, nodes and landmarks, are as useful inside a research environment as they are in his original discussion of cities (see the *Jump Associates: San Mateo* case study for an example of 'neighbourhoods' for different kinds of work).

It is argued that such interpretations of space apply equally well to smaller spatial constructs – that the building is nothing more than a small city simply because it is made up of active spatial elements. While we do not propose that the full analogy of city to campus applies in every way, we argue that the creative situations within both are analogous. Both require people situated in contexts and both rely on the activity that arises from such situations. Indeed, it could be argued that it is precisely the activity that arises from such situations in a university that is its very reason for existence.

Characteristics of creative situations

From the above, a series of characteristics of creative situations emerge. They are necessarily incomplete by their own definition and act more to generate the idea of space, similar to Khan's analogy of the building archetype: "...a recognition of something which you can't define, but must be built" (Wuman, 1986).

It is the activity (event) that matters.
Without activity, there is no space. This is not a metaphysical statement, but a situated one. Different spaces allow different behaviours but these are not deterministic. One behaviour may emerge in a space intended for another, clearly indicating that the physical elements of that space are only a part of the place itself. What matters here is the situated activity, that is, activity that emerges or is activated within a context.

Experiment and play.
That by engaging in play and experimentation, creativity will naturally emerge (see Williams' paper: *The creative footprint*). From this creativity will arise active spaces as a natural outcome of this situated behaviour: by playing, we create; by creating, we change things. Moreover we must necessarily do this in a context and, as any designer will tell you, the very act of design has the potential to respond, engage, activate and change a context in itself.

The creative act is also a social act.
Constant sums up the Situationist difference between artist and situation well: "Among the New Babylonians, on the other hand, the creative act is also a social act: as a direct intervention in the social world, it elicits an immediate response" (Constant, 1974). More precisely, it is essential to realise the relevance of the social aspects of space and place with respect to creativity and to realise that these have an effect on the space itself.

Creative situations arise from action that engenders change.
This is, in many ways, a truism that follows from creative situations – by creating, we change things. The potential that any space has for adaptive change should be obvious (just look at the variety and richness of what people do to their homes). What is perhaps less obvious are the other factors that 'permit' change: individual agency, social constructs, economic models, cultural habits, etc. As such, the creative situation relies as much on the wider social context as it does on the immediate physical one.

EXAMPLES OF CREATIVE SITUATIONS

With these outline characteristics, the following creative situations are presented. They are intended to provoke thought in terms of activity and situations, providing interesting and alternative ways of considering any space. Each is illustrated with examples from this book.

Improvisational space

The Situationists proposed a new experimental theatre where a universal integration of players and audience, performance space and spectator space, theatrical experience and 'real' experience existed together (Sadler, 1999). Beyond the Situationists, the city as theatre is a well-used metaphor. Mumford suggests: "It is in the city, the city as theatre, that man's most purposive activities are focused..." (Mumford, 1996). Goodman and Goodman's 'carnival' was not simply a zone within a city for entertainment: "No one can resist the thrill of a blizzard as it piles up in the streets" (Goodman & Goodman, 1996).

Improvisational space emerges from shared human activity in space. Like Jan van Pelt & Westfall's 'theatre: imagining' (Jan van Pelt & Westfall, 1991, p. 160), these are essentially socio-political spaces that shape and are shaped by the social activity enacted in that space. But there is a starting point or event that is characteristic of this space: be it part of the space itself (perhaps a focal point), an activity as starting point (such as a social gathering), or simply a serendipitous occurrence (such as Goodman and Goodman's blizzard).

Improvisational space is by nature loose, formless space. The space arises from social activity around some shared focus. The engendered change is explicitly enacted publicly in an open way – both the performer and audience change in an embodied, mutual space of active creativity.

In this book, the recipes *#32 Serendipity on the back of a napkin*, *#22 Sharing food* and *#34 Popup whitespace hubs* are a few examples with the potential for improvisational space. That is, they rely on emergent behaviour through social interaction around some focal point. In each, the potential is simply waiting for the actors to begin the performance.

Stitch space

For the Situationist movement, labyrinths seemed to be the ideal environment in which to induce the social relationships and encounters necessary to provoke situations. Situationists often used the drawings of Piranesi as a vital source of geographic inspiration, with his fantastical drawings of overlapping and intertwined staircases and bridges. These very interstices offered the emergence of situations.

The overlap and interaction of elements in a city is, like the city as theatre, not a new concept. Alexander (1965) gives us the example of the newsstand and traffic light, where pedestrians stop at the traffic lights and naturally interact with the newsstand that happens to be there. This interaction between two apparently disparate elements (traffic light and newsstand), make up an example of Alexander's 'city unit'.

In many ways, this interaction creates a 'third space' and it is what we propose to call *stitch space*, arguing that it applies to buildings and even rooms just as it does cities. Stitch space has no landmark quality, meaning that it is not explicitly defined in itself. Rather it arises from the convergence, confluence and overlap of other spaces and activities, creating a situation through the relationships it brings together.

The social creativity of this space is vital since without the 'agreement' of its users it simply cannot exist. To recognise stitch space, the user has to agree to it existing by actively engaging with it. *#59 Attractor spaces*, *#45 Lowbrow powwow*, and *#49 Get into the zone* all present grounded examples of stitch space, where the overlap of different active spaces induces a potential 'third space'. Each of these spaces also depends on an agreement or 'contract' between users that the behaviour and activity can take place. For example, someone might use the *Attractor spaces* recipe as it was originally intended - without actually engaging with the extended use it offers. For others, the space is a stitch space that emerges from what else they do with it.

Cloud space

The Situationists recognised that technology is an indispensable tool for realising an experimental collectivism. Without a fixed physical space, a fluctuating creative community can still be maintained through intensive virtual communications (Constant, 1974). Situationist social theory proposed that social groups are not only created by location, but by community of interest and through physical and psychological interdependence.

As before, this is not only a Situationist idea. Smithson and Smithson (1970) noted that a family can still be tight-knit and possessive even when its members are thousands of miles apart. They argued that real social groups cut across geographical barriers and the most important factor of social cohesion is the looseness of groupings and the effortlessness of communication, rather than the isolation of arbitrary portions of a community with exceedingly difficult communications. Therefore, Smithson and Smithson argued that the creation of non-arbitrary groupings and providing means of effective communications are the primary functions of the planner.

Cloud space is the 'space' created by these social groupings, relying on the interaction of people around some organising identity. The shape of cloud space is formed by the active situations that emerge. As with many other active themes, the interaction with and within the space necessarily engenders change in that space – indeed, it may be that the cloud space offers the greatest potential for such change. Whether these spaces are simply groups we associate ourselves with, an online social network or remote working research groups, the active spatial component cannot be ignored.

#20 Share what you made, #25 Research group as extended family and *#19 Digital scholarship – start here* are all recipes that make active use of cloud space. Some of these make use of social identity that overlaps with physical location and some of them are independent of the physical. But they all share the same active, creative element – the people that make up the groups coalesce around some shared, active identity.

Play space

The Situationists described a play-spirit – the freedom to dérive, or drift. The free spirit is also described by Benjamin (2002) in his Arcades Project, as the *flâneur* for whom strolling in a locale is essential to experiencing it. Play spaces are free, unhindered sequences of spaces that allow for playful constructive behaviour to occur within a context (situation).

Turning to Alexander once again, he provides an important understanding of play: "[the asphalted and fenced-in playground] has nothing to do with the life of play itself" and that "play takes place in a thousand places – it fills the interstices of adult life. As they play, children become full of their surroundings" (Alexander, 1965).

This suggests that play can (and perhaps should) take place anywhere so we present play space as any space in which this occurs. Its essential ingredient is the active, creative mind that brings to it the activity of playfulness, whether this is simple observation and curiosity or physical experimentation with the space itself. In many ways, play space is a state of mind: an attitude and approach rather than a set of physical properties.

Many of the recipes in this book require an element of play in some sense or other. Play is essentially a creative activity and one that lends itself to the enquiring researcher. The recipes *#40 Creative spaces for interdisciplinary research, #61 Workshop space* and *#41 Idea room* are all direct examples of play spaces, providing the space is approached with the attitude of play itself. In each of these, we 'allow' ourselves to play, perhaps an indictment of current places of research by Alexander's warning.

Regenerative space

In *New Babylon*, use must be made of every empty space (Constant, 1974). Sadler observes that the need for creation has always been intimately associated with the need to play through the elements of architecture, time and space (Sadler, 1999). The need for constructing situations was one of the fundamental desires on which the next civilisation would be founded – therefore the architecture of tomorrow should be a means of modifying present conceptions of time and space (Ivain, 1953).

We live in an era where the pace of change is increasing. We are designing spaces for professions that do not yet exist, hospitals that require change as soon as construction is complete and homes that 'want' to adapt, just as they always have (Brand, 1995). Therefore space must be created, and allowed to be recreated, continuously. In order to respond to dynamic, shifting and evolving creative communities, we must develop different ways of viewing our physical built environment as an adaptive rather than static object (Schnädelbach, 2010). This also requires a fundamental reconceptualisation of what such adaption might be. For example, instead of updating a research building every 10 or 15 years, dynamic and agile spaces should allow a reformulation of current models of research in collaboration with the space itself. The question changes from 'what space do we need to do research?' to 'how might the research and space adapt together to engender an embodied research space?'

Regenerative space is limited by its physical nature but this constraint is still eclipsed by social, economic and psychological barriers, where change and unpredictability are difficult. The recipes *#50 Make do and mend*, *#51 Work that space* and *#52 Rebel space* all present examples of adaptive space and behaviour that can be applied by anyone. Perhaps the key to regenerative space, as with play space, is the state of mind required to recognise that it is possible.

Informal settlements – (favela space)

For the Situationists, the concept of the dérive (or drift) existed not in city centres, but on the margins of the city. The labyrinth became a metaphor for a meandering maze of organic paths negotiated by the drifter, as opposed to the logic of rationalist planning and modern urbanism (Sadler, 1999). The word *favela* comes from the unplanned settlements that emerged in Brazil, created by the inhabitants themselves without formal planning systems.

The notion of peripheral elements in a city is not new, whether this is Sassen's marginality, where "economic globalisation has contributed to a new geography of centrality and marginality" (Sassen, 1996) or Edge Cities (Garreau, 2011). Inhabiting the edges in a city blurs the boundaries between planned and emergent development. Marshall's 'border crossings' mediated by 'free radicals' occupy a similar function - interstitial elements where the crossing of boundaries can be achieved physically and culturally (Marshall, 2013).

Favela space emerges in boundary spaces (edges, overlaps and 'in-between' spaces) and is constructed from local, diverse, and meaningful organisational identities. It is a creative space where its occupants can: 1) react to a given structure – accept it or reject it; 2) bypass the presence of the structure; 3) displace the structure; or 4) create a new structure that displaces or transforms the original structure. In some ways, favela space is the ultimate regenerative space. Favela space is the antithesis of the planned city, so the social creative activity becomes essential in creating the space against the 'grain' of the deterministic context, analogous to Alexander's 'unselfconscious design' (Alexander, 1965).

In this book, recipes such as *#52 Rebel Space* and *#34 Popup whitespace hubs* are favela spaces, where the use of these spaces is determined by the activity of the group using them. Even at a personal level, the favela space can still be created as an individual 'space within a space': *#53 Bus as research environment* and *#54 A mobile thinking shrine* both demonstrate examples of this. In all of these examples the use is applied to the existing space, which in turn changes the space itself.

CONCLUSION

Through this brief set of examples we have introduced a potential spectrum of themes for creative situations. It is important to realise that these are themes only – they are necessarily descriptive rather than prescriptive. In that sense, they are more akin to Alexander's patterns (Alexander, 1979) or, interestingly perhaps, Jan van Pelt and Westfall's socio-political types (Jan van Pelt & Westfall, 1991). They describe the underlying human value of these spaces through their situated use, highlighting the importance of activity over form or intended function.

What we might conclude is that the spatial constructs of creative spaces and situations must amplify, enable, and elicit the complexity, contradictory, difficult and interesting – the diverse and conflicting, the inconsistent and ambiguous nature of modern thinking and problem solving. Echoing what Robert Venturi described as complexity and contradiction in architecture – that which has a richness of meaning based on the richness and ambiguity of a modern experience: "I prefer 'both-and' to 'either-or,' black and white, and sometimes gray, to black or white. A valid architecture evokes many levels of meaning and combinations of focus: its space and its elements become readable and workable in several ways at once" (Venturi, 1984, p. 16)

It is also the charge of creative individuals (planners, architects, and occupants alike) to re-invent, re-interpret, and propose alternative constructs of creativity that do not yet exist. The very emergent nature of these themes requires that this is so. The responsibility for these allowances is not simply in the hands of the designer. By viewing space as an active situation, every user has an opportunity to effect change.

But the most important summary point might be that considering space in terms of creative situations allows us to rethink space itself – as an embodied conception of active and creative situations. That the space we inhabit is as much a product of ourselves is an empowering alternative conceptualisation of it. At the very least, space should allow the emergence of such situations – not prevent them.

CONCLUSIONS

CONCLUSIONS AND INVITATION

EDITORS

Alison Williams
Derek Jones
Judy Robertson

CONCLUSIONS

This volume sought to address some of the questions that have emerged from three years of SPIRES' work: What does a great research space look like? Feel like? What are its core elements? What are the social factors that make a difference to us as researchers and to our work? How do we know when they are in place – and how do we know when they aren't, or are undeveloped? What technological factors are helpful, and what are not?

Three major questioning themes have come out of the recipes, case studies and papers in this volume to become part of the book's structure: What is needed for great research work on one's own (*Working solo*)? How do we work well collaboratively (*Working together*)? And how do we build, hack, and design appropriate environments within which to produce remarkable research (*Working environment*)?

Two foundational premises emerge from the contributions: firstly, that unless and until we ask questions our understanding remains covert or tacit, and the status quo continues. Once the questions are raised, then so is our awareness of the circumstances. The big questions underlying this are: What are we missing? What is not being spoken about? Where do we need to put our attention? Only once the questions are asked can we become aware of what IS, and what is needed. Awareness comes first. The second emergent premise is that as researchers we have agency and can make changes. We can make changes intrapersonally i.e. cognitively and emotionally; interpersonally in how we interact and collaborate with others; and materially in how we view and interact with our physical environment.

As editors we have sought to work using these and other points arising from the text. The importance, for example, of play and experimentation, and of serendipity has been central to how the volume came together, as the SPIRES members, guests and Travel Scholars played with the data they had collected (*Why recipes?*). The integral role of collaboration in producing remarkable research has informed how we worked together (*Introduction*) with its varied and challenging emotional, as well as coolly professional, moments.

A host of sub-themes run through the work: the role of motivation, particularly motivation driven by small wins, permeates the recipes. Small changes can make a significant difference to how and where we work. Larger physical changes build connections with colleagues and changes in attitude can make life and research significantly smoother (ideas for building trust, connections and joie de vivre abound).

It is notable that the original EPSRC funding was to explore 'effective' research. Through the book's authors this has metamorphosed into 'creative' research – an inspirational shift that offers a contrast to the world of bibliometrics and impact factors.

INVITATION

So we would like to extend an invitation to you to start using this book – if you haven't already – in a variety of ways:

1. Ask the questions. How do I feel when I come into my research environment? Why? What does it say about how I am working solo, working with colleagues, and where I am working?
2. Become aware. What works? And what doesn't? What do I want to address? Change?
3. Take action. Find the recipes that work for you and try them out.
4. Spread the word. Start a BITE group for encouraging remarkable research
5. Write your own. We feel certain that there are many more recipes, case studies and papers about creative and remarkable research out there in the wide and fascinating landscape of research.

If you would like to participate in potential future editions of BITE: Recipes for remarkable research, here are some suggested ways of doing this (and we look forward to hearing about the unexpected ways you use the material in this book):

Use the *Grammar of creative workplaces* at the end of the book to audit your physical workspace and give pointers to beneficial changes. If you prefer an electronic version, email us at **biteresearchrecipes@gmail.com**

- Send us your scores so that we can add it to the database. We will send you back a report of how your space benchmarks against 1) the average and 2) the best

By contributing to potential future editions:

- Writing your own recipes. You have seen the format – write your own and send it to us

- Propose academic papers – send us a 500 word abstract

- Contribute a case study of your own research environment pre- and post- any changes you make as a result of a grammar audit, or of implementing any of the recipes

Above all, have fun, play and experiment, collaborate with your peers and enjoy the unexpected serendipitous moments that – along with all the hard work – make for remarkable creative research.

#63

AUTHOR
Alison Williams

SERVE TO

Researchers and
decision-makers;
designers and architects

COST

Free

BENCHMARK YOUR SPACE

Using the **Grammar of creative workplaces** to improve your space

BACKGROUND —

Until we are prompted to think about our physical surroundings – by discomfort or a well-timed question – most of us take them for granted and just accept how they are. Once we become aware of them, and how they are affecting us, then the picture changes. Grumbling is fun for a little while, but it doesn't change anything – "they" don't listen. This book is all about agency – doing things for ourselves.

That is what the grammar of creative workplaces is: an instrument for assessing how well – or otherwise – a work environment is supporting your own and your colleagues' good thinking. We invite you to audit your own workplace, and see how well it measures up to the best practice set out in Table 7 of the paper *The creative footprint*.

The grammar audits four aspects of the physical environment:

- Place: the range of places needed for different creative behaviours

- Properties: the places' sensory properties of comfort, sight, sound, spaciousness, movement and aliveness that support good thinking

- Behaviours: that are possible within the places for engaging with or disengaging from people, ideas and information

- Affordances : materials and equipment that support creative behaviours

Each of these is set out in the pages that follow, with a scale of between 0 – 4 for you to score the different aspects of your workplace.

INGREDIENTS

- **A research environment**

- **A researcher/research team/research colleagues who sense that things could be better in their research environment**

- One or more copies of the *Grammar of creative workplaces* (in this book or request online from **biteresearchrecipes@gmail.com**)

METHOD

1. Decide on the area to be audited
   a. Involve your colleagues – tell them what you are doing, and why. Gather support and suggest that they might want to do their own grammar audit – that will give you an interesting take on
   b. Look at the research places section first, and decide which one you want to focus on – your core space. The others are ancillary: important in how they support the core space and fill in any gaps. You may want to do the audit twice – once for the core space, and again for the ancillary spaces.

2. Carry out the audit
   a. Assess each aspect in turn, section by section, marking the scores (between 0 and 4) for each statement as you go. You will find that there are a lot of deliberate crossovers between *behaviours* and *affordances*.
   b. Make notes in the margin against the prompts to remind yourself what you have and have not got in each sub-category
   c. You may need to go round a second time at a different time of day when there are more (or less) people there.

3. Total the scores
   a. You don't score the places section. It is included as a prompt to see what the ideal number and kind of spaces might be
   b. Add up the scores in each section and enter them into the final table at the back of the grammar
   c. Look for any scores of less than 3: these are the areas that will need working on. If you have a whole cluster of 3s in one section, that gives you a clear idea of where you should focus
   d. Refer to Table 7 in The creative footprint to benchmark your scores against the database average, and the highest (to date) audit

4. Take action
   a. There are recipes for most of the aspects in the grammar. Look through the book for ideas
   b. Involve your colleagues (if you haven't already done so). There's nothing like a beer and pizza or tea and buns session to get walls painted, or furniture moved, or pictures hung or whiteboard walls put up

5. What next.....
   If you would like your spaces benchmarked against the SPIRES database, send your audit to **biteresearchrecipes@gmail.com**. We will add it to the database and send a report back to you. Make sure you fill out the front form fully, so that we can compare like with like as well as the average.

COOK'S TIPS

Remember: it is better to ask forgiveness than beg permission...

If you want to find out more, you can download my thesis at:
http://roar.uel.ac.uk/3077/

PLACES

CORE SPACE	DESCRIPTION AND COMMENTS
	E.g. Open-plan office 50-100 people, 10-50 people; flor of single offices etc
Core space	
Ancillary space 1	E.g. Small meeting room(s) How many?
Ancillary space 2	E.g. Large meeting or Board room(s) How many?
Ancillary space 3	E.g. Informal meeting area. How many?
Ancillary space 4	E.g. Office kitchen space(s), water coolers, coffee machines etc. How many?
Ancillary space 5	E.g. Canteen/works cafe. How many?
Ancillary space 6	E.g. Chill-out area(s). How many?
Ancillary space 7	E.g. Privacy space/secluded small table etc. How many?
Ancillary space 8	E.g. Communal area, foyer/reception, anywhere people congregate. How many?

LINKING SPACES: DESCRIPTION AND COMMENTS

How each ancillary space is linked to the core space being evaluated: E.g. By corridors, open walkways, route through workstations, etc

Linked to core space by:

Linked to core space by:

Linked to core space by:

Linked to core space by:

Linked to core space by:

Linked to core space by:

Linked to core space by:

Linked to core space by:

PROPERTIES OF THE SPACE

IN THIS SPACE (WHEN IN USE)		0	1	2	3	4	
The smell is	Unpleasant	○	○	○	○	○	Fresh
The atmosphere feels	Stuffy and airless	○	○	○	○	○	Fresh without being draughty
The temperature for desk work is	Extreme (too hot/ too cold)	○	○	○	○	○	Just right
It feels lively	Not at all	○	○	○	○	○	Strong impression given of liveliness
The sound levels are	Completely silent	○	○	○	○	○	Quiet buzz
The environment is	Very messy	○	○	○	○	○	Orderly
The sound levels are	Distractingly noisy	○	○	○	○	○	Quiet buzz
People can walk about	Very little	○	○	○	○	○	Extensively
People can chat	Not at all	○	○	○	○	○	Easily
Quiet thought is possible	Not at all	○	○	○	○	○	Easily

IN THIS SPACE		0	1	2	3	4	
Team spaces contain team artefacts	Not at all	○	○	○	○	○	Amost all the teams
Individual workstations are personalised	Not at all	○	○	○	○	○	Almost everyone
The ceiling height is	Below 10 ft approx	○	○	○	○	○	Above 10ft approx
Workstation desks and chairs are	Extremely uncomfortable	○	○	○	○	○	Very comfortable
Views of the outside are	None: no windows	○	○	○	○	○	Wide/far-reaching views
Natural light is	Non-existent	○	○	○	○	○	Floods the space
The sunlight glare is	Very strong	○	○	○	○	○	Non-existent
The artificial light is	Glaring	○	○	○	○	○	Replicates daylight
The colour scheme is	Monotonous (drab)	○	○	○	○	○	Cheerful
The colour scheme is	Extremely bright	○	○	○	○	○	Calm
Line-of-sight from workstations is	Less than 2 ft	○	○	○	○	○	Long (over 20ft approx)

COMMENTS AND DESCRIPTIONS

COMMENTS AND DESCRIPTIONS

BEHAVIOURS

IN THIS SPACE THERE ARE PLACES WHERE IT IS POSSIBLE TO		0	1	2	3	4	
Have formal/planned work conversations	Difficult	○	○	○	○	○	Very easy
Have informal/unscheduled work conversations	Impossible	○	○	○	○	○	Very easy
See formal information	None	○	○	○	○	○	Plentiful
See informal information	None	○	○	○	○	○	Plentiful
Experiment, play, try things out, craft, review	None	○	○	○	○	○	Plentiful
Bump into people by chance	Impossible	○	○	○	○	○	Highly likely
Encounter unexpected information and ideas	Impossible	○	○	○	○	○	Highly likely
Encounter unexpected information and ideas from people from outside the site	Impossible	○	○	○	○	○	Highly likely
Take short walks	Difficult	○	○	○	○	○	Many

IN THIS SPACE THERE ARE PLACES WHERE IT IS POSSIBLE TO		0	1	2	3	4	
Exercise for long periods of time	Not at all	○	○	○	○	○	Amost all the teams
Have the facilities that support exercise	Not at all	○	○	○	○	○	Almost everyone
Have access to transport	Below 10 ft approx	○	○	○	○	○	Above 10ft approx
Think and reflect quietly on one's own	Extremely uncomfortable	○	○	○	○	○	Very comfortable
Work without interruption	None: no windows	○	○	○	○	○	Wide/far-reaching views
Work on one's own	Non-existent	○	○	○	○	○	Floods the space

E.g. Meeting rooms

E.g. Chill-out areas, kitchen spaces, informal meeting spaces, corridors

E.g. Posters, screens

E.g. Post-it notes, team display boards, whiteboards

E.g Workshop areas, 'sandpits', football table play spaces

E.g. Coffee machine, water cooler, canteen etc

E.g. Displays, journals, screens, bookshelves, etc

E.g. Seminars, visits, showing people around etc

E.g. To photocopier, kitchen, other offices etc

E.g. Gym, jogging tracks, cycle paths

E.g. showers, bicycle racks

For travelling to work e.g. bus, train, car parking

E.g. Privacy space/secluded small table etc (observed)

E.g. Configuration of workstation (observed)

E.g. Configuration of workstation (observed)

AFFORDANCES

IN THIS PLACE THERE ARE AFFORDANCES TO SUPPORT...		0	1	2	3	4	
Making thinking visible and accessible inside teams	None	◯	◯	◯	◯	◯	Rich
Making thinking visible and accessible between teams	None	◯	◯	◯	◯	◯	Rich
Thinking visually together	None	◯	◯	◯	◯	◯	Rich
Collaborating with others/other teams	None	◯	◯	◯	◯	◯	Rich
Informal conversations	None	◯	◯	◯	◯	◯	Rich
Productive thinking	None	◯	◯	◯	◯	◯	Rich
Bumping into unexpected information and ideas	None	◯	◯	◯	◯	◯	Rich
Bumping into people unexpectedly	None	◯	◯	◯	◯	◯	Rich
Experimenting, playing with ideas, trying things out, crafting, reviewing	None	◯	◯	◯	◯	◯	Rich

IN THIS PLACE THERE ARE AFFORDANCES TO SUPPORT...		0	1	2	3	4	
Casual physical movement inside the building	None	◯	◯	◯	◯	◯	Rich
Intense physical activity	None	◯	◯	◯	◯	◯	Rich
Mechanical movement	None	◯	◯	◯	◯	◯	Rich
Daydreaming and reflection	None	◯	◯	◯	◯	◯	Rich
Thinking and writing solo	None	◯	◯	◯	◯	◯	Rich
Generating ideas solo	None	◯	◯	◯	◯	◯	Rich
Generating ideas in a group	None	◯	◯	◯	◯	◯	Rich

E.g. Whiteboards, flipcharts, writing walls, post-it boards etc

E.g. Multi-touch electronic tables, video-conferencing, whiteboards, flipcharts, writing walls, post-it boards, posters etc

E.g. Whiteboards, flipcharts, writing walls, post-it boards etc

E.g. Multi-touch electronic tables, video-conferencing, whiteboards, flipcharts, writing walls, post-it boards

E.g. Coffee machine, water cooler, chill-out area etc

E.g. Access to other people, information and ideas

E.g. Seminars, visits, showing people around etc (observed)

E.g. Coffee machine, water cooler, chill-out area etc (observed)

E.g. Whiteboards, flipcharts, writing walls, post-it boards etc (observed)

E.g. Walk to canteen, kitchen, photocopier, printer, other offices, workshop etc (observed)

E.g. Gym, jogging track etc

E.g. Easy access to car parking, bus, train

E.g. Chill-out space, sofa, easy chairs, secluded small table etc (observed)

E.g. Unoccupied small office, screens, secluded small table/desk; chill-out area, table in canteen etc (observed)

E.g. Chill-out space, sofa, easy chairs, secluded small table etc (observed)

E.g. Meeting room (large or small), dedicated thinking space, chill-out area etc (observed)

GRAMMAR AUDIT SCORE SHEET

SCORING THE GRAMMAR OF CREATIVE WORKPLACES	SCORE (0-4)	ANY SCORES OF 2, 1, OR 0

PROPERTIES OF THE SPACES

Smell		
Atmosphere		
Temperature		
Lively feel		
Sound levels (1)		
Environment orderliness		
Sound levels (2)		
Movement		
Sense of speech/chat		
Sense of quiet thought		
Team artefacts		
Personalised workstations		
Ceiling height		
Comfy furniture		
Views to the outside		
Natural light		
Sunlight glare		
Artificial light		
Colour scheme (1)		
Colour scheme (2)		
Line-of-sight		

SUBTOTAL

SCORING THE GRAMMAR OF CREATIVE WORKPLACES	SCORE (0-4)	ANY SCORES OF 2, 1, OR 0

BEHAVIOURS POSSIBLE IN THE SPACES

Formal conversations

Informal conversations

Formal information

Informal information

Experiment, play, try things out, craft, review

Bump into people by chance

Encounter unexpected info and ideas

Encounter unexpected info from external people

Take short walks

Take sustained exercise

Facilities to support exercise

Access to transport

Think quietly on one's own

Work without interruption

Work on one's own

SUBTOTAL

GRAMMAR AUDIT SCORE SHEET

SCORING THE GRAMMAR OF CREATIVE WORKPLACES	SCORE (0-4)	ANY SCORES OF 2, 1, OR 0

AFFORDANCES THAT SUPPORT THE BEHAVIOURS

Thinking is visible inside teams

Thinking is visible between teams

Thinking visually together

Collaborating with others

Informal conversations

Productive thinking

Bumping into unexpected info and ideas

Bumping into people unexpectedly

Experiment, play, try things out, craft, review

Casual physical movement inside the building

Intense physical activity

Mechanical movement (transport)

Daydreaming and reflection

Thinking and writing solo

Generating ideas solo

Generating ideas in a group

SUBTOTAL

TOTAL SCORE
(SUM OF THE THREE SUBTOTALS)

BENCHMARKING
YOUR AUDIT

If you want us to benchmark your audit, please fill in this sheet and send it to us along with your score sheet and/or the grammar including comments.

_____

Name of assessor

University, School or Department, organisation, institution

Contact details

_____

Space/facility being assessed

Name

Sector (academic/commercial/other (what)

Location (city centre/suburbs/campus/other (what)

Sole use of building/Shared building

Core space: single room/building

No. of people using the core space

No. of people in the entire organisation (estimate)

_____

Date of assessment

___

SIGNATURE

___

Send to **biteresearchrecipes@gmail.com**

BIOGRAPHIES

Peter Aspinall

Peter Aspinall is Emeritus Professor of Environmental Studies in the School of Built Environment at Heriot Watt University, UK. He has taught environmental psychology to building and architecture students, and is currently involved in two research groups he co-founded – VisionCentre3 and OPENspace.

Serkan Ayan

Mvy name is Serkan Ayan and I'm a Research Student in Centre for Interaction Design Edinburgh Napier University. My research topic includes layered experience of users in physical spaces especially in cityscape. I'm interested in user engagement in those interactions and the pervasiveness of the technology used. I have done most of my field research in Digital Tourism. So far I have designed and implemented augmented experiences for different spaces such as parks, galleries, woods and cities. Currently I am interested in different evaluation metehods of such experiences, specifically evaluating the transition of physical towards digital.

Madeline Balaam

Madeline Balaam is a lecturer in Interaction Design at Newcastle University. Much of her work focuses on the design of digital interactions within healthcare and wellbeing, and has included for example the participatory design of bespoke technologies to motivate rehabilitation post-stroke through to the design of interactive tabletop "toys" for use within play therapy. Madeline is currently working on a diverse range of projects, including consultancy work at the Edinburgh Royal Hospital for Sick Children exploring future technologies of play through to the design of an augmented kitchen which provides a task-based second language learning experience. Madeline completed her PhD at the University of Sussex where she developed a tangible technology to support the secret communication of emotion between school children and their teacher.

Peter Barrett

Peter Barrett has been in the School of the Built Environment, University of Salford since 1988. In 1992 he became a professor; from 1993-6 was Head of School and Director of the Research Institute for the Built and Human Environment; and in 1998 became faculty Dean and in 2001 Pro-Vice Chancellor for Research and Graduate Studies for the whole University. From 2007-10 he was President of the International Council for Construction and Building Research and Innovation (CIB) and has recently been External Examiner at University of Cambridge for their MSc in Interdisciplinary Design for the Built Environment.

He is now a research professor in the School ; Member of UK High Level Group of the Construction Technology Platform and of the High Level Group of the European Construction Platform.

Peter's main teaching input is as part of the Research Methods Team that provides programmed support to all MSc students as they address their dissertations. He also supervises a number of doctoral students and makes occasional presentations to other groups within the School. His research interests are: Briefing, facilities management, construction management, practice management and, especially, the sensory impact of building design on users' well-being and effectiveness.

Evgenij Belikov

Evgenij Belikov is a PhD candidate in Computer Science at Heriot-Watt University, working on improving adaptive control of paralleism for parallel functional languages to improve performance portability across heterogeneous and hierarchical architectures. He is member of SPIRES and is also interested in ways to improve social and physical aspects of research spaces.

Diana Bental

Diana Bental is a research associate on SerenA (The Serendipity Arena), Chance Encounters in the Space of Ideas. I am interested in using computer-based representations and reasoning methods, such as the Semantic Web, to support researchers in making connections with other researchers and with new ideas in unexpected ways.

Simon Biggs

Simon Biggs is a new media artist, writer and curator interested in digital poetics, autopoietic systems, interactive and performance environments, interdisciplinary research and co-creation. His work has been widely presented, including at Tate Modern, ICA, CCA, Kettles Yard, Pompidou Centre, Academy de Kunste Berlin, Kulturforum Berlin, Rijksmuseum Twenthe, Maxxi Rome, Macau Arts Museum, San Francisco Cameraworks, Walker Art Center Minneapolis and the Art Gallery of New South Wales Sydney. Publications include Remediating the Social (2012), Autopoiesis (with James Leach, 2004)

Meredith Bostwick-Lorenzo Eiroa

As a thought-leader in the design and planning of academic science and research spaces, Meredith is a Strategic Planner and Process Manager at Skidmore, Owings & Merrill LLP (SOM). Her current work is focused on a diverse palette of laboratory projects for academic research and institutional/industry partnerships. As a "Lab Creative" her work strives to bridge both like-minded research and un-common collaboration with the aim to spark innovation and the creative process. Her work with researchers and conversations with cognitive scientists has inspired her writings on a series of 'Types and Typologies' as a creative spatial framework for academic research institutions. Meredith has presented at regional conferences for Society of College and University Planners (SCUP), Project Kaleidoscope and the Laboratory Design Conference. She has been published in R&D Magazine's 2012 issue, "The Ups and Downs of Modern Laboratory Design" and Laboratory Design Newsletter's April 2013 issue, "Expanding Science Research and Teaching in a Single City Block." She is a Registered Architect in the State of New York and a LEED® Accredited Professional. Mrs. Bostwick-Lorenzo Eiroa received her B.S. with Honors in Architecture from Georgia Institute of Technology and her M.A. in Architecture from Princeton University.

George Buchanan

George Buchanan is a Reader in the Centre for Human-Computer Interaction Design at City University London. Dr. Buchanan has published extensively on digital libraries, mobile interaction and hypertext, and his recent research has focussed on the impact of place on information seeking. Previously, George has worked at Swansea University, University College London, University of Waikato (New Zealand) and Middlesex University. Before returning to academia, he owned and directed a successful desktop publishing software house.

Richard Coyne

Richard Coyne is Professor of Architectural Computing at the University of Edinburgh, UK. He is an architect who researches and teaches in theories and practices of architecture, design and digital media, on which he has published eight books. At Edinburgh University, he has served as Head of the Department of Architecture, and Head of the School of Arts, Culture and Environment, and is now Dean of Postgraduate Research in the College of Humanities and Social Science

Martyn Dade-Robertson

Martyn Dade-Robertson is a lecturer in Architecture at Newcastle University. He has published more than 20 peer reviewed publications including the book *The Architecture of Information* (Routledge 2011) and received more than £400,000 in research income working on projects which span architectural design and digital technologies. His research group ArchaID is the basis form both his research and teaching. The group specialises in computation and architecture with projects ranging from Synthetic Biology to Interaction Design and I formation Architecture. Through the development of core research programs in technology his aim is to develop a rigorous intellectual engagement with new types of material systems and practices.

Marian Dörk

Marian Dörk is a postdoc working in Culture Lab, Newcastle University on the PATINA project exploring new ways of interacting with digital information. With a background in computer science, Marian's particular interest lies in information visualization. During his PhD research at the University of Calgary (2008-2012), Marian designed and studied visual interfaces to support exploratory information practices. He has also undertaken related work at Google, Microsoft Research, and IBM Research, and before his PhD, he studied Computational Visualistics at Universität Magdeburg (2003-2008). Marian's website has videos, demos, and papers of his work: http://mariandoerk.de

Rosamund Davis

Rosamund Davies has a background of professional practice in the film and television industries and lectures in creative and media writing at the University of Greenwich. Rosamund is co-author of the book *Introducing the Creative Industries: theory into practice* (SAGE 2012). Further publications include articles and book chapters on screenwriting, hypertext and online video. In her recent media practice, she has explored the intersection between narrative and archive as cultural forms and transmedia storytelling approaches to dramatic narrative. As As co-investigator on the interdisciplinary research project 'PATINA' (Personal Architectonics Through Interaction with Artefacts), funded by the RCUK Digital Economy programme, Rosamund has brought narrative enquiry to the context of 'Designing Effective Research Spaces', collaborating with colleagues in computer science, human computer interaction, archeology and architecture.

Ema Findley

Ema's initial research interests are rooted in user-centered design and interactions. Her current work as part of the PATINA project (EPSRC/AHRC PATINA (£1.72m) Designing Effective Research Spaces, EPSRC Digital Economy Programme http://www.patina.ac.uk) includes the strategic design and development of learning and research space and its relationships to creative pedagogic practice.

Mike Fraser

Mike Fraser is a Professor of Human-Computer Interaction in the Department of Computer Science at the University of Bristol. His research draws on studies of personal and social interaction to inspire the design of novel technologies. Over the past five years he has obtained over two million pounds of funding from EPSRC, ESRC, EU and industry. Prof Fraser sits on the steering committee for the ACM TEI conference and has served on the program committees of a number of international conferences. He has published numerous papers in ACM Transactions on CHI, Personal and Ubiquitous Computing, CSCW Journal, and at ACM CHI, ACM CSCW, ACM UIST and UbiComp.

Maria João Grade Godinho

Maria is a Portuguese biologist. She has over a decade of research experience in various areas of the life sciences, having worked in laboratories in Portugal, New Zealand and Australia. While conducting doctoral research, investigating nerve regeneration, Maria became involved with artists developing biological artworks, and she found such experiences fascinating. Consequently, in 2012 she became a Research Fellow at the ESRC Genomics Policy and Research Forum, University of Edinburgh, to examine interdisciplinary collaborations between arts and biological sciences. While at the Forum she presented her work at international conferences and co-organised the symposium Evaporation of Things (http://www.evaporationofthings.com/). Maria is currently a member of CIRCLE and Invited Lecturer in Interdisciplinary Creative Practices at the Edinburgh Colleague of Art.

Dorothy Hardy

Dorothy Hardy is passionate about renewable energy, and intrigued by the process of enthusing others about renewable energy, in the most enticing and exciting ways possible. She studied both Mechanical Engineering and Glass Art, and is now completing a PhD at Heriot-Watt University, looking into ways of making solar cells look better in architecture. She creates intriguing structures incorporating solar cells. More available on request!

Jim Hensman

Jim works as a researcher at Coventry University and is an Associate of the Serious Games Institute based there. His recent work has focused on projects in the area of collective intelligence and collaborative research and innovation, including the development of Virtual Research Environments and on facilitating cross-disciplinary, Citizen Science and research-business communities. He has a particular interest in virtual worlds and games in learning and research, including the use of immersive environments to facilitate collective thinking, creativity and interaction. He previously was based in the Innovation Group at the University which he set up, working on investigating, prototyping and advising on strategy for new ICT related developments and managing major initiatives, including large EU projects working with business and the community. He has a background in the electronics, computer and games industries, and was responsible for the design and development of a number of major innovations in these sectors.

Nicole Lotz

Nicole is a Lecturer in Design at the Open University, UK. She graduated as a Communication Designer in Germany and has earned her PhD from The Hong Kong Polytechnic University. She has been researching the relationship of designing and culture in Europe, Asia and Africa. For years she has been developing design patterns and pedagogical patterns that can be shared and used by others, just like recipes in cooking, to improve design education and practice.

Anita McKeown

Anita is an interdisciplinary artist, producer and researcher working in the public domain with research interests in open source culture and the impact of technology. As Co-founder and Creative Director of Art Services Unincorporated she continues to have her work exhibited and performed nationally and internationally winning the prestigious Bravo Award, for a digital public art project in Memphis, TN. She was elected by invitation to the Royal Society of Arts and recently invited to the inaugural Placemaking Leadership Council convened by Project for Public Spaces, in Detroit, 2013.

Bruce Mackh

Bruce Mackh earned a BFA from the School of the Art Institute of Chicago, an MFA from Tulane University, and a PhD in Critical Studies in Fine Art from Texas Tech University. While at Texas Tech, he was awarded a TEACH Fellowship, and was the only Fellow from the School of Art to earn this distinction. Bruce has a strong interest in curriculum development, pedagogy, and faculty development, all of which inform his present work as the Mellon Research Project Director at the University of Michigan, ArtsEngine. The goal of this project is to compile the first comprehensive guide to best practices in the integration of the arts into the research university, central to which is a focus on the idea of arts practice as research—perhaps one of the most crucial debates concerning the future of the arts in academia. Bruce is also an accomplished photographer, and his largest collection of images is part of the permanent collection of the Louisiana State Museum, illustrating the lasting impact of Hurricane Katrina on the city of New Orleans.

Andrew Macvean

Andrew Macvean is a PhD student in HCI at Heriot-Watt University in Edinburgh. Andrew's research interests are in the area of understanding and explaining behavior within interactive systems, through the application of theories from behavioral psychology. Andrew has researched enjoyment, motivation, goal-setting, creativity, and the role of context within serious games, alternate reality games, game authoring tools, and professional software development environments. Andrew's PhD thesis looks at understanding the motivation levels and goal-setting behavior of children within a serious game, through the use and application of Bandura's theory of self-efficacy. At the center of Andrew's work is a mobile, location-aware exercise game which is used to promote physical activity and behaviour change within an adolescent demographic. As well as working at Heriot-Watt University, Andrew has worked as a User Experience Researcher at Google, and as a visiting scholar at the Georgia Institute of Technology.

Panos Mavros

Panos is a PhD student in the Centre for Advanced Spatial Analysis, UCL, researching the role of emotions in urban behaviour. Emotions are a critical component of human cognitive functions. Panos uses emerging technologies, such as mobile EEG, to study the role of emotions in urban behaviour and the interactions between the individuals and their environment. This has implications in the study of way finding and spatial decision making mechanisms, but also raises questions about the impact of the environment and architecture on individual and collective experience.

Debbie Maxwell

Dr Deborah Maxwell is a researcher at Edinburgh College of Art, University of Edinburgh, on the Arts and Humanities Knowledge Exchange hub, Design in Action. Her research interests are around the ways that people interact with and reshape technology and the roles that storytelling can play across media. Past research includes her doctoral research working with traditional storytellers in Scotland, mobile digital interpretation projects in rural Northumberland, and the design of digital tools to facilitate and encourage serendipitous encounters in research.

Inger Mewburn

I am a researcher, specialising in research education since 2006. Prior to this I lectured in architecture and worked in architecture offices for around a decade.

I am currently the Director of Research Training at The Australian National University where I am responsible for co-ordinating, communicating and measuring all the centrally run research training activities and doing research on student experience to inform practice.

Aside from editing and contributing to the Thesis Whisperer, I write scholarly papers, books and book chapters about research student experiences. I am a regular guest speaker at other universities and do occassional media interviews. Some details of these other activites are below. For further information, view my Linkedin Profile, contact me by email on inger.mewburn@anu.edu.au or visit my Google Scholar page. I often visit other universities and do workshops on publishing, writing, social media and presentation skills: if you are interested, please send me an email.

Negin Moghim

I am a final stage Computer Science PhD candidate at Heriot-Watt University, Edinburgh with a keen passion for applying research to real life problems. I have dedicated my research to a cause very dear to my heart: improving the quality of life of individuals whom suffer from epilepsy through improving automatic seizure detection and prediction systems.

Jeanne Narum

Jeanne L. Narum, Principal—Learning Spaces Collaboratory (LSC) & Founding Director—Project Kaleidoscope (PKAL). Since 1991, under the aegesis of PKAL Narum has been involved with conversations and initiatives exploring the relationship of the quality of learning to the quality of learning spaces—with specific attention to the process of planning. With PKAL colleagues, in 1995 she published a major resource for campus planners—*Structures for Science: What Works*. Narum has orchestrated twenty years of workshops for academics and architects on best practices in classrooms, laboratory and library planning. With LSC colleagues and NSF support, she is preparing a guide for *Planning for Assessing 21st Century Learning Spaces*. With support from the Sloan Foundation, a LSC group developed a working paper on Cognition and Creativity—Planning Learning Spaces. An LSC website is evolving (www.pkallsc.org). Narum also consults with campuses at early stages in the planning process.

Anitra Nottingham

Anitra Nottingham is a graphic designer and Monash University Design School graduate. She has been a Creative director for the design studio London Road Design, and has previously worked for Oxford University Press, Penguin Books, and Intuit (USA) where she was Design Director. Anitra has taught graphic design for 10 years, and is currently Online Director for the School of Graphic Design at the Academy of Art University, San Francisco, where she oversees their extensive online graphic design program.

Pawel Orzechowski

Pawel Orzechowski is a self described digital anthropologist. He has been creating paper and digital tools to empower communities for about a decade and is currently finishing his PhD and working for a creative agency StormIdeas in Edinburgh. For SPIRES, Pawel traveled to Sydney to plunge into uncharted intersections of jungle and concrete, creativity and structure, future and present, brain and heart, personal and public. Pawel is a driven by unusual insights, prototyping reality and observing organic interactions we have with the world around us. "Professionally I'm an overexcited puppy playing with confetti"

Nick Pearce

Nick Pearce is a teaching fellow at Durham University's Foundation Centre, teaching courses in anthropology and sociology. His research interests include the use of social media in education and research and he has worked on projects relating to YouTube, Pinterest, Weibo amongst other things. He has previously worked at the Open University and Lancaster University.

Sapna Ramnani

I have been a documentary filmmaker since completing a Masters in 2000 and will be completing a PhD in 2014. My interest lies in providing a voice for people who are under represented and will be focusing some of my future documentaries on human rights issues from the personal perspective of victims and survivors. I am developing techniques to treat my tinnitus and will be writing a book about my experiences as well as treatments, exercises and techniques that have worked for me.

Sian Robinson Davies

I graduated from Fine Art at Goldsmiths College, and later from Linguistic Studies at Birkbeck College, University of London. My interests are writing and performing comedy and theatre and more specifically, humour, sincerity and structures of storytelling.

Jenny Roe

Dr Jenny Roe is a Senior Research Leader for the Stockholm Environment Institute, University of York and formerly a Lecturer at Heriot Watt University. She is an Environmental Psychologist and Landscape Architect with expertise in restorative and salutogenic (health-improving) environments - indoors and out - and health and behaviour in relation to climate change. www.jennyjroe.com

Mel Woods

Mel Woods is an artist and researcher based at Duncan of Jordanstone College of Art and Design, University of Dundee. Her work has explored problems and opportunities associated with convergence of technologies for communication and interaction between people and for ideas. She is interested in the challenges we face in designing interfaces, creating prototypes and provocations for the future. Currently she is PI for the RCUK 'SerenA' investigating serendipity, and the tools to support chance encounters in the research environment; PI for 'StoryStorm' appropriating methods such as hacking to technology for communities with an urgent story to tell and is CoI for 'Design in Action' AHRC Knowledge Exchange Hub.

REFERENCES

Abraham, A. & Windmann, S. (2007). Creative cognition: The diverse operations and the prospect of applying a cognitive neuroscience perspective. *Methods (San Diego, Calif.), 42*(1), 38–48.

Adams, A., Fitzgerald, E. & Priestnall, G. (2013). Of catwalk technologies and boundary creatures. In *ACM Transactions of Computer-Human Interaction, special issue on 'the turn to the wild', 20*(3), ACM.

Alberti, R. E. & Emmons, M. L. (1974). *Your perfect right: A guide to assertive behaviour.* San Luis Obispo, CA: Impact.

Alexander, C. (1964). Notes on the synthesis of form. Cambridge, Mass: Harvard University Press.

Alexander, C. (1965). A City is Not a Tree. *Architectural Forum, 122*(1).

Alexander, C. (1979). *The timeless way of building.* New York: Oxford University Press.

Alexander, C. (1996). The origins of pattern theory - the future of the theory, and the generation of a living world. Retrieved from http://www.patternlanguage.com/archive/ieee/ieeetext.htm

Alexander, C., Ishikawa, S., Silverstein, M., Jacobson, M., Fiksdahl-King, I. & Angel, S. (1977). *A pattern language* (1st ed.). New York: Oxford University Press.

Allen, D. (2002). *Getting things done.* London: Piatkus.

Alloway, L., (1959). City notes. *Architectural Design, 29*, pp.34–35.

André, P., Teevan, J., Dumais, S. (2009). Discovery is never by chance: Designing for (un)serendipity. In *Proceedings of Creativity and Cognition*, 305–314. Berkley, CA: ACM.

Amabile, T. M. (1983). *The social psychology of creativity.* New York: Springer-Verlag.

Amabile, T. M. (1996). *Creativity in context.* Oxford: Westview Press.

Amabile, T. M. & Kramer, S. J. (2011). *The progress principle: Using small wins to ignite joy, engagement, and creativity at work.* Boston, MA: Harvard Business Press.

Amabile, T. M. & Kramer, S. J. (2012). How leaders kill meaning at work. *McKinsey Quarterly.* Retrieved 13 November 2013 from http://mckinsey.com/insights/leading_in_the_21st_century/how_leaders_kill_meaning_at_work

Andrade, J. (2009). What does doodling do? *Applied Cognitive Psychology,* doi: 10.1002/acp.1561. [See also: *Applied Cognitive Psychology, 24*(1), 100–106.]

Anon. (2010). Stay on target. *The Economist.* Retrieved 28 August 2013 from http://www.economist.com/node/16295664

Anthes, E. (2009). Building around the mind. *Scientific American Mind, 20*(2), 52–59.

Aragon, C. R., Poon, S. S. & Aragon, D. (2009). *A tale of two online communities: Fostering collaboration and creativity in scientists and children.*

Aspinall, P., Mavros, P., Coyne, R. & Roe, J. (2013). The urban brain: Analysing outdoor physical activity with mobile EEG. *British Journal of Sports Medicine,* doi:10.1136/bjsports-2012-091877.

Bachelard, G. (1984). *The poetics of space.* Boston: Beacon Press Books.

Bakewell, S. (2010). *How to live: A life of Montaigne in one question and twenty attempts at an answer.* London: Chatto & Windus.

Bandura, A. (2000). Self-efficacy: The foundation of agency. In W. J. Perrig & A. Grob (Eds.) *Control of human behaviour, mental processes and consciousness* (pp. 17–33). Mahwak, NJ: Erlbaum.

Barrett, P. (2010). Creating sensory-sensitive creative spaces. In: P. Zennaro (Ed.) *Colour and Light in Architecture – First International Conference Proceedings,* pp.187–192.

Barrett, P. & Barrett, L. (2010). The potential of positive places: Senses, brain and spaces. *Intelligent Buildings International 2,* pp. 218–228.

Barrett, P., Barrett, L. & Davies, F. (2013). Achieving a step change in the optimal sensory design of buildings for users at all life-stages. *Building & Environment, 67,* pp. 97–104.

Barrett, P. & Zhang, Y. (2009). Optimal learning spaces: Design implications for primary schools. In *SCRI Research Report Series.* Salford, UK: University of Salford.

Barrett, P.S., Zhang, Y., Moffat, J. & Kobaccy, K.A.H. (2013). An holistic, multi-level analysis identifying the impact of classroom design on pupils' learning. *Building and Environment, 59:* pp. 678–689.

Bartle, R. A. (2003). *Designing Virtual Worlds.* Indianapolis: New Riders.

Beatty, E. L. & Ball, L. J. (2011). Investigating exceptional poets to inform an understanding of the relationship between poetry and design. *Conference Proceedings: DESIRE 11.*

Belcastro, S-M. (2013). *The home of mathematical knitting.* Retrieved 21 July 2013 from http://www.toroidalsnark.net/mathknit.html

Benjamin, W. (2002). The Arcades Project. [Rolf Tiedemann (Ed.). Translated by Howard Eiland & Kevin McLaughlin.] New York: Belknap Press.

Berardi, F. (2009). *The soul at work: From alienation to autonomy.* Los Angeles: Semiotext(e).

Berger, W. (2012). The secret phrase top innovators use. *Harvard Business Review Blog.* Retrieved 13 November 2013 from http://blogs.hbr.org/2012/09/the-secret-phrase-top-innovato/

Bergson, H. (2002). *Henri Bergson: Key writings* (1st ed.). London: Continuum.

Berne, E. (1964). *Games people play: The psychology of human relationships.* New York: Grove Press.

Blanchette, D. M., Ramocki, S. P., O'Del, J. N., & Casey, M. S. (2005). Aerobic exercise and creative potential: Immediate and residual effects. *Creativity Research Journal, 17*(2 & 3), 257–264.

Bohm, D. (2004). *On dialogue* (2nd ed.). Oxford & New York: Routledge.

Boyce, R. (2000). *Advice for new faculty members.* Pearson.

Brand, S. (1995). *How buildings learn: What happens after they're built.* Penguin Books.

Brey, P. (2005). The epistemology and ontology of human-computer interaction. In *Minds and Machines, 15* (3-4), 383–398.

Brill, M., Margulis, S. & Konar, E. (1984). *Using office design to increase productivity,* Vol. 1 & 2. Buffalo, NY: Workplace Design and Productivity, Inc.

Brill, M., Weidemann, S., Alard, L., Olson, J., Keable, E. (2001). *Disproving widespread myths about workplace design.* Jasper, IN: Kimball International.

Brown, S. (2011). Sunni Brown: Doodlers, unite! Video on TED.com. Retrieved 21 July 2013 from http://www.ted.com/talks/sunni_brown.html

Bryan, T. (2010). *The mind map book.* London: Pearson.

Businessweek (n.d.) [Images of Jump Associates work spaces.] Retrieved 21 November 2013 from http://images.businessweek.com/ss/06/07/jump/index_01.htm

Buzan, T. (2002). *How to mind map.* Thorsons: London.

Cai, D.J., Mednick, S.A., Harrison, E.M., Kanady, J.C. & Mednick, S.C. (2009). REM, not incubation, improves creativity by priming associative networks. *PNAS 2009 106*(25) 10130-10134; doi:10.1073/pnas.0900271106.

Carlsson, C. (2008). *Nowtopia: How pirate programmers, outlaw bicyclists, and vacant-lot gardeners are inventing the future today!* Oakland: AK Press.

Carr, S. (1992). *Public space.* Cambridge University Press.

Carroll, J. M. & Ganoe, C. H. (2008). Designing for creativity in cooperative Work. *International Journal of e-Collaboration, 4*(December), pp. 51–75.

Carusi, A., & Reimer, T. (2010). *Virtual research environment collaborative landscape study.* Retrieved from http://www.jisc.ac.uk/publications/reports/2010/vrelandscapestudy

Ceylan, C., Dul, J. & Aytac, S. (2008). Can the office environment stimulate a manager's creativity? *ERIM Report Series: Research in Management,* Ref. No. ERS-2008-059-LIS.

Chapman, J. (2005). *Emotionally durable design: Objects, experiences and empathy.* London: Earthscan.

Chapman, J. (2009). Design for (emotional) durability. *Design Issues, 25*(4), 29–35.

Charmaz, K. (2000). Grounded theory: Objectivist and constructivist methods. In N. K. Denzin, & Y. S. Lincoln (Eds.) *Handbook of qualitative research* (2nd ed.). London: Sage.

Chatwin, B. (n.d.) *Bruce Chatwin - The songlines.* Moleskine website. Retrieved from http://www.moleskine.com/bruce-chatwin-the-songlines

Chellappa, S.L., Steiner, R., Blattner, P., Oelhafen, P., Götz, T. & Cajochen, C. (2011). 'Non-visual effects of light on melatonin, alertness and cognitive performance: can blue-enriched light keep us alert?' *PLoS ONE 6*(1): e16429. doi:10.1371/journal.pone.0016429

Chenail, R. J. (2008). "But is it research?": A review of Patricia Leavy's Method Meets Art: Arts-Based Research Practice. *The Weekly Qualitative Report, 1*(2), 7–12.

Ching, F.D.K. (1979). *Architecture: Form, space and order* (1st ed.). New York: Van Nostrand Reinhold.

Chipchase, J. (2013). *Future perfect » Everything's Rosy.* Retrieved 20 August 2013 from http://janchipchase.com/

Chomsky, N. (1957). *Syntactic structures.* The Hague: Mouton.

Clark, S. & Maher, M. L. (2001). The role of place in designing a learner-centred virtual learning environment. *CAAD Futures,* 1–14.

Claxton, G. (1997). *Hare brain, tortoise mind.* UK: Fourth Estate.

Constant (1974). New Babylon. [Nieuwenhuys, C.] The Hague: Gemeentenmuseum den Haag.

Costello, F. J. & Keane, M. T. (2000). Efficient creativity: Constraint-guided conceptual combination. *Cognitive Science, 24*(2), 299–349.

Cougar, J. D. (1994). *Creative problem solving and opportunity finding (Decision making and operations management).* London: Boyd & Fraser.

Coyne, R. (2007). Thinking through virtual reality: Place, non-place and situated cognition. *Techne: Research in Philosophy and Technology, 10*(3), 26–80.

Coyne, R. (2013). Reflections on digital media & culture. Retrieved from http://richardcoyne.com/

Craft, A. (2001). *An analysis of research and literature on creativity in education.* Prepared for the Qualifications and Curriculum Authority, UK.

Creative Education Foundation (2013). *Brainstorming - Where brainstorming began.* Retrieved 18 August 2013 from http://www.creativeeducationfoundation.org/our-process/brainstorming

Cross, N. (1982). Designerly ways of knowing. *Design Studies, 3*(4), 221–227. Retrieved from http://linkinghub.elsevier.com/retrieve/pii/0142694X82900400

Cross, N. (2006). *Designerly ways of knowing* (1st ed.). London: Springer-Verlag.

Csikszentmihalyi, M. (1975). *Beyond boredom and anxiety*. San Francisco: Jossey-Bass.

Csikszentmihalyi, M. (1996). *Creativity: flow and the psychology of discovery and invention*. New York: HarperCollins.

Damasio, A. (2006). *Descartes' error: Emotion, reason, and the human brain*. London: Vintage.

Dandekar, H.C. (1994). Farm type in the American midwest: A reflection on government policy. In K. A. Franck & L. H. Schneekloth (Eds.) *Ordering space: types in architecture and design*. Van Nostrand Reinhold.

Darlaston-Jones, D. (2007). Making connections: The relationship between epistemology and research methods. *The Australian Community Psychologist, 19*(1).

Debord, G. (1956) [1958, December]. Theory of the dérive. *Internationale Situationniste #2*.

Debord, G. (1957). *Report on the construction of situations and on the international situationist tendency's conditions of organization and action*. Retrieved from http://www.bopsecrets.org/SI/report.htm.

Debord, G. (1994) [1967]. *The society of the spectacle*. [Translation by Donald Nicholson-Smith.] New York: Zone Books.

De Botton, A. (2006). *The architecture of happiness*. NY: Pantheon.

de Certeau, M. (1984). *The practice of everyday life*. Berkeley: University of California Press.

De Dreu, C.K., Baas, M. & Nijstad, B. A. (2008). Hedonic tone and activation level in the mood-creativity link: Toward a dual pathway to creativity model. *Journal of Personality and Social Psychology, 94*(5), 739–756.

de Vries, E., Lund, K. and Baker, M. (2002). Computer-mediated epistemic dialogue: Explanation and argumentation as vehicles for understanding scientific notions. *Journal of the Learning Sciences, 11*(1), 63–103.

Deleuze, G. & Guattari, F. (1987). *A thousand plateaus: Capitalism and schizophrenia*. Vol. 2. London: The Athlone Press.

Dietrich, A. (2004). The cognitive neuroscience of creativity. *Psychonomic Bulletin & Review*.

Dix, A., Rodden, T., Davies, N., Trevor, J., Friday, A. & Palfreyman, K. (2000). Exploiting space and location as a design framework for interactive mobile systems. 7 ACM Trans. Comput.-Hum. Interact. 3, pp. 285–321.

Dourish, P. (2001). *Where the action is: The foundations of embodied interaction*. Cambridge: MIT Press.

Dul, J. & Ceylan, C. (2011). Work environments for employee creativity. *Ergonomics, 54*(1), 12–20.

Elbow, P. (1998). *Writing without teachers*. USA: Oxford University Press.

Ellspermann, S.J., Evans, G.W. & Basadur, M. (2007). The impact of training on the formulation of ill-structured problems. *Omega, 35*(2), 221–236.

Evans, R. & Russell, P. (1989). *The creative manager*. London: Unwin Hyman.

Fayard, A-L. & Weeks, J. (2007). Photocopiers and water-coolers: The affordances of information interaction. *Organisation Studies, 28*, pp. 605–634.

Fayard, A-L. & Weeks, J. (2011). Who moved my cube? Creating workspaces that actually foster collaboration. *Harvard Business Review, 89*(7), 103–110.

Franck, K. A. (1984). Exorcising the ghost of physical determinism. *Environment and Behavior, 16*, pp. 411–435.

Fleming, N. D. (2006). *VARK Visual, Aural/Auditory, Read/Write, Kinesthetic*. New Zealand: Bonwell Green Mountain Falls.

Fleming, N. & Baume, D. (2006). Learning styles again: VARKing up the right tree! *Educational Developments*. SEDA, Issue 7.4, pp. 4–7.

Flyvbjerg, B. (2001). *Making social science matter: Why social inquiry fails and how it can succeed again*. Cambridge University Press.

Florida, R. (2002). *The rise of the creative class: And how it's transforming work, leisure, community and everyday life*. New York: Basic Books.

Forty, A. (2004). *Words and buildings: A vocabulary of modern architecture* (1st ed.). London: Thames & Hudson.

Foucault, M. (1970). *The order of things: An archaeology of the human sciences*. Tavistock.

Foucault, M. (2002). *The archaeology of knowledge*. London: Routledge.

Foy, N. (1994). *Empowering people at work*. London: Gower.

Franck, K.A. & Schneekloth, L.H. (1994). Type: prison or promise. In K. A. Franck & L. H. Schneekloth, (Eds.) *Ordering space: Types in architecture and design*. New York: Van Nostrand Reinhold.

Franz, G. (2004). Physical and affective correlates to perceived order in open-plan architecture. *Dresden International Symposium of Architecture*.

Franz, G. & Wiener, J. M. (2008). From space syntax to space semantics: a behaviourally and perceptually oriented methodology for the efficient description of the geometry and topology of environments. *Environment and Planning B: Planning and Design, 35*, pp. 574–592.

Fromm, E. (1964). *The heart of man*. New York: Harper & Row.

Garner, S. (2008). *Writing on drawing: Essays on drawing practice and research*. Intellect Books.

Garreau, J. (2011). *Edge city: Life on the new frontier*. Google eBook: Random House LLC.

Gibson, J. J. (1977). The theory of affordances. In R. Shaw & J. Bransford (Eds.) *Perceiving, acting, and knowing*. New Jersey: Lawrence Erlbaum Associates.

Glei, J.K. (2012). What it takes to innovate: Wrong-thinking, tinkering & intuiting. *99U*. Retrieved from http://99u.com/articles/7158/what-it-takes-to-innovate-wrong-thinking-tinkering-intuiting

Glei, J.K. (2013). *Manage your day-to-day: Build your routine, find your focus, and sharpen your creative mind*. Las Vegas, NV: Amazon Publishing.

Goodfellow, R. & Lea, M. R. (Eds.) (2013). *Literacy in the digital university: Critical perspectives on learning, scholarship and technology*. London: Routledge.

Goodman, P. & Goodman, P. (1996). A city of efficient consumption. In R. T. LeGates & F. Stout (Eds.) *The city reader*. London: Routledge.

Grasswick, H. E. (2010). Scientific and lay communities: earning epistemic trust through knowledge sharing, in *Synthese, 177*(1), 387–409.

Groom, J. (2011). *DS106 digital storytelling MOOC, 2011*(August). Retrieved from http://ds106.us/.

Groves, K. & Knight, W. (2010). *I wish I worked there! A look inside the most creative spaces in business*. Chichester: Wiley.

Grudin, J. (2012). A moving target - The evolution of human-computer interaction. In J. Jacko (Ed.), *Human-computer interaction handbook* (3rd ed.). Taylor & Francis.

Guilford, J.P. (1967). *The nature of human intelligence*. New York: McGraw-Hill.

Haner, U-E. (2005). Spaces for creativity and innovation in two established organisations. *Creativity and Innovation Management, 14*(3), 288–298.

Harrison, N. B. (1999). The language of shepherding: A pattern language for shepherds and sheep - setting the stage. In *Proceedings of PLoP*.

Harrison, S., Sengers, P. & Tatar, D. (2011). Making epistemological trouble: Third-paradigm HCI as successor science. *Interacting with Computers, 23* (1), 385–392.

Hathaway, W. E., Hargreaves, J.A., Thompson, G.W. & Novitsky, D. (1992). *A study into the effects of light on children of elementary school-age: A case of daylight robbery*. Retrieved 12 November 2013 from http://www.centerfor greenschools.org/docs/study- into-the-effects-of-light.pdf

Hatwell, Y., Streri, A. & Gentaz, E. (Eds.) (2003). *Touching for knowing: Cognitive psychology of haptic manual perception*. John Benjamins Publishing.

Heap, T. & Minocha, S. (2012). An empirically grounded framework to guide blogging for digital scholarship. *Research in Learning Technology, 20*.

Heidegger, M. (1962). *Being and time*. Oxford: Wiley-Blackwell.

Heilman, K. M., Nadeau, S. E. & Beversdorf, D. O. (2003). Creative innovation: Possible brain mechanisms. *Neurocase, 9*(5), 369–379.

Hennessey, B.A. (2003). The social psychology of creativity. *Scandinavian Journal of Educational Research, 47*(3).

Hensman, J. (2012). *JISC final report: Inspires (Innovative Networks Supporting People Who Investigate Research Environments and Spaces)*. Retrieved from http://repository.jisc.ac.uk/4985/1/Inspires_Project_Final_Report_Dec_2012.pdf

Heritage, J. (2012). Epistemics in action: Action formation and territories of knowledge. *Research on Language and Social Interaction, 45*(1), 1–29.

Herzberg, F. I. (1959). *The motivation to work*. New York: John Wiley & Sons.

Herzberg, F. I. (1987). One more time: How do you motivate employees? *Harvard Business Review, 65*(5), 109–120.

Heschong Mahone Group (1999). *Daylighting in schools*. Fair Oaks, CA: Californian Energy Commission.

Huppert, F., Baylis, N. & Keverne, B. (Eds.) (2005). *The science of well-being*. Oxford University Press.

Ito, J. (2012). *Innovation on the edges in 1925 - 3M*. Retrieved 15 September 2013 from http://www.linkedin.com/today/post/article/20121104164030-1391-innovation-on-the-edges-in-1925-3m

Ivain, G. (1953). *Formulary for a new urbanism. Internationale Situationniste #1*. Retrieved from http://www.cddc.vt.edu/sionline/presitu/formulary.html

Jan van Pelt, R. & Westfall, C.W. (1991). *Architectural principles in the age of historicism*. New Haven; London: Yale University Press.

Janis, I. L. (1971). Groupthink. *Psychology Today, 5*(6), 43-46, 74-76.

Janis, I. L. (1982). *Groupthink: Psychological studies of policy decisions and fiascos* (2nd ed.). New York: Houghton Mifflin.

Jeffers, S. (1993). *Feel the fear and do it anyway*. London: Arrow.

Jindal-Snape, D., Davies, D., Collier, C., Howe, A., Digby, R. & Hay, P. (2013). The impact of creative learning environments on learners: A systematic literature review. *Improving Schools, 16*(1), 21–31. Retrieved 6 September 2013 from http://imp.sagepub.com/cgi/doi/10.1177/1365480213478461.

Jobs, S. (2000). *Macworld San Francisco 2000 –The Mac OS X introduction (pt.1)*. Retrieved 11 July 2013 from: http://www.youtube.com/watch?v=Ko4V3G4NqII

Jump Associates (n.d.) [Official website About page.] Retrieved 12 April 2013 from http://www.jumpassociates.com/about

Kämpfe, J., Sedlmeier, P. & Renkewitz, F. (2010). The impact of background music on adult listeners: A meta-analysis. *Psychology of Music, 39*(4), 424–448. doi:10.1177/0305735610376261

Kaplan, R. & Kaplan, S. (1989). *The experience of nature: A psychological perspective*. Cambridge University Press.

Kaplan, S. (1995). The restorative benefits of nature: Toward an integrative framework. *Journal of Environmental Psychology, 15*, pp. 169–182.

Kaplan, S., Talbot, J. & Kaplan, R. (1988). *Coping with daily hassles: The impact of nearby nature on the work environment*. Project Report, U.S. Forest Service, North Central Experiment Station, Urban Forestry Unit Cooperative Agreement 23-85-09.

Kelly, T. (2001). *The art of innovation*. New York: Random House.

Kitto, H.D.F. (1996). The Polis. In R. T. LeGates & F. Stout (Eds.) *The city reader*. London: Routledge.

Knez, I. (1995). Effects of indoor lighting on mood and cognition. *Journal of Environmental Psychology 15*(1), 39– 51.

Knorr-Cetina, K. (1999). *Epistemic cultures: How the sciences make knowledge*. New York: Cambridge University Press.

Koestler, A. (1964). *The act of creation*. New York: Dell.

Koskinen, I., Zimmerman, J., Binder, T., Redstrom, J. & Wensveen, S. (2011). *Design research through practice* (1st ed.). Waltham: Elsevier.

Kostelanetz, R. (2003). *Conversing with Cage*. London: Routledge Chapman & Hall.

Kratzer, J., Leenders, R. & Van Engelen, J. (2006). Managing creative team performance in virtual environments: an empirical study in 44 R&D teams. *Technovation, 26*, pp. 42–49. doi:10.1016/j.technovation.2004.07.016

Kristensen, T. (2004). The physical context of creativity. *Creativity and Innovation Management, 13*(2), 89–92.

Kruft, H-W. (1994). *A history of architectural theory: From Vitruvius to the present* (2nd ed.). New York and London: Zwemmer and Princeton Architectural Press.

Lakoff, G. & Johnson, M. (1980). *Metaphors we live by*. Chicago: University of Chicago Press.

Laseau, P. (2001). *Graphic thinking for architects & designers*. John Wiley & Sons.

Latour, B. (1992). Where are the missing masses? The sociology of a few mundane artifacts. In W. Bijker & J. Law (Eds.) *Shaping technology. Studies in sociotechnical change*, pp. 151–179. Cambridge: MIT Press.

Latour, B. (2005). *Reassembling the social*. New York: Oxford University Press.

Latour, B. & Woolgar, S. (1979). *Laboratory life: The construction of scientific facts*. Sage.

Law, J. (2004). *After method: Mess in social science research*. New York: Routledge.

Lefebvre, H. (1991) [1974]. *The production of space*. Oxford: Basil Blackwell.

Lepper, M.R. & Greene, D. (1973). Undermining children's intrinsic interest with extrinsic reward: A test of the 'overjustification' hypothesis. *Social Psychology, 28*(1), 129–137.

Leisch, F. (2002). Sweave: Dynamic generation of statistical reports using literate data analysis. In W. Härdle & B. Rönz (Eds.) *Compstat 2002 – Proceedings in Computational Statistics*. Heidelberg, pp. 575–580.

Leshed, G. & Sengers, P. (2011). "I lie to myself that I have freedom in my own schedule": Productivity tools and experiences of busyness. Proceedings of CHI 2011, Vancouver, Canada, 905–914.

Levine, B. (2011). *Get up, stand up: Uniting populists, energizing the defeated, and battling the corporate elite*. White River Junction, VT: Chelsea Green Publishing.

Licklider, J. (1960). Man-computer symbiosis. In *Transactions on Human Factors in Electronics*. HFE-1, pp. 4–11.

Licklider, J. (1965). *Libraries of the future*. Cambridge, Mass: MIT Press.

Lindsay, G. & Kasarda, J. (2011). *Aerotropolis: The way we'll live next*. New York: Farrar, Straus and Giroux.

Lynch, K. (1960). *The image of the city* (1st ed.). Massachusetts: MIT press.

Lyons, J. (1970). *Chomsky*. In F. Kermode (Ed.) Fontana Modern Masters. London: Fontana.

Mahnke, F. (1996). *Colour, environment, & human response*. New York: John Wiley & Sons.

Makri, S. & Blandford, A. (2012). Coming across information serendipitously: Part 1: a process model. *Journal of Documentation, 68*(5).

Malhotra, Y. (2000). *Knowledge management and virtual organizations*. London: Idea Group Publishing.

Marshall, J. (2013). *Free radicals*. Retrieved from http://www.pkallsc.org/sites/all/modules/ckeditor/ckfinder/userfiles/files/FreeRadicals--jjm.pdf

Mavros, P., Coyne, R., Roe, J. & Aspinall, P. (2012). Engaging the brain: Implications of mobile EEG for spatial representation. In H. Achten, J. Pavlicek, J. Hulin & D. Matejdan (Eds.) *Digital Physicality – Proceedings of the 30th eCAADe Conference*, pp. 657–665. Czech Technical University in Prague: Molab.

Mayer, R. E. (1999). Fifty years of creativity research. In R. J. Sternberg (Ed.) *Handbook of creativity*. New York: Cambridge University Press.

McCoy, J. M. (2000). *The creative work environment: The relationship of the physical environment and creative teamwork at a state agency – a case study*. PhD thesis: University of Wisconsin, Milwaukee.

McCoy, J. M. & Evans, G. W. (2002). The potential role of the physical environment in fostering creativity. *Creativity Research Journal, 14*(3 & 4), 409–426.

McDougall, G., Kelly, J., Hinks, J. & Bitichi, U. S. (2002). A review of the leading performance measurement tools for assessing buildings. *Journal of Facilities Management, 1*(2).

Meades, J. (2012). *Museums without walls*. London: Unbound.

Meadows, D. H. (1998). *Indicators and information systems for sustainable development. A report to the Balaton Group*. Hartland Four Corners, VT: The Sustainability Institute.

Mehrabian, A. & Russell, J. A. (1974). *An approach to environmental psychology*. Cambridge, MA, USA; London, UK: MIT Press.

Merleau-Ponty, M. (1962). *Phenomenology of perception*. London: Routledge & Kegan Paul.

Mewburn, I. (2011). What if your CV is not enough? (part one). *The Thesis Whisperer*. Retrieved 17 November 2013 from http://thesiswhisperer.com/ 2011/05/26/what-if-your-cv-is-not-enough-part-one/

Milton, D. K., Glencross, P. M. & Walters, M. C. (2000). Risk of sick leave associated with outdoor air supply rate, humidification, and occupant complaints. *Indoor Air, 10*, pp. 212-221.

Mor, Y., Warburton, S. & Winters, N. (2012). Participatory pattern workshops: a methodology for open learning design inquiry. *Research in Learning Technology, 20*.

Moultrie, J., Nilsson, M., Dissel, M., Haner, U-E., Janssen, S. & van der Lugt, R. (2007). Innovation spaces: Towards a framework for understanding the role of the physical environment in innovation. *Creativity and Innovation Management, 16*(1), 53–64.

Muhl, A.M. (1930) *Automatic writing*. [See also Kessinger Publishing, 2003.]

Mumford, L. (1996). What is a city? (1st ed.) In R. T. LeGates & F. Stout (Eds.) *The city reader*. London: Routledge.

Najafi, M. & Shariff, M.K.B.M. (2011). The concept of place and sense of place in architectural studies. *World Academy of Science, Engineering & Technology, 56*, pp. 1100–1107.

Nelson, H. & Stolterman, E. (2003). *The design way – Intentional change in an unpredictable world*. New Jersey: Educational Technology Publications.

Nemeth, C. J. & Nemeth-Brown, B. (2003). Better than individuals? The potential benefits of dissent and diversity for group creativity. In P. Paulus & B. Nijstad (Eds.) *Group Creativity*. Oxford: Oxford University Press.

Newport, C. (2012). *So good they can't ignore you: Why skills trump passion in the quest for work you love*. Business Plus. ISBN: 978-1455509126.

Newstetter, W. (2006). Fostering integrative problem solving in biomedical engineering: The PBL approach. *Annals of Biomedical Engineering, 34*(2).

Norberg-Schulz, C. (1980). *Genius loci: Towards a phenomenology of architecture*. Academy Editions.

Norman, D. (2004). *Emotional design: Why we love (or hate) everyday things*. New York: Basic Books.

Oldenburg, R. (1989). *The great good place: Cafes, coffee shops, community centers, beauty parlors, general stores, bars, hangouts, and how they get you through the day*. New York: Paragon House.

Olsen, E. M., Cooper, R. & Slater, S. F. (1998). Design strategy and competitive advantage. *Business Horizons, 41*, pp. 55–61.

Online PhD. Program (2013). *101 Twitter accounts every #PhD should follow*. Retrieved 9 July 2013 from http://onlinephdprogram.org/twitter-accounts/

Ophir, E., Nass, C., & Wagner, A.D. (2009). *Cognitive control in media multitaskers*. PNAS 2009 106 (37) 15583-15587. doi:10.1073/pnas.0903620106.

Osborn, A.F. (1953). *Applied imagination*. New York: Scribner's.

Pasteur, L. (1954). Inaugural lecture, University of Lille, December 7, 1954. In Houston Peterson (Ed.) *A treasury of the world's great speeches*, p. 473.

Pearce, N., Weller, M., Scanlon, E. & Kinsley, S. (2010). Digital scholarship considered: How new technologies could transform academic work. *Education, 16*(1).

Pederson, T. (2003). *From conceptual links to causal relations physical-virtual artefacts in mixed-reality space*. PhD Thesis. Umea University.

Procter, R., Poschen, M., & Wilson, R. (2013) *VRE Synthesis – JISC Final Report* (Unpublished).

Rea, M.S. (2003). *The IESNA lighting handbook: Reference & application (9th ed.)*. Illuminating Engineering Society of North America.

Rego. A., Machado, F., Leal, S. & Cunha, M.P.E. (2009). Are hopeful employees more creative? An empirical study. *Creativity Research Journal, 21*(2-3), 223–231.

Resnick, M. (2007). Sowing the seeds for a more creative society. *Learning and Leading With Technology, 35*(4), 18-22.

Reverberi, C., Toraldo, A., D'Agostini, S. & Skrap, M. (2005). Better without (lateral) frontal cortex? Insight problems solved by frontal patients. *Brain*, pp. 2882-2890.

Rheingold, H. (1985). *Tools for thought: The history and future of mind-expanding technology.* Cambridge, Mass: MIT Press.

Richard Murphy Architects (2000). *Dundee Contemporary Arts.* Retrieved 12 November 2013 from http://www.richardmurphyarchitects.com/50304

Riley, J., Corkhill, B. & Morris, C. (2013). The benefits of knitting for personal and social wellbeing in adulthood: findings from an international survey. *The British Journal of Occupational Therapy, 76*(2), 50-57.

Rittel, H.W.J. & Webber, M.M. (1973). Dilemmas in a general theory of planning. *Policy Sciences, 4*, pp. 155-169.

Riverdale & IDEO (2011).
Design thinking for educators. *Evolution,* (April). Retrieved from http://designthinkingfor educators.com/

Robey, D. & Azevedo, A. (1994). Cultural analysis of the organizational consequences of information technology. *Accting., Mgmt & Info. Tech, 4*(1), 23–37.

Roderick, L. (1987). *Housing, dwellings and home: Design theory, research and practice* (1st ed.). Chichester: John Wiley & Sons.

Roessler, G. (1980). The psychological function of windows for the visual communication between the interior of rooms with permanent supplementary artificial lighting and the exterior. *Light Research and Technology, 12*(3), 201–216.

Rolls, E. T. (2007). *Emotion explained.* Oxford: Oxford University Press.

Rosen, L. D. (2012). *iDisorder: Understanding our obsession with technology and overcoming its hold on us.* New York: Palgrave MacMillan.

Russell, B. (1969). *The autobiography of Bertrand Russell 1944-1969 – Volume 3.* Simon & Schuster.

Russell, J. A. & Snodgrass, J. (1987). Emotion and the environment. In D. Stokols & I. Altman (Eds.) *Handbook of environmental psychology.* New York: John Wiley & Sons.

Sadler, S. (1999). *The situationist city* (1st ed.). Massachusetts: MIT Press.

Sassen, A. (1996). A new geography of centers and margins: Summary and implications. In R. T. LeGates & F. Stout (Eds.) *The city reader.* London.

Sawyer, R.K. (2003). *Group creativity.* NJ: Lawrence Erlbaum.

Sawyer, K. (2011). The cognitive neuroscience of creativity: A critical review. *Creativity Research Journal, 23*(2), 137–154.

Schmid, H. B. (2012). Sharing in truth: Phenomenology of epistemic commonality. In D. Zahavi (Ed.) *The Oxford handbook of contemporary phenomenology.* OUP.

Schmidt, A. (2000). Implicit human-computer interaction through context. *Personal Technologies 4*(2-3), 191–199.

Schnädelbach, H. (2010). Adaptive architecture – A conceptual framework. In *Proceedings of MediaCity 2010.* Weimar, Germany. Retrieved 22 September 2013 from http://www.academia.edu/download/30405634/MediaCity-2010_sm.pdf#page=523

Schön, D. A. (1980). Policy planning as a design process. *Human Settlement Issues: Occasional Papers, 12*(26).

Schön, D. A. (1987). *Educating the reflective practitioner.* San Francisco: John Wiley and Sons.

Schott, G. (2011). Doodling and the default network of the brain. *The Lancet, 378*(9797), 1133–1134.

Schultz, S.E., Kleine, R.E. & Kernan, J.B. (1989). 'These are a few of my favorite things': Toward an explication of attachment as a consumer behavior construct. *Association for Consumer Research, Conference Proceedings, 16*(1988).

Sears, A. & Jacko, J. A. (2007). *The human-computer interaction handbook: Fundamentals, evolving technologies and emerging applications.* CRC Press.

Selhub, E. M. & Logan, A.C. (2012). *Your brain on nature: The science of nature's influence on your health, happiness and vitality.* John Wiley.

Seligman, M. (2011). *Flourish: A new understanding of happiness and well-being – and how to achieve them!* Boston & London: Nicholas Brealey Publishing.

Sellen, A.J., Murphy, R. & Shaw, K.L. (2002). How knowledge workers use the web. In Proc. CHI '02, 4, 227.

Sellier, A-L. & Dahl, D.W. (2011). Focus! Creative success is enjoyed through restricted choice. *Journal of Marketing Research, 48*(December), 996–1007.

Shaw, J. (2001). 'Winning territory': Changing place to change pace. In J. May & N. Thrift (Eds.) *Timespace: Geographies of temporality.* London: Routledge.

Simonton, D. K. (2005). Creativity. In C. R. Snyder & S. J. Lopez (Eds.) *Handbook of positive psychology.* US: Oxford University Press.

Singh, S. (1998). *Fermat's last theorem* (1st ed.). London: Fourth Estate.

Nemiro, J., Beyerlein, M. M., Bradley, L., & Beyerlein, S. (Eds.). (2008). *The Handbook of High Performance Virtual Teams: A Toolkit for Collaborating Across Boundaries* (1st ed., p. 800). San Francisco: Jossey Bass.

Smithson, A. & Smithson, P. (1970). *Ordinariness and light: Urban theories, 1952-1960 and their application in a building project, 1963-1970* (1st ed.). Massachusetts: MIT Press.

Solomon, C. (2003). Transactional analysis theory: The basics. *Transactional Analysis Journal, 33*(1), 15–22.

Spence, C. & Gallace, A. (2011). Multisensory design: Reaching out to touch. *Psychology and Marketing, 28*(3), 267–308.

Spors, K. K. (2008). Top small workplaces 2008. *Wall Street Journal.* Retrieved 23 November 2013 from http://online.wsj.com/news/articles/SB122347733961315417

Stamps, A. E. III (2005). Isovists, enclosure, and permeability theory. *Environment and Planning B: Planning and Design, 32*(5), 735–762.

Stamps, A. E. III & Krishnan, V. V. (2006). Spaciousness and boundary roughness. *Environment and Behaviour, 38*(6), 841–872.

Steiner, R. (1916). The twelve human senses. From *Toward imagination: Culture and the individual.* [Lecture Three, Berlin, 20 June 1916. Pub. 1990.] Hudson, NY: Anthroposophic Press.

Sternberg, R.J. (2006). The nature of creativity. *Creativity Research Journal, 18*(1), 87–98.

Stiny, G. (1980). Introduction to shape and shape grammars. *Environment and Planning B: Planning and Design 7,* pp. 343–351.

Stiny, G. (2006). *Shape: Talking and seeing and doing.* London: MIT Press.

Stokes, P. D. (2001). Variability, constraints, and creativity: Shedding light on Claude Monet. *American Psychologist, 56*(4), 355–359.

Strayer, D. L., Drews, F. A. & Johnston, W. A. (2003). Cell phone-induced failures of visual attention during simulated driving. *Journal of Experimental Psychology: Applied, 9*(1), 23–32.

Sun, X., Sharples, S. & Makri, S. (2011). A user-centred mobile diary study approach to understanding serendipity in information research. *Information Research, 16*(3), paper 492. Retrieved from http://InformationR.net/ir/16-3/paper492.html

Szalma, J.L. & Hancock, P. A. (2011). Noise effects on human performance: A meta-analytic synthesis. *Psychological Bulletin, 137*(4), 682–707.

Taylor, L.H. & Socov, E.W. (1974). The movement of people towards light. *Journal of the Illuminating Engineering Society, 3*, pp. 237–241.

Tett, G. (2012). The plan behind open-plan. *Financial Times Magazine*, 11/12 February 2012.

The D.School (2010). Stanford D.School students prototype on the cheap in 'extreme affordability' class. Retrieved from http://www.fastcompany.com/1638669/stanford-dschool-students-prototype-cheap-extreme-affordability-class

Thesis Whisperer (2011). The top 5 #phdemotions. *The Thesis Whisperer.* Retrieved 10 September 2013 from http://thesiswhisperer.com/2011/01/19/the-top-5-phdemotions/

Thiis-Evensen, T., 1987. *Archetypes in Architecture* (1st ed.). Norwegian University Press.

Toplyn, G. & Maguire, W. (1991). The differential effect of noise on creative task performance. *Creativity Research Journal, 4*(4), 337–347.

Treadaway, C. & Smith, K. (2012). No time like the present. In A. Duffy, Y. Nagai & T. Taura (Eds.) *2nd International Conference on Design Creativity*, Glasgow, UK, 18-20 September 2012, Electronic Conference Proceedings. The Design Society. ISBN:978-1-904670-40-7

Tschumi, B. (1996). Architecture and Disjunction. Massachusetts: MIT Press.

Tuan, Y-F. (2001). *Space and place: The perspective of experience.* Minnesota: University of Minnesota Press.

U101 Course Team (2013). *U101: The design thinking blog: Jugaad.* Retrieved 9 July 2013 from http://designthinking.typepad.com/dialogues/2013/01/jugaad.html

Ulrich, R. (1984). View from the window may influence recovery from surgery. *Science, 224,* pp. 420–421.

Ulrich, R. (1993). Biophilia, biophobia, and natural landscapes. In S. Kellert & E. Wilson (Eds.) *The biophilia hypothesis*. Washington, DC: Island Press.

Unsworth, J. (2000). *Scholarly primitives: What methods do humanities researchers have in common, and how might our tools reflect this?* Retrieved 3 August 2012 from http://people.lis.illinois.edu/~unsworth/Kings.5-00/primitives.html

Uzzi, B. & Spiro, J. (2005). Collaboration and creativity: The small world problem. *American Journal of Sociology, 111,* pp. 447–504.

Van Andel, P. (1994). Anatomy of the unsought finding. Serendipity: Origin, history, domains, traditions, appearances, patterns and programmability. *British Journal for the Philosophy of Science, 45*(2), 631–648.

Van de Ven, A. H., Polley, D. E., Garud, R. & Venkataraman, S. (1999). *The innovation journey.* Oxford: Oxford University Press.

Venturi, R. (1984). Complexity and contradiction in architecture. *Museum of Modern Art papers on architecture* (2nd ed.). New York: The Museum of Modern Art, New York.

Vidler, A. (1994). *The architectural uncanny: Essays in the modern unhomely* (1st ed.). Massachusetts: MIT Press.

Waks, L. J. (2001). Donald Schon's philosophy of design and design education. *International Journal of Technology and Design Education, 11*, pp. 37–51.

Wallas, G. (1926). *The art of thought*. New York: Harcourt, Brace.

Wargocki, P., Wyon, D. P., Sundell, J., Clausen, G. & Fanger, P. O. (2000). The effects of outdoor air supply rate in an office on perceived air quality, sick building syndrome (SBS) symptoms and productivity. *Indoor Air, 10*, pp. 222–236.

Weeks, J. & Fayard, A-L. (2007). *The affordances of practice: the influence of structure and setting on practice*. INSEAD: Faculty & Research Working Paper.

Weller, M. (2011a). The digital scholar: How technology is transforming scholarly practice. London: Bloomsbury Academic.

Weller, M. (2011b). A pedagogy of abundance. *Spanish Journal of Pedagogy, 249*, pp. 223–236.

Wheatley, M. & Kellner-Rogers, M. (1996). *A Simpler Way*. San Francisco: Berrett-Koehler.

Williams, A. (2009a). Creativity syntax: An emerging concept for creativity in the workplace. *Design Principles & Practices, 3*(5), 193–202.

Williams, A. (2009b). The creative footprint: the impact of physical space on workplace creativity. In *Conference Proceedings, Creativity & Cognition 2009*.

Williams, A. (2013). *A grammar of creative workplaces*. PhD thesis. University of East London.

Wilson, F.R. (1998). *The hand: How its use shapes the brain, language, and human culture*. Pantheon Books.

Wilson, M. (2002). Six views of embodied cognition. *Psychonomic Bulletin & Review, 9*(4), 625–636. Retrieved from http://www.ncbi.nlm.nih.gov/pubmed/12613670

Wittgenstein, L. (1922). *Tractatus Logico-Philosophicus*. (C. K. Ogden, Trans.) (eBook, 2010.). (original) Kegan Paul, Trench, Trubner. Retrieved from http://www.gutenberg.org/ebooks/5740

Witthoft, S. & Geehr, C. (2010). Bodystorming. *The k12 lab wiki*. Retrieved 18 August 2013 from https://dschool.stanford.edu/groups/k12/wiki/48c54/

Wuman, R.S. (1986). *What will be has always been: The words of Louis Khan*. New York: Rizzoli International Publications.

Wurtman, R.J. (1975). The effects of light on the human body. *Scientific American*, pp.69–77.

Wyon, D. & Nilsson, I. (1980). Human experience of windowless environments in factories, offices, shops and colleges in Sweden. *Proceedings of the Symposium on Daylight, Commission Internationale de L'Eclairage*.

Young, J.W. (2003). *A technique for producing ideas*. New York: McGraw-Hill.

Zhao, S., Grasmuck, S. & Martin, J. (2008). Identity construction on Facebook: Digital empowerment in anchored relationships. *Computers in Human Behavior, 24*, pp. 1816–1836.

Printed in the United States
By Bookmasters